Rabbi Levi A. Olan
(An Untired Liberal)

Melvin H. Weinberg
BBA, MBA, MSJS, DSJS

©Copyright 2020, Melvin H. Weinberg

All Rights Reserved.

No part of this book may be reproduced, stored in electronic format, or transmitted without written permission from the author.

ISBN: 978-1-60414-923-4

PUBLISHED BY:
Fideli Publishing Inc.
119 W. Morgan St.
Martinsville, IN 46151

www.FideliPublishing.com

Contents

Acknowledgements .... *v*
Preface .... *vii*

Chapter 1   Worcester and Dallas — The Pulpit Years 1

Chapter 2   Reform Judaism 31

Chapter 3   An Untired Liberal 51

Chapter 4   Religion and the Social Problem 71

Chapter 5   The State of Israel 105

Chapter 6   Judaism and Modern Theology 115

Chapter 7   Religious Truth 133

Chapter 8   A Polarity of Thought — God and Sin 151

Chapter 9   The Nature and Destiny of Man 179

Chapter 10 Judaism and Immortality 197

Chapter 11 Epilogue 215

End Notes 223

General Resource List and Bibliography 277

Acknowledgements

This text is a culmination of my years as a student of Spertus Institute for Jewish Learning and Leadership which began in 1999. From my very first course, "The Religion of Biblical Israel," the exuberance of Dr. Rachel Dulin was instrumental in fostering a continuing and significant yearning for pursuing further Jewish studies.

The achievement of my doctoral goal would not have been successful without the assistance of numerous individuals. Appreciation goes to Gerry Cristol, archivist for Temple Emanu-El in Dallas and Tim Binkley, archivist for the Perkins School of Theology of Southern Methodist University, for providing access to the Olan collection of materials at their respective facilities. From the Jacob Rader Marcus Center of the American Jewish Archives, special recognitions go to Kevin Proffitt, Senior Archivist for Research and Collections and his proficient staff, and Dr. Gary P. Zola, Executive Director, for their assistance and encouragement during the course of my research of the Olan Collection at the Archives in Cincinnati.

The completion of my doctoral aspirations and this dissertation would not have been possible without the assistance of my doctoral advisor, Rabbi Dr. Byron L. Sherwin *z'l*. His continued encouragement, suggestions, and observations were instrumental in cementing the structure and content of this manuscript. Exceptional recognition goes to Spertus Provost and Vice-president Dr. Dean Phillip Bell, Dr. Peter Haas, and Dr.

Ellen LeVee, members of my dissertation committee, for their tireless efforts in reading and commenting on this manuscript during the concluding phase of my doctoral program. Along with Dr. Sherwin, their input challenged me to continue to focus and substantively improve, where necessary, this manuscript.

Additional gratitude goes to my Temple Emanu-El rabbis David Stern and Debbie Robbins for their teaching, friendship, and continued encouragement during these past many years.

In the final analysis, my objectives would not have been possible without the support and love of my wife Ettie for her continuous encouragement while allowing me the time devoted to the Spertus course of study and this project. Thanks to our children Sheila and Neal, and our grandchildren Danielle and Aaron, for their continued interest and support in the pursuit of my Judaic goals.

Preface

This manuscript represents the *Final Project* and is being submitted in accordance with the requirements of the Doctor of Science in Jewish Studies (DSJS) Program of the Spertus Institute for Jewish Learning and Leadership. The subject of this discourse is Rabbi Levi A. Olan, a prominent liberal mind in American Reform Judaism from the decades of the 1930s through the 1970s, who spoke out on the issues of the day, while struggling to correct the dilemmas that society was inflicting upon its less fortunate members. Like innumerable religious leaders of past centuries, Olan was troubled by the injustices of life in a world where a just and compassionate God is Creator.[1] He was a staunch supporter of human equality, especially with respect to social, political, and economic rights and privileges, and his social justice philosophy advocated removal of the disparities and injustices among people. As reflected in his monographs and sermons, Olan's three basic doctrines of faith were rooted "in the family of man, the demands of justice, and the dignity of the human personality," principles that he believed could not be taught without relating them to existent conditions.[2] Simply stated, this meant the strong must help the weak, the rich care for the poor, and the gifted support the simple.[3] This premise was often repeated in Olan's scholarly papers and addresses centering on social justice issues, and was in keeping with his view that God blessed some of His children so that they might help others who need it.

One may inquire, "Who was Levi A. Olan and why was he so important in the communities in which he preached and lived?" This is a simple question, yet the answer can only come from one's analysis and interpretation of the many essays and addresses spanning Olan's many years in the pulpit. To begin with it must be stressed that Rabbi Olan was a man of eminent intellectual strength and considerable charm, a distinguished and forceful public speaker — "despite his diminutive statute (five foot five)"[4] — with incredible energy and an admirable sense of responsibility, determination, and commitment. When reading Olan's essays and hearing his addresses, one frequently encounters various other scholars mentioned, and an issue is seldom addressed without providing some historical background. In his articles describing the Dallas Jewish establishment, American author and literary critic David Ritz described Olan's inspirational sermons as follows:

> "Like a black gospel preacher, Olan could shout with the best of them. At once he elevated, impressed, intimidated, shamed, scolded, forgave, and motivated. He was a testifier, a witness, whose carefully written sermons — some of them took 20 hours to write — could shake the most complacent listener. His was a voice that could evoke the memory of thunder from ancient mountains."[5]

Throughout the twentieth century, many spokesmen for religious liberalism have cited the Hebrew prophets to frame their charges of social ills and their pleas for reform.[6] Like many religious thinkers of his generation, the teachings of the biblical prophets provided the foundation of Olan's religious philosophy. The prophets of the Hebrew Bible, "the moral conscience of ancient Israel,"[7] spoke out against many issues of injustice, corruption, and immorality within their communities, a tradition that Olan saw fit to continually pursue. The prophetic faith, he said, permeated all elements of individual existence as the prophets were concerned with not only individual behavior but also with the actions necessary to make the good society — "to do good and not evil that they may live."[8] The prophets were not men prophesying doom, but spokesmen of a realistic hope stemming from the demands of justice, condemning oppression of the poor, and the exploitation of the underprivileged. "To ignore them is to court death and destruction in any era. To accept their message and apply it individually, nationally, and internationally, is to embrace salvation and survival."[9] Simply stated, and as evidenced by his scholarly pursuits devoted to numerous social justice issues, Olan taught the messages of the Biblical Prophets through his writings, extensive sermonic engagements, and actions. He demonstrated the teachings of the prophets and their concern for the human condition through his commitment to social action rather than an inflexible religious doctrine. Referring to the prophetic writings, he noted: "Their significance today is their assertion that men and nations are subject to universal moral laws which are an integral part of creation."[10] The prophets, proclaiming an ethical monotheism to the world, revealed a God whose relation to men was one of moral demands, asking them to join Him in building a kingdom where "men shall beat their swords into plowshares...and none shall make them afraid."[11]

Religion for Olan was much more than just theological devotion and the good life. He equated religion to life itself, in that conditions inherent in both religion and life reveal similarities that are comparable to one another. "The essence of religion," he wrote, "was and is the attempt to relate man's life to the meaning of existence. A man who does not know how to seek a response to his basic needs, no matter how exemplary his moral life, is not a religious man."[12] In his radio sermon of April 27, 1952, Olan ascribed the essential beliefs for all religions to: a belief in God, which "can be achieved rationally, mystically, morally, psychologically, or revelation;" the moral law, which requires a commitment to God and moral living; the freedom of will, where "man is free to choose between good and evil, right and wrong;" the meaning or purpose of life, for "without the belief that life has some purpose in the scheme of things there can be no religion"; and conceivably the most controversial, the eternal nature of a purposeful life and the "illogical" assertion "that there is a God who asks us to live in accordance with His will because there is a purpose to all of it, and then have it end in the grave."[13] These essential beliefs are further analyzed and discussed in subsequent chapters of this document.

During his rabbinic career Olan campaigned for religious liberalism as he spoke out for and expressed dedication to the core liberal values essential to Reform Judaism. These important principles of Reform Judaism encompass early American Reform prescribed by the Pittsburg Platform of 1885, under which Olan's rabbinic training occurred, and the "Classical" phase advocated by the Columbus Platform of 1937, which represented the official version of Reform during the greater part of Olan's rabbinate. Both platforms are discussed in depth in Chapter 2.

Olan repeatedly emphasized the social message, preaching what he called "the social justice part of religion."[14] His concerns for social justice were grounded on the concept of people ruled by the law of God, the Creator, who he believed to be fundamental to the theology of the Bible. "There shall be but one law for you and the stranger who sojourns among you."[15] Like many of his contemporaries, this meant that all of us, black and white, Jew and Gentile, rich and poor, strong and weak, American and non-American, are all part of one family as co-workers with God as the Father in the divine pattern of history.[16] He continually sermonized on the relationship of religion to key societal issues by focusing on numerous modern ethical and moral dilemmas that included poverty, segregation and race relations, ignorance, unemployment, education, housing, the elderly, disease, and such global issues as the potential for nuclear holocaust, environmental pollution, the promise and challenge of scientific discoveries, commercial effects of big business, and exhaustion of natural resources. During his years in the pulpit, Olan opposed McCarthyism and its arbitrary assertions of defamation, anti-Semitism, and racism as he championed federal public housing and the integration of public schools. In his depiction of America as the land of plenty, he continually spoke out against the want and desperation of societies' less privileged classes.

As demonstrated on subsequent pages, Olan had a profound effect on the religious and secular communities in both Worcester, Massachusetts and Dallas, Texas, and he created a climate of respect and social concern throughout those communities and the two congregations in which he served. Although the first twenty years of his rabbinic career occurred in Worcester, Massachusetts, this document primarily reflects his tenure in Dallas, "the religious capital of Texas,"[17] which includes the years beginning in 1949 and ending with his death in 1984.

Upon his arrival in Dallas, Olan stepped into the role of his predecessor, Rabbi David Lefkowitz, who had been on the radio for years, by continuing the Sunday morning radio sermons. Olan soon became known as a powerful preacher and scholar, and "by 1951, he was already a media star; Christians driving to church on Sunday morning would listen to Rabbi Olan preach at them through the car radio. He was an instant hit."[18] His weekly radio sermons drew from numerous Jewish sources, as well as covering such topics as politics, philosophy, psychology, art, ethics and morality, social justice issues, and interfaith relations. There were many requests for copies of his sermons, some of which were read at Sabbath services at small synagogues having no rabbi.[19]

Religious congregations were plentiful in Dallas in the 1950s, suggesting that one might have considered the city to be the home of religious people trying to obey the rules of their religion and living in a manner that is considered morally right. In other words, it appeared to be a God-fearing community. This was a time when Dallas possessed one of the largest Presbyterian churches and the biggest Methodist and Baptist churches in the United States.[20] From the time of his appointment as Senior Rabbi of Temple Emanu-El in Dallas in 1949, until well past his retirement in 1970, Olan was the dominant voice of Judaism and the Jewish community in Dallas and the State of Texas. He was not only rabbi to his congregation, but in numerous ways the most prominent religious leader of the community. With such significant and/or distressing events occurring during his Dallas years — the Korean War (1950-1953), the 1954 desegregation decision of the United States Supreme Court, the assassination of President John F. Kennedy (1963), Israel's Six-Day War of 1967, and the Vietnam War (1965-1973) — it was Rabbi Olan that the people of Dallas turned for insight, analysis, and guidance.[21] A July 1964 *Fortune Magazine* article entitled "How Business

Failed Dallas" noted: "Dallas churches, for all their affluence, have been criticized for being singularly unrealistic about the urgent problems of the city. Accordingly, the most powerful religious voice in the area is undoubtedly that of Levi Olan, rabbi of Temple Emanu-El."[22] And later, in a 1976 *Dallas Times Herald* newspaper article, Olan was characterized as "the conscience of the city."[23] Without any reservations, he preached on how to cure the ills of society while gaining the respect and admiration of many leading businessmen and women because of the soundness of his criticisms and the courage with which he defended them.[24] He was a man of great integrity, willing to stand for his beliefs; and no one could possibly suspect him of any self-seeking motives. As one with purposes and goals in which he believed, a commitment in pursuit of those goals, and the patience to sacrifice in order to achieve their success, Olan demonstrated all of the characteristics of a leader. These leadership characteristics were exemplified throughout his career by his writings and passionate preaching and continual immersion in social justice causes.

Olan was rewarded by his contemporaries by being elected president (1967-1969) of the Central Conference of American Rabbis, the national body of American Reform rabbis. In addition, he was active in community affairs, serving on many local, state, and national boards and associations that are noted in Chapter 1. Furthermore, Olan's hunger for education manifested itself in his service as visiting professor at the Perkins School of Theology of Southern Methodist University in Dallas, the University of Texas at Arlington, the University of Texas at Austin, Emory University in Atlanta, and Leo Baeck College in London, and a visiting lecturer at Texas Christian University in Fort Worth. Honorary doctorates were bestowed upon him from Hebrew Union College in Cincinnati (1955), Austin College in Sherman, Texas (1967), and Southern Methodist University in Dallas (1968). He also held the prestigious position of regent (1963-1969) on the Board of Regents of the University of Texas, an appointment made by Texas Governor John Connally.

The monographs, writings, sermons, addresses, and correspondence of Rabbi Levi A. Olan are numerous, and are housed primarily at the Jacob Rader Marcus Center of the American Jewish Archives in Cincinnati, Ohio. Some of his writings and related documents, as well as over 200 radio sermons included in a digital collection, are located at the Bridwell Library of the Perkins School of Theology of Southern Methodist University, and selected papers and audio recordings of sermons and addresses are located in the library and archives of Temple Emanu-El in Dallas. This writer has been given access to the aforementioned information by those organizations housing the papers and collections, and those materials have been utilized in the research, analyses, interpretation, and explanation of the dominant issues included within this paper and addressed by Olan over the course of his rabbinic career. This study will highlight the affirmations and concerns that Olan saw central to Reform Judaism and Jewish life. As illustrated from his writings and sermons, the following chapters will show how Olan's religious thinking and philosophy were influenced by his desire to conform to and strengthen Reform Judaism while, at the same time, live, preach, and correlate his doctrines of faith to their relationship to social justice issues.

While other scholarly writers have provided brief noteworthy discussions or comments concerning Rabbi Olan's liberal religious philosophy and social justice activities, there does not appear to be an in-depth study of his religious views during the course of his rabbinic career and how his views were translated into social justice action.[25] One may consider this project to be an "intellectual biography" of Rabbi Levi A. Olan as its goal is to disseminate his philosophy and theology of Jewish religious thinking and Jewish life.

A broad concept of Olan's religious and social philosophy throughout his rabbinic career is presented in the following chapters and include his central topics of religious liberalism, social justice and theism. In order to achieve a consistent flow of discourse within this manuscript, the writer begins with a brief biography featuring Olan's rabbinic successes in Worcester and Dallas, followed by a short history of Reform Judaism that previews his introduction and commitment to the Reform Movement. Subsequent chapter titles stem from major headings of specific sermons and writings over the course of Olan's career. Chapters succeeding the short history of Reform are arranged in a natural progression with each chapter focusing on a fundamental theme significant to Olan and the Reform Movement during his rabbinate. One of Olan's favorite and frequent titles, "An Untired Liberal," focuses on his religious liberalism and its core tenets of freedom, reason, and progress, and is followed by a chapter dealing with his conceptions of and resolutions to issues of social justice experienced and envisioned by him throughout his life. Olan's sentiments of Zionism and the State of Israel are then presented, followed by a chapter that surveys the theological market place of Jewish theology and its meaning and significance in the understanding of Judaism. The methodology of obtaining religious truth and ultimate reality is followed by Olan' views of theism, omniscience and omnipresence of God and the question of evil, followed by the nature and destiny of man that reflects the desperation of humanity and the societal effects of secularism. Spiritual redemption and immortality of the soul (supported by his text, *Judaism and Immortality*, published in 1971) precede the concluding chapter that reflects Olan's place in the history of American Reform Judaism and Jewish theology, and his impact on the communities and congregations in which he lived and worked.

CHAPTER 1

Worcester and Dallas— The Pulpit Years

In the Beginning

Levi Arthur Olan was born Lemel Olanovsky (Ulanowsky) on March 22, 1903, in a small *shtetl* (town) near the city of Kiev in the Russian Ukraine. In 1907, like his father Mardchan (Max) Olanovsky did three years earlier, Lemel and his mother, Basse (Bessie) Leshinsk, left Russia for the United States to escape the persecutions of Czar Nicholas II (Bloody Nicholas) who ruled Russia from 1894 to 1917.[1] The massacre on "bloody Sunday," January 9, 1905, marked the beginning of open revolution in which social, economic, and political demands ultimately ended in tragedy for many victims.[2] It was a favorable time for the Olanovsky family to immigrate to a country where they could live in freedom and security. After entering the United States through Ellis Island, the family arrived in Rochester, New York to be near relatives. Like thousands of other immigrants arriving before and after them, and at the suggestion of immigration officials, the Olanovsky name was changed to Olan.[3]

Levi Olan grew up in a Yiddish-speaking home while attending the public schools of Rochester. His father became a peddler, buying clothing and other items in order to sell to local citizenry door to door while traveling on a bicycle. After a while his father opened a store selling a variety of clothing to both men and women. This was the vocational route taken by many immigrant Jews in other American communities. Olan's initial Hebrew learning came from a "bearded elderly man who came to our house and received fifty cents, a glass of tea, and Mother's delicious cookies."[4]

A significant influence in Olan's early life was the social center of the neighborhood, the Baden Street Settlement House, established by German Jews in the ghetto area of Rochester where the Olan family lived.[5] It was at this settlement house where the Boys' Literary Club was formed to bring community leaders to speak to its young members. Milton Steinberg (1903-1950) and Sidney Regner (1903-1993), two club members and friends of Olan, later played an important role in his choice of the rabbinate as a career. Further encouragement came from Minister William Gannett (from the distinguished family of newspaper publishers) of the Rochester Unitarian Church. Pastor Gannett took an interest in Olan's vocational future, encouraging him to pursue a rabbinic career, suggesting that Olan visit with Horace J. Wolf, spiritual leader of Rochester's Reform Temple (B'rith Kodesh) and the first chairman of the Conference Commission on Social Justice.[6] Wolf's friendliness put Olan at ease and he decided to attend one of the Temple services, which were held on Sunday. The meeting with Wolf and Olan's subsequent attendance at his services were two events that influenced his ultimate embrace of Reform Judaism, even though the service was almost entirely in English with little Hebrew and the *Shema* was recited with uncovered heads. "It was a congregation composed almost entirely of German Jews who to us were goyim."[7] Olan believed that only in the Hebrew language does one experience the soul of the Jewish people.

> "There is a world of difference between 'Shema Yisrael' and 'Hear O Israel.' In the latter, it is the universal declaration of monotheism, the declaration that God is one. But in the Hebrew, one hears the voice of the Prophets, the wisdom of the Talmud, the cry of the persecuted, and the undying faith of

an undying people. The Jew is most fully his Jewish self when he speaks and hears in the language which his people have always used to express their deepest faith."[8]

After graduating from Rochester High School, and lacking the financial resources to go away to college, Olan remained at home and enrolled at the University of Rochester.[9] "His classes exposed him to challenging ideas, such as Darwin's theory of evolution, which made the Orthodox views of his home 'no longer meaningful' in the way they had been."[10] With a strong desire to attend school away from home, as well as financial considerations and the encouragement of Wolf, Olan was directed to the Hebrew Union College (HUC) which offered free tuition and scholarships for room and board.[11]

He left for Cincinnati in 1923 to enroll in both the University of Cincinnati, where he attended classes in the mornings, and the HUC for classes in the afternoon. Olan's leaning toward Judaic pursuits came partly from the encouragement of his boyhood friends and fellow students at the Rochester Talmud Torah, Milton Steinberg and Sidney Regner, who were both preparing to enter rabbinic institutions.[12] Steinberg, who encouraged Olan to study Hebrew, became an important scholar in the Reconstructionist movement while Regner pursued the rabbinate through study at the HUC in Cincinnati, later becoming the executive director of the Central Conference of American Rabbis for many years.[13]

Horace Wolf was also instrumental in the ultimate decision by Olan that shaped the balance of his life. When questioned about the effect on his life of Horace Wolf's guidance in suggesting the HUC, Olan's explanation centered on his lack of financial resources and free tuition. "At Hebrew Union College I could go without any tuition. Since I had no money that was a very important incentive. That played a part of my becoming a rabbi."[14] When questioned by the admissions committee about his reason for being there, Olan playfully replied: "because I have a friend (Sidney Regner) here."[15] "Behind that astounding answer lay a childhood and youth which led to anything but the choice of the Rabbinate as a life's career."[16] But it would be misleading to assume that Olan's rabbinic career was founded wholly on the lack of financial resources or because he was following in the footsteps of his friends. His Orthodox background and early Hebrew environment, the Baden Street Settlement House and Boys Literary Club, and the roles of Steinberg and Regner, as well as the encouragement of Gannett and the prodding of Wolf, provided Olan with the enthusiasm to pursue the rabbinate. His academic environment at the College interrelated with the dilution of his earlier Orthodox upbringing, as well as his desire to assimilate into the American way of life, deeply influenced his responsibilities as a Jew, and his commitment to social justice and the Reform Movement.

One particular experience remembered by Olan at the HUC was the class on Jewish history taught by Dr. Jacob Mann, who had a limited English vocabulary. Mann once asked: "Olan, vat did de Jews vage against the Philistines?" Olan, displaying his avid sense of humor, replied: "I'll bite, doctor." To which Mann responded: "vat do you mean you will bite?"[17] From the academic curriculum, Olan was influenced by the courses on the prophets, especially those courses taught by Dr. Moses Buttenwieser. Prophetic Judaism was significant in the curriculum at the HUC and Moses Buttenwieser "taught the prophetic literature with critical competence and great enthusiasm for the subject."[18] Olan said that Buttenwieser's course about the Biblical prophet Amos, "influenced and to a large measure defined" his rabbinate throughout his career.[19] Amos' influence on Olan came from the prophet's brave and daring condemnation for those communities violating the laws of social justice; and, even though Israel was designated as the "Chosen People," they were not immune to punishment.[20] "Amos did not desire to replace religion by morality; he desired to moralize religion."[21] This concept prevailed over the totality of Olan's rabbinate and his outspoken messages, like those of Amos' brave and daring condemnations, centered upon the timeless moral laws at the center of life which society must learn and by which it is to be guided. His book, *Prophetic Faith and the Secular Age*, published in 1982, applied the faith of the prophets to the issues of the period. "Their (prophetic teachings) significance today," Olan wrote, "is their assertion that men and nations are subject to universal moral laws which are an integral part of creation."[22] With this view, "the prophetic message was based upon a theology which viewed God as a law-giver and the world as morally abiding. Men must live by law if they would survive; physical law such as that of gravity, and moral law such as that of justice."[23] A clear statement of this view, Olan preached, derives from Amos 5:14: "do (seek) good and not evil, that you may live."

Olan graduated from the University of Cincinnati in 1925, and, after completing his rabbinic courses in six years, he was ordained by the Hebrew Union College in 1929, the year of the Great Depression "confident that I possessed the sure cure for the world's ills."[24] Years later, during his Presidential Address to the 80th Annual Convention of the CCAR, June 16, 1969, he recalled the 1929 ordination of his class of eleven: "We were told that we are very fortunate to begin our rabbinical careers at a time when unending prosperity and enduring peace would bless our vineyard."[25] The "unending prosperity" and "enduring peace" proved to be an incongruity with the impending stock market crash of 1929 marking the end of several years of unparalleled prosperity, followed by the 1933 election of Adolf Hitler as Chancellor of Germany. Later, when asked by others why he became a rabbi, his response, again in his whimsical fashion and non-serious vein, was always: "I made a survey, and it came out if you want to make the most money and do the least work, you became a rabbi. I end up saying that was the worst survey ever made."[26] Following his ordination Olan ascended to prominence in the Reform Movement as an active pulpit rabbi, serving only two congregations (Temple Emanuel in Worcester, Massachusetts and Temple Emanu-El in Dallas, Texas) spanning a period of forty-one years, from 1929 through 1970. During his retirement years, and until his death in 1984, Olan continued to remain actively involved in the Reform Movement and American Jewish religion through his lectures and literary activities.

Worcester, Massachusetts

Olan's first rabbinic position was Temple Emanuel in Worcester, Massachusetts, where he remained for 20 years until his move to Dallas.

During his term as the third rabbi of the 27 year old synagogue, the congregation grew from 100 to more than 600 families.[27] His philosophy was influenced by Professor Harry Wolfson (1887-1974) of Harvard University, the first chairman of a Jewish studies center in the United States, and Rabbi William Braude (1907-1988) in Providence, Rhode Island. Through weekly study sessions with Wolfson and Braude, Olan acquired the discipline of spending mornings studying some of the things they talked about, particularly philosophy; then he would go to the temple in the afternoons where he became very active in the community and civic life of Worcester, Massachusetts.[28] Olan's independent program of study included the works of American educator John Dewey (1859-1952), who influenced his reasoning and thinking, with additional inspiration coming from Friedrich Hegel (1770-1831), who emphasized the progress of history and ideas, and American psychologist and philosopher William James (1842-1910), who proposed the idea that progress makes a life significant. Olan also became friendly with Rabbi Hyman Silver, an Orthodox rabbi with whom he periodically studied Talmud, engaging its ancient theological judgements with modern philosophy. "Despite our friendship he (Silver) denounced me as a goy at every public occasion."[29]

In 1931, soon after his arrival in Worcester, Olan married Sarita Messer, daughter of Frank Messer, a Cincinnati builder, and Rose Hauben Messer. They met at a dance at the Hebrew Union College. Later he jokingly told Sarita: "I married you because I was hungry." This was in reference to his being invited to her parent's home for dinner. She taught school until their marriage and the move to Worcester, where she became a full-time homemaker.[30]

The 1930s and 1940s provided great challenges for young new rabbis and their congregations. It was during this period that Americans experienced Prohibition, during which time the sale, manufacture, and transportation of alcohol were banned nationally; nativism, the favoring of native inhabitants as opposed to immigrants; isolationism, the reluctance to become involved in European alliances; and anti-Semitism, the hostility toward or discrimination against Jews as a religious, ethnic, or racial group. With the ratification of the 21st Amendment to the U.S. Constitution, repealing the 18th Amendment, the era of national prohibition of alcohol in America came to an end in December 1933. Immigration concerns of the 1930s were influenced by the depression and resulted in a decline in the number of immigrants coming into the country. Isolationism and the reluctance of American leaders to deal with matters within the European countries came to a close with the rise of Nazism during the 1930s and America's entrance into the war in 1941.

American anti-Semitism had its roots in negative Jewish stereotypes fostered by traditional Christian anti-Judaic teachings and the association of Jews with money and financial success. The 1920s saw the revival of the Ku Klux Klan and, although the Klan directed most of its enmity against blacks and Catholics, it increased its violence in the 1930s against certain German-Americans and Jews.[31] The respectability of anti-Semitic attacks on American life was aided by automaker Henry Ford through his weekly newspaper, the *Dearborn Independent*, purporting to describe an international Jewish conspiracy based on the notorious anti-Semitic forgery known as *The Protocols of the Elders of Zion*.[32] Further fuel to anti-Semitism emanated in the national CBS network broadcasts by Father Charles E. Coughlin, a Catholic priest in Detroit, describing anti-Semitism as just another variant in the crusade against communism,[33] while at the same time denouncing bankers and Jews.[34] In March 1942, Coughlin declared that "Hitler's persecution (of the Jews in the death camps) was justified because it had been one of international Jewry's goals to involve the United States in another war against Germany."[35] The Jewish image had also been tarnished by unscrupulous Jews involved in criminal activities and corrupt practices before the repeal of Prohibition in 1933 and the scandal surrounding the 1919 World Series ("Black Sox"). "The massive damage inflicted on the Jewish image during the interwar years (between the First and Second World Wars)…was compounded by the damage wrought by educational quotas, restrictive covenants, occupational discrimination, and physical attacks."[36] These restrictive quotas limited the number of Jewish students at many major universities, private academies and preparatory schools, as well as harsher restrictions for fraternities, clubs, hotels, and resorts. In effect, the Jews were excluded by the educational quotas not on the basis of merit but simply because of their ancestry and faith.[37] "In addition, bigoted practices and 'restrictive covenants' excluded Jews from some of the most desirable neighborhoods in New York, Chicago, Washington, D.C., Los Angeles, Miami, Denver, Baltimore, Boston…as well as from many newly emerging suburbs."[38]

Hitler's rise to power in Germany, along with the subsequent arrival of Jewish refugees in America, provided both challenges and opportunities to Olan's rabbinate in Worcester. He viewed Hitler's rise to power as fostering a revival of anti-Semitism affecting not only German Jews, but Jews everywhere. He referred to Hitler as an "unbalanced, temperamental, neurasthenic actor who has the courage of his own banality."[39] Hitler, like Stalin, represented a deadly disease, and Olan compared them to "boils of an infection that we all carry to a greater or lesser degree."[40] The impact of Nazism was not confined solely to the community of German Jews, for, as Olan preached: "It reaches as well to the whole world of Jewry. For it has started a revival of anti-Semitism…spreading as any pestilence may spread, from land to land and from heart to heart."[41] "Let hatred be loosed anywhere, and like a fire it spreads and devours the world."[42] For Olan, the affliction of the Jew in Germany was also a problem for Christianity and free men everywhere for it infringed upon the rights of those in any minority group. Rabbi Olan said:

> "Wherever there are minority groups today, in some condition of race, religion, or social status different from their fellows — there is an insecurity which springs from the insecurity of the Jew in Germany. The affliction of the Jew, in other words, becomes the affliction of the Negro. The outlawry of the Jew becomes the outlawry of the Catholic, the pacifist, the liberal. So long as one man is in danger, we are all in danger. If the rights of one group are denied, then the rights of all groups, and in the end, the rights of humanity itself are in grave jeopardy. The supreme tragedy of the German Jew is to be found in the fact that his misery marks the downfall of the freedom

of our age and therewith the collapse, if it not be stayed, of civilization."[43]

Preaching that the Jews of Germany were a dilemma for world resolution, Olan helped inspire his congregation to become instrumental in assisting many immigrants from Germany and Europe. One of the refugees Olan assisted to immigrate to this country was Cantor Hugo Adler, who was welcomed to Olan's Temple in Worcester. Adler introduced synagogue music that retained the traditional cantorial music of Eastern Europe while writing many large-scale cantatas on biblical and other Judaic subjects.

The issue of civil rights for black Americans also began to force its way to the top of the Jewish social action agenda. Although lay and Jewish religious organizations were not deeply involved in civil rights issues prior to World War II, many Jewish leaders protested the injustice and cruelty taking place at that time. However, it was not until after the end of World War II that civil rights became a central religious issue and moral imperative for American Jews. The National Council of Churches, in which Jews took part, and the National Conference of Christians and Jews encouraged this trend, as did the American Jewish Committee and all three Jewish religious movements.[44]

Throughout his career, Olan addressed what he termed the social justice part of religion, continually emphasizing the social messages of justice for the oppressed and the injustice of the disparity between the wealthy and the poor. In Worcester, this was demonstrated by his courageous and energetic responses to the aforementioned challenges, validated by his orations and pro-active civic contributions, all of which aligned with the ideological pronouncements and tenets of Reform Judaism. In relation to the mission of the American Reform Movement, the Pittsburgh Platform of 1885, relevant at the time of Olan's ordination in 1929, called for the improvement of relations between the rich and poor and solution of problems on the basis of justice and righteousness.[45] The Columbus Platform of 1937, applicable to the majority of

Olan's career, expanded and clarified the Reform Movement's position on Judaism's commitment for the Jewish people.

> "Judaism seeks the attainment of a just society by the application of its teachings to the economic order, to industry and commerce, and to national and international affairs. It aims at the elimination of man-made misery and suffering, of poverty and degradation, of tyranny and slavery, of social inequality and prejudice, of ill-will and strife. It advocates the promotion of harmonious relations between warring classes on the basis of equality and justice, and the creation of conditions under which human personality may flourish…"[46]

Olan designed his preaching for society as a whole, the individual, the organization, and government, as he sought to emphasize the moral law as crucial to the attainment of a just society. Religion for Olan was not only a matter of personal faith, but also involved in other aspects of life. "No religion," Olan sermonized, "is worthy of its name which does not concern itself with the social, political, economic, and international problems of its time; likewise no religion can be acceptable which does not give men and women a philosophy of life for unsteady and uncertain times."[47]

His time in Worcester involved active participation in the life of the non-Jewish community as well as the Jewish community. He served on numerous boards and civic organizations, while at the same time often exchanging pulpits with various Christian ministers of the Methodist and Unitarian churches, as well as with his closest friend, Dr. Thomas Roy, Minister of a local Baptist Church. Olan was also instrumental in organizing a People Forum whose purpose was to provide speakers of numerous topics of interest. As the presiding officer, he introduced Norman Thomas (1884-1968), socialist, pacifist, and "perennial candidate (six times for the Socialist Party of America) for U. S. president who remained a friend until he died."[48] Another speaker was Clarence Darrow, with whom Olan debated the topic of religion, admitting he was no match for the captivating rhetoric of the elderly Darrow. Two thousand people came to the forum to hear Darrow, and Olan later declared "that while he (Darrow) denies God, his (Darrow's) life's work is evidence of his faith in a world in which God is a reality."[49]

The *Jewish Civic Leader* newspaper issue of December 10, 1948 was dedicated to Olan upon learning of his upcoming departure for Dallas. "It's difficult to write an 'editorial' on Rabbi Levi A. Olan. In fact, it's impossible. What should we emphasize — his efforts on behalf of all of us in Worcester, his spiritual contribution to the Jewry of the city, or the greatness of the man himself? Who are we to judge?"[50] Various editorials in the paper referred to him as a humanitarian, philosopher, and educator, paying many tributes to Olan for his many years of contributions to the total Worcester Community from 1929 to December 31, 1948. When asked about his greatest accomplishment in Worcester, Olan responded: "I feel my greatest work was in helping to organize the Jewish Community into what is now the Jewish Federation — the greatest instrument of the community toward the fulfillment of Jewish community needs."[51]

After Olan made public his decision to accept the Dallas move, numerous honors were bestowed on him by the Worcester community. At a December 5, 1948 banquet, he was honored by more than 1,200 people, congregational members and guests, at a major Worcester hotel. Previously, on November 27, 1948, he was honored at an informal dinner attended by one hundred and fifty representatives of 39 city organizations joining in a tribute highlighted by a presentation from local residents and a silver tray inscribed as follows:

> "Worcester, Massachusetts, November 27, 1948. To Rabbi Levi A. Olan with deep appreciation for his cooperation and leadership in the religious and social services of Worcester and his devotion to the betterment of our community, September 1929 — December 1948."[52]

The above tributes and honors acknowledge Olan's active involvement "in every important community organization as well as every Jewish organization"[53] during his 20 years in Worcester, Massachusetts, which included:[54]

- Past president of the New England Regional Council of Jewish Federations and Welfare Funds (United Jewish Charities);
- Past president of the Jewish Social Services Agency in Worcester;
- Director of the Foreign Policy Association;
- Director of the Worcester People's Forum;
- Director of the Massachusetts Mothers' Health Council;
- Vice President of the Worcester Red Cross Chapter and chairman of its Home Services Department;
- Vice President and member of the Board of Trustees of the Worcester Foundation for Experimental Biology;
- Former vice president of the Worcester Economics Club;
- Member of the Council of the YMCA;
- Director of the Massachusetts Society for the Prevention of Cruelty to Children;
- Member of the Executive Committee of the Worcester Community Council;
- Member of Executive Board of the Central Conference of American Rabbis;
- Member of Advisory Board of the State Department of Public Welfare;
- Member of the board of the Community Chest;
- President of the Worcester Ministers Association.

After twenty years at Temple Emanuel in Worcester, Olan's decision to leave was not an easy one to make. Mindful of his accomplishments and the success of Temple Emanuel in achieving its major program, Olan confessed the persuasive call to a greater challenge was impossible to refuse.[55] In the column "The Rabbi Speaks to You," of the December

10, 1948 issue of the *Jewish Civic Leader*, page 1, he said: "I have stood beside too many people in their hours of joy and tragedy, not to sense the ties that exist between us. All of this is difficult to leave behind, yet I know that my many friends understand that the call to greater duty must supersede my personal desires." As a revered New England community leader and religious scholar, his decision to leave Worcester for Dallas provoked numerous heartfelt accolades from congregants as well as non-Jewish residents of the area. Letters from two members of his Worcester congregation demonstrate the essence of the community's love and respect for Olan. "The feeling I had when you left Worcester, was not unlike what I felt when my dear mother passed away. There was no consolation in knowing hundreds of others felt the same way;"[56] and "in your leaving we lost a very useful and prominent citizen."[57]

Dallas, Texas

Olan was influenced to move to Dallas by two rabbinic leaders of the Reform Movement, rabbi and biblical archaeologist Nelson Glueck (1900-1971), president of the Hebrew Union College, and rabbi and Jewish historian Jacob Rader Marcus (1896-1995), founder of the American Jewish Archives.[58] With the population shift of Jews to the Southwest, leaders of the Reform Movement recognized the area's future importance to its growth. Olan was both encouraged and eager to accept the position as Senior Rabbi of Temple Emanu-El in Dallas in order to enhance the further development of the Reform Movement in this rapidly growing southwestern part of the United States. Temple Emanu-El, the first Jewish congregation in North Texas, was founded in 1875. It evolved from the Dallas Hebrew Benevolent Association (the first Jewish organization in the city) organized in 1872 by eleven men who established a cemetery and held the first Jewish services in Dallas.[59]

Rabbi Olan, with his wife, Sarita and their three children, arrived in Dallas on December 31, 1948. He recalled that his first great event was being taken to the Cotton Bowl Football game on January 1, 1949. He said "it was hot enough to sit in shirt sleeves." But the change from

Worcester was more than a change in the weather. His new congregation, with a membership approximating 900 family members in 1949 and an operating budget approaching $100,000,[60] was previously led by Rabbi David Lefkowitz, a *"classical"*[61] Reform Rabbi, who conducted services almost entirely in English with only the *Shema* in Hebrew. Like many Reform congregations throughout the country, Temple Emanu-El generally neglected celebrating bar mitzvahs to mark the obligation of thirteen year-old boys to fulfill Jewish laws. With the abandonment of the bar mitzvah ceremony, Reform congregations introduced confirmation ceremonies signaling graduation from the tenth grade of religious school. The Temple's Sunday school curriculum taught no Hebrew and very little Jewish history.[62] It was in the closing days of Rabbi Lefkowitz that Temple leadership began to realize the need to do a good deal more about the religious school as well as the role of the Temple as an institution in becoming part of the community life, developments that "flowered however in later years under Olan's rabbinate."[63] Remembering his early observations upon entering his new pulpit, Olan later wrote: "There was a choir and organist, all goyim. Dr. Lefkowitz was a kindly pastor who was beloved in the city by Gentiles and Jews...It occurred to me that in Worcester I had to make goyim out of Jews; in Dallas the job was to make Jews out of goyim."[64]

Dallas was viewed as "an ideal pulpit for introducing changes in liturgy, ritual, and direction that the Reform Movement had embraced but the South had largely ignored."[65] Olan's initial years in Dallas included the culmination of a period of great transformation of Judaism which had been occurring within the second and third quarters of the twentieth century. This transformation was aptly described by the noted Jewish theologian and social thinker, Will Herberg (1906-1977):

> "American Jewry first established itself in this country as an ethnic-immigrant group. In its earlier phases it seemed but little different from the other immigrant groups with whom it had made the overseas journey to the New World. But unlike the rest, it somehow did not lose its corporate identity with advancing Americanization; instead-largely within the last

quarter of a century-it underwent change of character and turned into an American religious community, retaining, even enhancing, it's Jewishness in the process."[66]

Olan made clear his concern with the larger picture, the relationship of Temple Emanu-El to both the local Jewish community and Reform Judaism as a whole. Like many Reform rabbis, believing that Reform Judaism met the needs of "modern thinking people," Olan reintroduced some of the traditional ritual practices that the reformers had abandoned, thereby enabling the congregation to begin strengthening the liberal movement in the Jewish community.[67] With his mindset, Olan was convinced that the temple should offer attractive opportunities for involvement to unaffiliated Jews and to those who were dissatisfied with the Conservative and Orthodox synagogues.[68]

In 1951, at the request of the Board of Trustees, Rabbi Olan was invited to express his views about the contributions the Temple should make to the lives of its members. Provided with the challenge of motivating progressive thinking and change, he fashioned the following guidelines and course of action for Temple leadership and for the congregation: the teaching of Judaism and its religious values from the pulpit and in adult classes, in the religious school for children, in the meetings of Brotherhood and Sisterhood, as well as at every possible time and place; counseling and guidance for members in time of sorrow and of joy (a pastor in the profound meaning of the word); expressing in art forms and in symbols the religious ideas of our faith by religious services that include moving emotional experiences and Hebrew liturgical music; and working with the other religious denominations in a unified effort to strengthen the religious faith of the community.[69]

This was the genesis of the rebuilding process under Olan's tenure. He was instrumental in the transformation of what was then called a Sunday school (currently referred to as Religious School) by instituting Hebrew study and hiring a professional director who devised a curriculum that added studies in Jewish history and readings in post biblical literature. Adult Jewish education became significant in the transformation process of Temple, as Olan explained its purpose:

> "It is almost futile for me to urge upon you the value or the importance of learning something about our faith and our history. A desire to know is not created by a word from me. But this much seems clear — we, as Jews, are the heirs to a great religious faith and philosophy, which can help us live our lives more fully. The courses are planned to make that faith more meaningful."[70]

Further changes included the return of the bar mitzvah celebration and the regular occurrence of the reading of the Torah among the lay members. And in keeping with Olan's social action pursuits, and at the time when Dallas was the largest city in the United States without public kindergartens, the Temple's Community Affairs Committee was successful in its efforts in 1965 to develop a pre-school center for disadvantaged children.[71]

As most of the membership considered themselves "classical reform," it is not too difficult to understand the members' concerns about these innovations, and many congregants accused Olan of leading the congregation towards Orthodoxy and Zionism. In response to this accusation Olan emphasized that the job of the rabbi is to teach Judaism rather than what laymen instructed him to teach. He believed Temple Emanu-El should be the kind of religious house in which an individual "entering would have the experience of the holy."[72] Any opposition among the members and Rabbi Olan was soon resolved when a leadership committee apologized to Olan stating their support of his position.[73]

But the Jewish faith issue represented only a portion of the total responsibility package of his rabbinate and the Temple community. It was Olan's obligation and the charge of Temple Emanu-El to also be concerned with and actively involved in their relationship to the community. "An enterprise worthy in itself must ultimately relate itself to the problem of human existence."[74] In this regard, Olan stressed the requirement that members of society must seek answers to the questions that matter most, "How should we live? How to act? How to look upon the community? To what shall we aspire?"[75]

One particular adult education program, the Significant Book Series launched by two members of the Sisterhood, became a unique platform for Olan to express many of his liberal ideas. His criterion for the books discussed was their "significance of our time."[76] This series was one method that provided Olan an outlet to interact with other religious and civic organizations and the broader community experienced a significant impact. His outspoken commentaries on existing racial inequalities and poverty nurtured the integration of his religious and social justice stances. "I think that it is fair to say that through the radio, television and the Book Series the Temple became the leading voice of social and religious liberalism."[77]

Early in his career at Temple Emanu-El, Olan was aware that racial segregation dominated the schools and every aspect of communal life in Dallas. It was a racially segregated city where African-Americans (Negroes in the vernacular of the 1950s through the 1970s) were not allowed: to drink from water fountains that whites used; to sit in restaurants where white people ate; to study in the same school where whites studied; or, to ride in the front portion of busses where the whites sat. A central issue of the 1950s involved the integration of public schools which resulted from the Supreme Court's unanimous rescinding of "separate but equal" Jim Crow laws in *Brown v. Topeka Board of Education* in 1954. This case outlawed segregation in public schools on the basis of race. As an outstanding proponent of liberal causes and social justice issues, Olan was a staunch supporter and acquaintance of Martin Luther King, Jr., meeting him on a Dallas visit that many local black pastors, fearing backlash from the larger white secular community, boycotted.[78] Olan affirmed that every citizen in America should share in the religiously committed life of Martin Luther King, Jr. who came to represent for all Americans and for the world some truths which were struggling for expression.[79] In his letter of March 11, 1970 to Reverend Peter Johnson, Regional Representative of the Southern Christian Leadership Conference, Olan referred to King as a "prophet" in his time.

> "Martin Luther King, Jr. was one of the prophets of our time. His conviction that justice can be achieved without violence is the necessary emphasis of this hour. If we are to move forward toward the good community, we should keep before ourselves the image of the man who stood for it, while raucous and riotous voices were calling for violence."[80]

The April 4, 1968 assassination of Martin Luther King, Jr. was described by Olan as the "epitome of tragedy" and a "senseless destruction of the good. It was at the same time a triumphant death because the man had never been as alive before...an event as to compel us to examine ourselves with a different perspective."[81] King's sudden death confirmed a common theme throughout Olan's rabbinic teachings — the indivisibility of humanity. In the religious tradition of monotheism, there is only God as the Father of one human family who are all His children, as Olan articulated in his Birmingham to Memphis sermon: "It is too late in history for anything but the brotherhood of man under the fatherhood of God."[82] King's death represented a profound impact on our society, slowly at first and ultimately in a direction leading to diminished integration issues well beyond the time of his assassination. Men mourned King's death, Olan said, for a variety of reasons.

> "The oppressed of the world shed real tears for the loss of a spokesman for their release. The humane in our midst mourned the passing of a dynamic humanitarian. Those who fear violence more than they care for brotherhood bemoaned the non-violent reformer even though they rejected his leadership for human rights. The politically ambitious formally mourned for political reasons."[83]

As a result of his deep concern with racial integration and its interrelated social problems, Olan urged his congregation to become more involved in projects having a genuine impact on those issues. Speaking vigorously on the racial issue proclaiming the moral integrity of the court's landmark decision, Olan said:

> "Segregation is immoral. It is immoral to say to any person, regardless of the color of his skin or the church of his faith, that he cannot sit where I sit, eat at my table, study in the same school as my children, apply for the job of work as I do. The question is not whether segregation shall continue but whether we shall voluntarily do what is right or be forced by experiences painful and damaging."[84]

Olan continually challenged the leadership of Dallas in regard to bringing about greater racial equality, integration, and social justice. He considered the innocent suffering of those people whose skins were black, or because they were born into poverty, to be "social sin." Olan attacked these evils and denounced school segregation through the continuation of radio sermons initiated by his predecessor, as well as from the pulpit and his activities in Dallas' civic affairs. He pointed to the agenda set out in the "Goals for Dallas," claiming that religion had failed the city and its community, ministering to the private needs of certain individuals and neglecting the injustices, the suffering, and the misery of many citizens.[85] Olan could not envision the city being turned over to the secularists who organized life without God. He continually questioned the meaning of human rights granted from his Creator to pursue life, liberty, and happiness.

> "If because of his color or creed he cannot live where others do even though he can pay for it, be responsible for the upkeep, and respect the property, then he is denied a right which is his by nature because he is human. The same may be said for the right to eat where other men freely go, or to work where one is as qualified as others. No man or group of men have the moral right to deny a man an equal chance with all other men. It is a violation of the spirit of our Founding Fathers and it is blasphemy against God. No one has the right to slander another person, to injure him, to deprive him of every opportunity to fulfill himself as a creature endowed by God with freedom to be a man."[86]

Because of his active support of black political goals, Olan suffered through bomb threats, hate mail, and eggs being thrown at Temple Emanu-El and his home.[87] He was joined by other prominent Jewish business leaders in persuading the Dallas community to react calmly when school desegregation began in 1961.[88] When questioned about the community's response to his preaching about the aforementioned issues, Olan recounted two types of responses to these sermons. "Two different responses began to arrive. One was vituperative and told me to go back where I came from. The other was not supportive of my position but tolerant and asked for a copy of the sermon."[89] These responses apparently suggested to Olan that there were individuals in Dallas and the state of Texas who were ready to consider a more progressive point of view regarding race relations. Any considerable resistance to civil rights demonstrations and rioting was mitigated by the influx of northern immigration to the state, increased sophistication of the Texas economy, and stronger ties to the national and global economies.[90] Although Dallas was not a model of racial equality, with the encouragement of business and religious leaders urging the acceptance of racial integration, civil disturbance and potential rioting was not a realistic option.

Dallas became the center of the universe on the fateful Friday of November 22, 1963. On that day massive crowds, including this writer, gathered to welcome the arrival of the President of the United States and his wife. While an enthusiastic throng gave the allegedly "too-liberal-for-Dallas president" an energetic welcome, some of the wealthy elite, surely a minority, charged Kennedy with treason.[91] To the extent that Memphis would not be accountable for the murder of Martin Luther King, Jr., nor Los Angeles for the killing of Robert F. Kennedy, Dallas was blamed for the assassination of President Kennedy and characterized as the "hate capital of the nation."[92] Called upon by the press to make a statement later that day, Olan said:

> "The tragedy of the assassination of the president of the United States has saddened the world. We of Dallas feel a special sense of shame that it happened in our city. Our grief is deep, and our sense of guilt is inescapable. We ask God's care for his fam-

ily and divine forgiveness for our sins. May we now learn that hate destroys and turn to the life giving blessing of love?"[93]

In so far as the whole community was concerned, Olan believed the mood of the citizens of Dallas to be one of rationalizing and justifying their behavior rather than taking responsibility for their actions. The evolution of American society, especially in the south, was taking place, gradually displacing previous behaviors and breaking down social barriers. Olan went on to "discuss the frustration and anxiety felt by many citizens who wanted to stop the rapidly progressing (social) revolution (of the 1960s) taking place in the country where the old values of religion, family, and society were in radical transition, thereby creating an ethical dilemma for the community."[94]

On November 22, 1964, the first anniversary of the death of President Kennedy, Olan addressed the community through his radio sermon appropriately titled "The First Anniversary of a Tragedy." Even though such a horrible event impacted our city, the nation, and the world, maybe some lessons may be learned. Perhaps foremost, Olan said, is the dramatic confrontation with the fact that death is an ever present reality for each of us. He reminded us that death is not only inevitable; it can come without advance notice at any moment. "It was, perhaps, the recognition of this somber reality which created the custom of the Synagogue Jew to affirm God's presence when he retired at night with the understanding that he may not awake in the morning. When he did arise, he thanked God for another day."[95] Kennedy's death is also a reminder of not only our own mortality, but also of the texture of our nation's life. In spite of the tragedy, the nation came together and found strength in the basic unity of the people, while at the same time catching a glimpse of the dangers of hate and bitterness to our existence.[96] During the year following the tragic death of Kennedy, Dallas was placed under a microscope and every blemish and action was available for the world to see. The citizens of Dallas could not hide their defects and "in a city where some of the largest churches and synagogues in the world are active, it was discovered that they were not concerned with slums, poverty, hatred, or ethical standards."[97] While the effort has been made to change the image, it is that city, "chosen by destiny for the tragic drama of our time," that must change to become a city of truth, goodness, and beauty.[98]

Olan fulfilled the role of "the conscience of the city" during the time when liberal voices preaching compassion and racial justice were depressingly scarce. When questioned about his individual contribution to the City of Dallas, Olan responded that he believed his role was to confront the city leaders, as well as his congregation, with the moral demands of the critical issues of his time — poverty, racism, education, and war — so that reason and faith could create the good society.[99] He continually called for many changes in the living conditions of people, while positing the view that there is something wrong with great wealth and great poverty living in the same area.

As he was in Worcester, Olan was an active communal leader serving as a member and on the boards of numerous city, state, and national organizations devoted to the expansion and improvement of the community. He was appointed to the Board of Regents of the University of Texas by Governor John Connally in 1963, making him the second Jewish regent from Dallas and the second rabbi; the first was Rabbi Maurice Faber of Tyler, who served in 1915 and 1916. As a regent, he was part of a Committee of 75 that conducted an intensive study of the university's policies resulting in the board of regent's decision in 1963 to desegregate the undergraduate division of the University of Texas. Olan also took it upon himself to urge the Board of Regents to emphasize that the purpose of a university education should be to humanize and cultivate the human being rather than preparing him or her to make a living by becoming an engineer, doctor, or something else.[100] During the same period, Olan was a member of the Advisory Committee of 50 at Southern Methodist University in Dallas, where he was a visiting lecturer and an almost daily visitor at his "hideaway" for study — a secluded area in Bridwell Library at SMU's Perkins School of Theology. In effect, Olan was the "conscience of clergy in Dallas" and instrumental in a regular gathering or circle of religious thinkers held at the Bridwell Library.[101] He was also feted in 1963 by SMU for his 60th birthday when many of his friends presented a valuable collection of rare books on the Judeo-Christian tradition to the Perkins School of Theology in his honor.[102]

In addition to the above honors, Rabbi Olan was actively involved as a board member or active participant in the following organizations:[103]

- Circle Ten Council of the Boy Scouts of America;
- Dallas Council of World Affairs;
- Dallas Housing Authority;
- Human Relations Commission;
- Area Educational Television Foundation;
- Dallas Symphony Orchestra Board;
- National Rehabilitation Association, Texas Chapter;
- Dallas Civic Music Association;
- Greater Dallas Community Relations Commission;
- Advisory Board of the Texas Psychiatric Foundation (1956);
- Dallas Girl Scout Council, Inc.;
- Honorary Advisory Committee of the Dallas County Committee for United Nations Week (October 24-30, 1955);
- Advisory Committee of the Dallas Pilot Institute for the Deaf;
- Ann Dalton Foundation;
- Dallas United Nations Association;
- Advisory Group of "The Association for Graduate Education and Research" (TAGER) in North Texas;
- Goals for Dallas;
- Southwest Intergroup Relations Council;
- Texas Philosophical Association;
- The John F. Kennedy Citizens Memorial Committee;
- Texas State Committee of the Sam Rayburn Foundation.

On the national stage, Olan was an active member and significant contributor in the American Reform Movement and the Central Conference of American Rabbis (CCAR). He delivered his first address, "Liberal Judaism in a Reactionary World," to the CCAR at its annual convention in 1942, and over the ensuing years presented numerous papers and monographs for CCAR publication. These included "On the Nature of Man" (1942); "An Introduction to a Philosophy of History" (1954); "Judaism and Modern Theology" (1956); "Mordecai Kaplan's Influence upon Reform Judaism" (1956); "Some Directions for Reform Judaism" (1958); New Resources for a Liberal Faith" (1962); "Freedom and Responsibility" (1965); and "Reform Judaism in a Post-Modern World" (1981). Olan was instrumental in establishing a Special Interest Group in Jewish Theology, which he chaired from 1961 to 1965. He also served on the executive board (1946-1948 and 1969-1971) and was elected vice president (1965-1967) and then president of the CCAR (1967-1968). In addition, Olan delivered the commencement address — "Judaism, A Religion of Realistic Hope for Man" — at the Hebrew Union College — Jewish Institute of Religion in 1953 and the presidential addresses to the Central Conference of American Rabbis annual conventions in 1968 and 1969. He was also vice president of the World Union for Progressive Judaism (1967-1968).[104] His teachings influenced numerous friends and scholars, many of whom wrote essays reflected in *A Rational Faith, Essays in Honor of Levi A. Olan (1984)* published in Olan's honor and as a tribute to his significant contributions to the concepts and practice of Reform Judaism. On his own account, Olan authored *Judaism and Immortality* (1942 and 1971), *Prophetic Faith in a Secular Age* (1982), and a selected collection of his radio sermons in *Maturity in an Immature World* (1984).

Olan maintained strong relationships with prominent Texas and national political leaders throughout his career. Senator Lyndon B. Johnson appreciated Olan's support (July 6, 1960 letter from Johnson) for the disarmament provisions in the Department of State budget; and in a January 7, 1961 letter, Johnson indicated his pleasure in working with Olan on a particular "hospitalization problem." Vice President Johnson, as chairman of the President's Committee on Equal Employment Opportunity, invited Olan via letter of October 22, 1963, to participate in a one day conference sponsored by the Committee in Los Angeles. Olan declined by letter of October 28, 1963 due to a burdensome schedule. Olan was also later invited by President Johnson to participate in the White House Conference on International Cooperation, also declined, via letter of November 10, 1965 to the President, due to scheduling conflicts. Olan was an active participant serving on The Sam Rayburn Foundation (with other prominent Texans to support the museum and home of Rayburn) with Chairman Lloyd M. Bentsen, Jr., future Congressman and Senator from the State of Texas. Moreover and possibly most notable, Olan maintained a lengthy relationship with Robert S. Strauss, a former board member and past president (1969-1971) of Temple Emanu-El. Strauss' career lead him to the chairmanship of the Democratic National Committee and ambassador to Russia.

Conclusion

In Olan's repertoire for presenting his religious and philosophic opinions and observations, the sermon, above all other commitments of his rabbinate, had first claim upon his time and strength. It is the first in order of priority, he said, because its aim is to win a response to the demands of the highest order.[105] In order to accomplish this, and like any great speaker, one must understand the composition of the audience while addressing the problems of those in attendance.[106] Olan believed the sermon should be a motivating factor for the mind, providing confidence and hope, while awakening ones moral feelings. "In essence, the sermon is a motivational tool, by which the preacher must make something happen to a listener."[107]

From the beginning, Olan's sermons centered on the injustices and the related sufferings of our society, suggesting it was God's law of justice and love which was needed to restore sanity and decency to the lives of the community. The trustees of the Hebrew Union College, believing religion to be a private matter rather than public, attempted to dissuade

Olan, and others, from preaching on the issues of social injustice and economic exploitation, explaining these issues to be practical matters that were better left to practical men. "The practice or request to keep the clergy away from secular public policy has not always been embraced by the clergy. Indeed, on many occasions, rabbis, acting as rabbis, have been particularly vocal about their involvement in areas considered to be the purview of *shtadlanim*" (medieval representatives of Jews in Germany), federations and defense organizations."[108] And for Olan, his traditional Jewish background, in conjunction with the bloody atrocities in Russia and his sensitivity of social injustices in America, cemented his prophetic belief that religion was essentially the recognition of God in life, both private and public, and man's responsibility to perform God's work. "Religion," he said, "is an awareness of the presence of a spiritual reality, or a faith in the being of God."[109]

While the sermon may have had first claim upon his time and strength, one cannot overlook the responsibilities placed on Olan by synagogue leadership and congregational members. Like the modern rabbi whose time is absorbed with the conduct of public worship, regular preaching, pastoral ministrations, and serving the community as an intermediary between the Jewish community and society-at-large,[110] Olan's congregational responsibilities also included education, administration, philanthropy, community, and interfaith relations. Included in these responsibilities are numerous life cycle events, an infinite number of staff meetings, board meetings, committee meetings, fund raising, public speaking, and teaching. Needless to say, his success at Worcester and Dallas was a collaborative effort between himself and synagogue leadership. Alluding to the growth of larger synagogues with more varied functions and activities not previously existing, the words of Arthur Hertzberg pointedly describe the increasing role of the rabbi during Olan's generation: "The obdurate fact remains that he is busy as institutional executive, and that his immediate constituents are justifiably demanding that he should not neglect his specific duties."[111]

As a religious liberal and prominent activist for American Reform Judaism, Olan repeatedly sought for the underlying causes of the injustices in the world while searching for their solutions. With an inquiring mind, and the desire to right the wrongs of society, he was dissatisfied with simple answers to the difficult questions of life. Although he was small in physical stature, Olan had a very strong and dynamic ego. He was blessed with tremendous physical and intellectual vitality and had a playful sparkle in his eye and a keen sense of humor, evidenced by his letter to Rabbi George Zepin: "For good or for ill, I am headed to the oil wells of Texas. Whether I can make those wells speak Hebrew is the big problem."[112] Olan appeared to enjoy saying the unpredictable by expressing his sentiments and beliefs in an elegant and concise manner. His voice resonated with authority and, once heard, it was never forgotten. He was called a "resident sage, an observer and commentator on life and letters"[113] as he continually alerted the community to the moral and ethical complexities of modern life.

As did his predecessor Rabbi David Lefkowitz, who had become a major presence in the Dallas community,[114] Levi Olan had a profound effect on the continuing evolution of Dallas into a religiously pluralistic city and its ongoing efforts in resolving issues of social justice and equality. Dallas continued its growth into a modern metropolitan area and, with Olan's influence along with the combined efforts of other prominent Jewish and non-Jewish civic and religious leaders, the Jews of Dallas were accepted by a society dominated overwhelmingly by Baptists and other Protestant denominations.

When asked how he would like to be remembered, Olan said: "I don't think I live my life by standards of what I will be remembered by. I live my life because I have to meet the issues of the day as well as I can as decently as I can. What will be remembered of me, if I were to pick something to put on my tombstone: 'He was the conscience of the city.'"[115] During his pulpit career in Dallas, he was not only rabbi to Temple Emanu-El, but in many ways the religious leader of the community, a connotation aptly described by his successor, Rabbi Gerald J. Klein:

> "What momentous and traumatic events have occurred during his Dallas Years! Whether it was the 1954 desegregation decision of the United States Supreme Court, the Vietnam War,

the assassination in Dallas of John F, Kennedy, it was Rabbi Olan that the people of Dallas turned for insight, analysis, and guidance. To this day (1977) the question 'What does Rabbi Olan think?' is an important and natural one."[116]

After retiring from Temple Emanu-El in 1970, Olan was invited to London for a year of teaching at the prestigious Leo Baeck College.[117] Upon his return to Dallas and Temple Emanu-El, he officiated at events or spoke only at the invitation of his successors, Rabbis Gerald J. Klein and Jack Bemporad.

Stanley Marcus (1905-2002), a Dallas resident, prominent civic leader, and longtime executive of luxury retailer Neiman-Marcus group, referred to Olan as "an ecumenical man;" and, in a letter to the editor of the Dallas Morning News, Adolphus Cummings (1917-2009), a retired Mobil Oil Corp. executive, quoted his Baptist minister who referred to Olan as 'best preacher in Dallas.'"[118] Throughout his productive life, Olan used his sermons to provide a window into the mind of the rabbi and the life of the community.[119] Sidney Regner, his lifelong friend, perhaps put it more succinctly in his memorial tribute to Olan: "preaching and teaching constituted for him the essential function of the rabbi and it was as preacher and teacher that he left his mark on his congregation and community."[120] Rabbi Levi A. Olan died in 1984, at the age of 81, and his wife, Sarita, died in 1989. Rabbi Olan's three children, Elizabeth Hirsch, David Olan, and Frances Olan, reside in Dallas, New York City, and Boston, respectively.

Bar Mitzvah of Levi Olan (circa 1916)

CHAPTER 2

Reform Judaism

Introduction

While it is not the intention of this writer to review the immense body of work encompassing the philosophies of German Reform and the development of twentieth century Reform Judaism in America, it is important to discuss the related historical events of the nineteenth and twentieth centuries before moving to the religious and social issues addressed by Olan in succeeding chapters. This entails a brief examination of the social, political, and religious environments in communities in which the Jews lived at the time when discontent with existing traditional Judaism began to appear. The following short historical sketch of the foundational concepts of the early reformers provides a sufficient background for comprehending American Reform Judaism in general, and "Classical" Reform Judaism in particular, the official version of Reform during the bulk of Olan's career.

German Reform

The ideology of Reform Judaism is grounded in the idealistic philosophy promulgated by George Wilhelm Friedrich Hegel (1770-1831), whose thinking dominated German philosophy in the first part of the nineteenth century.¹ "The key to his doctrine lies in the term *evolution*, whereby all existence is an integral part of a single unity or whole — the objective or Absolute Mind — which is itself in a perpetual flux and in a continuous process of unfolding, resulting from an inner drive to achieve self-realization…Human history, ethics, laws, religion, and social institutions are simply aspects of this process of development."[2] Furthermore, most "Jewish Hegelian thinkers of the nineteenth century believed, in one way or another, that Judaism differed from Christianity (and paganism) in that it preserved the discreteness of God from nature and, what amounts to the same thing, of the power of reason and moral freedom in the world."[3] Additionally, though their views differed in emphasis or detail, early scholarly leaders (Abraham Geiger, David Einhorn, and Kaufmann Kohler), and later teachers of the Reform rabbinate (David Neumark, Samuel Cohon, Henry Slonimsky, and Samuel Atlas) all spoke out of a German rational idealism.[4] It was this rationalism, Borowitz continues, "that validated liberal Judaism. Without it, there can be no right to reform."[5] The early reformers laid the foundation for what amounts to a liberalism whose significant aspects were freedom, reason, rationalism, and progress, all of which are addressed in subsequent chapters. This means that the historical process of development is an ongoing one and any generation, based on its environment and concept of understanding, could deviate from past traditions and embark on a new period of modification and creativity.

The motivation for changes in traditional (pre-reform) Jewish practice was partly encouraged by the Jewish community's response to political and social developments in Germany during the first half of the 1800s. It was during this period when the Jews of Germany slowly gained political emancipation and the status of civil equality. With the rise of German nationalism and the advancement of the German state and culture, Reform Jewish leaders were anxious for full acceptance within German society and sought to reduce the national and ethnic elements of Judaism and other characteristics separating the Jew from the non-Jew.[6] In search of alternatives to an established Jewish religious tradition, Reform Jewish leaders looked to Protestant churches, seeking to imitate their decorum: the hymns and prayers in the vernacular; the organ music and choir; and the sermons on universal moral themes.[7] They were concerned with creed and theology, the significance of ornate ritual and ceremonialism, and the extent of emphasis on the Bible, with the right of the individual to interpret Scripture according to his own conscious.[8]

Another factor instrumental in early Reform involved the nineteenth-century movement premised on modern critical intellectual and scientific studies expressed by the Science of Judaism (*Judische Wissenschaft*). This was a new emphasis on Jewish literature and culture leading to the emergence of German Jewish scholars who began to apply critical methods to the study and understanding of many areas of Jewish history. Through historical analysis, the scholars of the *Wissenschaft*, believing they found the "core" or "essence" of Judaism, separated those elements deemed insignificant from the historic traditions that safely could be reformed or dropped. The lessons of history benefitted religious leaders in determining which fundamentals of Jewish tradition were essential, therefore to be preserved, and which were nonessential and subject to removal. "By pointing to general and specific precedents from earlier ages, it could both hold in check arbitrary reforms motivated by assimilatory pressures and lessen resistance to more carefully considered innovations...showing that variety and change were characteristic of Jewish tradition assumed the highest priority for the Reformers."[9]

Freedom was an underlying proposition for the early reformers. In contrast with the historical Jewish tradition, the reformers were resistant, in a literal sense, to a fixed theology. They focused on the universalistic ethical teachings of biblical prophets, reinforcing the prophetic ideals of justice, freedom, and peace. This resulted in systematic changes affecting certain customs and ceremonies and, in the eyes of the reformers reflected a more advanced religious community that explained Jewish history as the history of "ethical monotheism." "They found the heart of the religion of the Jew," Olan said, "in ethical monotheism wherein God is free of all limitations of nature, and in which man derives his freedom from God in order to pursue the highest good."[10] And since other religions in Germany were considered to be monotheistic and ethical religions, this position was a polemic against those saying the Jews were different.

> "This basic teaching of a wholly free God, who is worshipped by a morally free human being, was for the early philosophers of Reform Judaism, the uniqueness of their faith. It was revealed to Israel, the Prophets, in the Scriptures, and is the peculiar treasure of the modern Jew. It endows the Jew with a mission to reveal this faith to the world and it establishes the essential cause for his survival as a people."[11]

As oppressive political and civil strife slowly developed in Germany during the late 1800s and early 1900s, Jews began to experience social regression and severe restrictions on equality previously granted. With considerably reduced opportunity many Germans, both Jews and non-Jews, chose to immigrate to the United States which offered political freedom and asylum, as well as economic opportunity.

American Reform

While the Jewish reformers had to struggle in Europe to achieve official recognition against deep-rooted traditionalist establishments, there was no preexistent Judaism in America, and the immigrants, as a freer and diverse community, had significant flexibility in determining their secular and religious relationships. The favorable political climate, along with a corresponding development in Christianity, made possible a redirection of religious energies toward improving inequities and addressing suffering in American society.[12] This allowed the immigrants the capacity to modify the actions of the German and European liberal reformers who failed to develop programs of social justice, which became a significant feature of American reform in the early 1900s[13] and continues to present times.

As evolution was an essential element for the reformers, the foundational period of Jewish reform involved fundamental changes in the domain of philosophy that challenged Jewish beliefs. "Reform Judaism in its intellectual character was distinguished from all previous movements of its kind by the fact that it recognized the evolutionary aspect of the tradition and was thus free to accept or reject the new winds of doctrine."[14] Viewed as revelation, this evolutionary aspect was ongoing and always open, coming in a variety of forms revealed throughout history.[15] This represented a "progressive revelation," influenced by Hegelian philosophy, claiming that as time passes people inevitably achieve a higher perception of truth than those before them. With this interpretation, succeeding generations attain higher levels of knowledge and understanding than previous generations, and therefore have the ability and authority to reform the teachings of the past and the historical imperative. "From this perspective, the later is always better."[16] Orthodoxy,[17] on the opposite side of the spectrum, maintains an opposing view of revelation and identifies the revelation at Sinai as the "apogee of revealed truth;" the more chronologically close a religious authority is to Sinai, the greater the authority.[18] With this viewpoint all authority ultimately goes back to God and Sinai. Between the Reform and Orthodox views, Conservative Judaism embraced the idea of "continuous revelation," in which the revelation of the divine will continues through the community of Israel.[19] This implies that the Jewish people are responsible in each generation for the development of Judaism taking the essential elements of the Sinai revelation and adapting them to the needs of the current generation.

In their eagerness for fresh or innovative religious practices and the emancipation of Judaism from their perception of numerous binding restrictions and regulations, leaders of the Reform Movement tended to move toward what was effectively the subordinated observance of Jewish law to moral or spiritual considerations. *Halachah* (the law) and *halakhic* authority were reinterpreted and reformulated by the reformers to be no longer binding or authoritative. In discarding old practices and creating new ones, they used *halachah* as guidance rather than governance. Actions of the reformers were designed to bring Judaism into harmony with modernity along with encouraging increased Jewish assimilation into American secular society. Their desire to complement Judaism with modernity obviated numerous aspects of Jewish law and traditions, inviting "nothing less than a version of Judaism compatible with full integration into American society."[20] In his presidential message to the 80th annual convention of the CCAR, Olan stated that "Reform Judaism dared to free the tradition from the ephemeral and recreate it for a living people."[21] The need to abandon any semblance of fixed formulae and an invariable creed was integral to the philosophy of the early reformers. This was an evolutionary way of thinking and an attempt by religiously minded Jews to meet the intellectual challenge of the new freedom of the mind. In Olan's view, it saved many Jews from complete irreligion by establishing a faith founded on reason and subject to study by the methods of science.[22] This view was shared by most members of the Reform rabbinate, including Olan's prominent contemporary Roland Gittelsohn: "To me, science and reason provide the most useful strainers I know for the necessary removal of that which was essential to Judaism at an earlier stage of its development but which may now need to be removed or at least refined if our faith is to be kept viable for the future."[23]

American Reform had been moving away from traditional Jewish belief and practice since the end of the American Civil War, and some of its leading rabbis had declared liberation from Orthodox dogma at a conference held in Philadelphia as early as 1869.[24] But a "clear and decisive commitment" to the classical position occurred later in 1885 with the adoption of the significant Pittsburgh Platform whose principals were generally accepted as the foundation of American Reform Judaism for more than fifty years.[25] The Pittsburgh assembly adopting these principles consisted of nineteen rabbis with Kaufmann Kohler, who wrote "the first systematic work on Jewish theology in English,"[26] presiding as their religious conscience. This period in the history of Reform Judaism later became known as "classical" Reform, in order to distinguish it from those seeking to support more traditional Judaism.[27] This was a Classical Reform theology that, in Kohler's view, included ethical monotheism, the Jewish mission, and the ultimate development of religious universalism.[28] Kohler's philosophy, especially in the areas of religious and social ethics, truth and justice, and progressive intellectualism, as reflected in the Pittsburgh Platform, influenced much of Olan's views of religious liberalism, social justice, and the nature of man's responsibility to society.

Many of the religious debates during the early years of American Reform Judaism, and also thereafter, took place within the newly formed Central Conference of American Rabbis, whose annual conventions comprise the framework for differing rabbinic opinions. In his desire to forge an "American Judaism," Dr. Isaac Mayer Wise (1819-1900), also a prominent religious scholar in the development of American Reform Judaism, presented the following message to the first convention of the Conference in Cleveland in 1890:

> "We are furthermore agreed, I trust, that this spirit of Judaism, made intelligible to us in its literary monuments and its historical revelations, is the essence of universal religion, the future religion of mankind…With this Conference we enter upon a new phase of American Judaism as the free messenger of God to a free people, a kingdom of priests to anoint a holy nation."[29]

The Pittsburgh Platform of 1885 and the subsequent Columbus Platform of 1937 represented the fundamental ideological pronouncements and guiding principles of American Reform Judaism during Olan's active years in the pulpit. Consequently, a brief summary of their principles is in order for the reader to grasp not only the primary objectives of the Reform Movement, but also the foundation of Olan's philosophical and religious beliefs during his tenure in the rabbinate. These statements of principle, along with the 1976 Centenary Perspective and 1999 Pittsburgh Principles, both of which were subsequent to Olan's pulpit years, shared a common purpose:

> "They all aspired to make their case for a Judaism that acknowledged the necessity and desirability of religious innovation, change in praxis, and ideological reformation. The changes in American Reform Judaism over the past 175 years are embedded within the various statements and manifestos that have sought to express the essence of Reform."[30]

Fundamentally, each successive platform in American Reform Judaism represents a religious philosophy that affirms a continuing process of change, innovation, and transformation, not as fixed dogma but as a guide for the progressive elements of American Reform Jewry. Statements and principles included in one platform and reversed or modified in another serve to present the developing nature and changing religious requirements of the Reform Movement. Principles of the Pittsburgh Platform of 1885 and Columbus Platform of 1937, each of which comprises several sections, are discussed in the following paragraphs.

The Pittsburgh Platform

The Pittsburgh Platform of 1885, under which Olan trained while at the HUC and during the first eight years of his rabbinate, "literally served as a watershed in the history of Reform Judaism in the United States. No statement or platform — before or since — can challenge its preeminent role as the metaphoric midwife in the process that brought about Jewish denominationalism in the United States."[31] Fundamentally, the document contained only a statement of "broad principles of ideology that spoke too many of the congregants in Reform synagogues and appealed to their interests and prejudices."[32] The Platform was an attempt to clarify the position of the Reform Movement on basic issues that would distinguish Reform Judaism from other expressions of Judaism. Isaac Mayer Wise called it a "Declaration of Independence" in which the Reform Movement became a distinct and separate movement within American Judaism.[33] The Platform consisted of eight principles and are described in the following paragraphs.[34]

The first principle states the superior religious belief, recognizing other religions but insisting "Judaism presents the highest conception of the God-idea as taught in our Holy Scriptures," a God-idea that remains as the "central religious truth for the human race."

The second principle declared that the Bible is not a literal record of the revelation at Sinai but rather characterized it as "the record of the consecration of the Jewish people to its mission as priest of the one God" and as "the most potent instrument of religious and moral instruction." In addition, although the Bible reflects "the primitive ideas of its own age," "modern discoveries of scientific researches in the domains of nature and history are not antagonistic to the doctrines of Judaism."

The third and fourth principles, possibly partially written with the Trefa Banquet[35] in mind, clarified the Reform position to "accept as binding only the moral laws and maintain only such ceremonies as elevate and sanctify our lives, but reject all such as are not adapted to the views and habits of modern civilization." Furthermore, and as it concerns religious practice, laws regulating "diet, priestly purity, and dress," were "altogether foreign to our present mental and spiritual state," declaring their observance "in our day is apt rather to obstruct than to further modern spiritual elevation."[36]

The fifth principle, perhaps the most famous of the Platform's principles, interpreted "the modern era of universal heart and intellect" as a sign of "the approach of the realization of Israel's great Messianic hope for the establishment of the kingdom of truth, justice, and peace among all men." This principle, in its attempt to eliminate distinctiveness and nationhood from peoplehood, continued with a statement that the movement would later partly retract, declaring "we consider ourselves no longer a nation, but a religious community, and therefore expect neither a return to Palestine, nor a sacrificial worship under the administration of the sons of Aaron, nor the restoration of any of the laws concerning the Jewish state." This antinationalist expression, the reason why early American Reform Jews did not support the Zionist Movement or the foundation of the State of Israel, remained the official position of the Reform Movement for the following four decades.

The sixth principle continued with the same emphasis on religion over peoplehood as Judaism is defined as a "progressive religion, ever striving to be in accord with the postulates of reason…in the establishment of the reign of truth and righteousness among men," while expressing "the utmost necessity of preserving the historical identity with our great past." Judaism is allied with "the spirit of broad humanity of our age," extending the "hand of fellowship" to "daughter religions of Judaism," Christianity and Islam, and "to all who cooperate with us in the establishment of the reign of truth and righteousness among men."

The seventh principle affirms Judaism's belief in the immortality of the soul while rejecting the ideas of bodily resurrection, and heaven and hell as abodes for everlasting reward and punishment. And the Platform's final principle, and perhaps the fundamental core of Olan's religious philosophy, linked Judaism with the demands for social justice: "the great task of modern times, to solve on the basis of justice and righteousness the problems presented by the contrasts and evils of the present organization of society."[37] The rabbis reasoned that moral conduct and social justice, rather than faith, laws, and ritual practices, formed the essence of their Judaism, and they reflected their beliefs in the manner in which they preached, taught, and wrote.[38] Olan stressed this great task of modern times and this pronouncement represented the firm foundation upon which modern Reform Judaism built a social justice program crucial to the identity of the Reform Movement as a permanent feature of its religious life.

The Pittsburgh Platform represented a "Classical" Reform Judaism that clearly intended to minimize the role of symbol and ritual.[39] "Classical" Reform was distinguished in part from other early twentieth century Jewish religious movements by, among other things: men and women sitting together in mixed pews; bareheaded men without prayer shawls; organ music accompanied by a mixed choir that included women and sometimes non-Jews; prayer books, containing only minimal amounts of Hebrew, opening from left to right, rather than right to left as do traditional Hebrew prayer books; and the majority of the service in English.[40] Even on the Sabbath, when traditional Jews do not light fire, cigarette and cigar smoke permeated the halls of the synagogue and food served at many congregational functions did not follow Jewish dietary laws.[41] And finally, the height of assimilation was reached by numerous congregations when Shabbat, the major service of the week, was not held on Saturday morning, as among the more traditional Jews, but on Friday night, or less commonly on Sunday mornings in order to accommodate worshippers who worked on Saturday.⁴²

The Pittsburgh Platform provided the American Reform Movement a greater comprehension of its own distinctiveness as it began to distinguish itself more clearly from East European traditionalism and emerging American Conservatism. Reform Judaism came to represent the particular religious affiliation of American Jews of German descent for the first, second, and third generation immigrants. In its move to what some might refer to as extremism and "testing the outer limits of Jewish identity,"⁴³ Reform leaders had to explain how and why Reform differed from more traditional Judaism and from Unitarian Christianity. The rabbis debated numerous religious issues as well as addressing such hot topics as science, evolution, social justice, and ethics. The rabbis taught and preached not on Judaism alone, but also biblical criticism, science and technology, as well as the ethical and moral aspects of social justice which was considered more significant than certain rituals and practices.

But the Pittsburgh Platform incited some degree of protest among particular religious leaders. The platform was criticized for its negative stand as it was perceived as neither an affirmative nor a constructive approach to doctrine or practice. Simply stated, it was a statement of beliefs rather than action. Those religious leaders seeking a more traditional Judaism of Europe and Germany, or those adopting the conservative approach, formed their own movements resulting in the establishment of the Orthodox Union in 1898 and the Jewish Theological Seminary in New York in 1887. In addition, further criticism came from the New York Society for Ethical Culture, an evolving movement focused on establishing universalistic social justice reforms. The Society's founder was Felix Adler, the son of Rabbi Samuel Adler who occupied the pulpit of the prestigious Reform Temple Emanuel in New York. From the late 1800s to the early years of the twentieth century, Felix Adler publically abandoned Judaism in favor of what he called Ethical Culture. Renouncing belief in a theistic God and in the particularities of the Jewish religion, he promoted instead a universalistic faith focused on ethics and the teachings of world religions.⁴⁴ The society was open to people of various religious heritages and those who held diverse convictions concerning matters theological and philosophical. And as Olan pointed out, this would include not only Jews, Christians, and Muslims, but everyone, together with theists, atheists, agnostics, materialists, and idealists.[45] Though Adler received much attention, he spoke for only a minute segment of American Jews. The society, unable to achieve enduring success, never became a popular movement. In 1945 it counted about 2,500 members in the U.S., scattered among six chapters in the larger cities.[46] Yet it must be noted that Adler was instrumental in encouraging social reform in public education, decent housing for workers, abolition of child labor, improving the status of the Negro, and assistance to refugees. In this regard, Olan viewed Adler as a "modern precursor of the social justice program of Reform Judaism and the social gospel of the Christian Church."[47]

Between World Wars

With the conclusion of World War I, the United States, preoccupied with the alleged dangers of foreign influence, turned from international responsibility to narrow self-interest and virtually closed its doors to immigrants.[48] This resulted in conflicted feelings within the American Jewish community as many non-Jewish Americans feared the atmosphere of cultural immigration. "Nativism, xenophobia, racism, anti-Catholicism, and anti-Semitism — all characterized the 'tribal twenties.'"[49] The economic depression in the United States, the rise of Hitler in Germany, and the initial stages of World War II occupied peoples' thoughts and minds during the decade of the 1930s. Yet, there was much to be joyful about even though American Jews had some cause for apprehension. The Jewish children of pre-war immigrants benefited from new opportunities in higher education and from the economic effects of wartime prosperity and postwar investment. Many American Jews became part of the broad middle class, living in new and better neighborhoods that reflected their improved economic conditions.

Assimilation into western society resulted in American Jews having to confront critical choices: one in the nature and extent of their participation in the majority society; and another in the nature and extent of their engagement in an individual Jewish religious life as well as community life. During the past two centuries these choices altered the character of modern Jewish existence that includes many, if not all, of the following features:[50]

- "The undeniable desire to enter or integrate into a larger society;
- Enduring insecurities and anxieties about Jewish acceptance, occasioned by and stimulating continued social separation, and necessitating organized collective action in defense of Jewish rights, interests, and culture;
- Rebellion against segregationist pre-modern features of Jewish life and culture, with accompanying rejection of religious rituals perceived as fostering exclusivity or precluding Gentile acceptance;
- Innovation in religious and cultural life to bring both in line with prevailing norms;
- Protection among the various religious and secular ideological camps from their adversaries;
- And, individual freedoms to choose among the various Jewish ideologies offered by modern tradition."

As evidenced by the aforementioned critical choices required of assimilated American Jews, their liberal, political, and social situation during the interwar years of the twentieth century gave rise to various contradictions within the very essence of Jewish life and Judaism. Culturally and spiritually, American Jews had access to a variety of Jewish religious movements that included Orthodoxy, Conservatism, and Reform, all of which were striving to find, or were believed to have found, their places in American Jewish religious life. The three Jewish religious movements of the interwar years represented a contrast between multiple extremes. On the one hand, many in the Orthodox community were representative of those groups that were sealed off from much of the world, refusing, to a great extent, to come to terms with the reality of modernity, and who continued to demand significant influence over the private and public life of the individual Jew. At the other extreme, Reform, and currently other liberal Jewish groups, willingly and consciously gave up much of the earlier Jewish religious tradition of former German and East European Jews as they pursued assimilation within the larger secular community. In between the two extremes, the Conservative Movement sought a limited reform of traditional Judaism within the framework of Jewish law.

As the optimism of the twentieth century began to decline as a result of World War I, the rise of Nazism, and the impending economic depression of 1929, the Central Conference of American Rabbis were called upon to issue a new set of "Guiding Principles of Reform Judaism." This document, approved in 1937, became known as the Columbus Platform, and, with the increased influence of those previously involved with earlier Eastern European and German reforms, dedicated Reform Judaism to a greater emphasis on Jewish observances, social justice, and limited support of Zionism.

The Columbus Platform

The 1937 Guiding Principles of Reform Judaism, whose principal architect was Samuel S. Cohon (1888-1959), the leading reform theologian at that time, was approved in Columbus, Ohio and represented a comprehensive religious transformation of Reform Judaism when compared to the earlier Pittsburgh Platform. This was the "first 'platform' officially framed and adopted by the CCAR."[51] These principles were the official version of Reform during the greater portion of Olan's rabbinate, and this new document, unlike Pittsburgh which emphasized ideological beliefs rather than action, reintroduced the question of ritual practice stating emphatically that Reform Judaism demands more from its adherents than loyalty to a creed or set of beliefs. It is a "comprehensive but concise liberal interpretation of religious Judaism"[52] that required a more affirmative approach toward traditional observance and practice than the Pittsburgh declaration. This involvement included participation in synagogue attendance and Jewish communal affairs; the transmission of Jewish knowledge through improved education; the use of Hebrew prayer in the home and the synagogue; the celebration of Jewish festivals and holidays; and the retention and development of Jewish customs, symbols and ceremonies possessing inspirational values.[53] While the Classical Reform of the earlier Pittsburgh Platform emphasized that Judaism was a religion and not peoplehood, the new Columbus document frequently referred to the "Jewish people," as if to stress that Judaism embraced both ethnicity and faith,[54] rather than "faith versus people."[55]

Two of the largest sections of the 1937 Columbus Platform were devoted to "religious practice" and "Israel." It called for faithful participation in the life of the Jewish community as it finds expression in home, synagogue and school. It stressed "Judaism as a way of life" that, "in addition to moral and spiritual demands," required "the preservation of the Sabbath, festivals, and Holy Days, the retention and development of such customs, symbols and ceremonies as possess inspirational value, the cultivation of distinctive forms of religious art and music, and the use of Hebrew, together with the vernacular, in worship and instruction."[56] In contrast with the earlier Pittsburgh Platform, the Columbus statement called for a rehabilitation of Palestine and affirmed the obligation of all Jewry to assist in the "up building" of a Jewish homeland not only as a refuge for the oppressed "but also a center of Jewish culture and spiritual life."[57] In the areas of ethics and religion, the Columbus Platform recognized Judaism as the blending of religion and morality into one concrete unit: "Seeking God means to strive after holiness, righteousness and goodness;" emphasizing "the kinship of the human race, the sanctity and worth of human life and personality and the right of the individual to freedom and to the pursuit of his chosen vocation."[58]

Additional provisions in the Columbus Platform declared Judaism as a historical religious experience of the Jewish people with a universal message aimed at the union and perfection of mankind under the sovereignty of God. It affirmed Reform Judaism's principle of progressive development in religion as a continuous process and consciously applied this principle to spiritual as well as to cultural and social life. The platform continued to affirm the doctrine of the One, living God, asserting man's creation in the Divine image, endowed with moral freedom and charged with the responsibility of overcoming evil and striving after ideal ends.

In connection with the Reform Movement's continued quest for assimilation, and in conjunction with recognition of its responsibility to the community, the Columbus statement included a social justice program that reflected the great depression of the 1930s and the rise of strong labor unions. The task of social justice was significantly broadened: "Judaism seeks the attainment of a just society by the application of its teachings to the economic order, to industry and commerce, and to national and international affairs...elimination of man-made misery and suffering, of poverty and degradation, of tyranny and slavery, of social inequality and prejudice, of ill-will and strife. It advocated the promotion of harmonious relations between warring classes on the basis of equity and justice, and the creation of conditions under which human personality may flourish...and the safeguarding of childhood against exploitation. It champions the cause of all who work and their right to an adequate standard of living, as prior to the rights of property. Judaism emphasizes the duty of charity, and strives for a social order which will protect men against the material disabilities of old age, sickness and unemployment."[59]

It is interesting to note that both the Pittsburgh and Columbus formulation of guiding principles for Reform Judaism affirmed the theistic nature of Judaism in their declaration of the centrality of God. The earlier statement acknowledged that every religion "attempts to grasp the infinite One" while affirming "that Judaism represents the highest conception of the God-idea as taught in our Holy Scriptures," maintaining "this God-idea as the central religious truth for the human race." The Columbus account focused on "the heart of Judaism and its chief contribution to religion" being "the doctrine of the One, living God, who rules the world through law and love."

Post World Wars

Following World War II, America experienced a renaissance of religious activity. This period included a rapidly changing intellectual and spiritual environment, and an urgent need for change occurred. In his comprehensive *A Religious History of the American People*, Sydney E. Ahlstrom presents the post war years through the 1960s as a time when "new scientific views forced adjustments of older conceptions of the natural world. A new profoundly altered social system brought changes in moral values that robbed old habitudes of their comfort."[60] "Against this background of rapid change American religious communities of nearly every type were favored during the postwar decade and a half by an increase of commitment and a remarkable popular desire for institutional participation. This popular resurgence of piety was a major subject of discussion in newspapers, popular magazines, and learned journals."[61]

This was a Jewish religious renewal that was encouraged by a favorable atmosphere that existed in America following the end of the war. Even though the theological ramifications of the Holocaust were hardly discussed until the Six-Day War, Jewish awareness was raised, creating a sense of American Jewry's special responsibility to maintain Jewish survival while focusing on the recapture of traditional Jewish values and practices. The efforts to establish the state of Israel aroused significant interest on the part of previous unconcerned individuals, but who now identified actively and contributed to the financial needs to settle the refugees. After the Jewish state had become a reality, Holocaust awareness and Israeli consciousness flourished while membership in Zionist organizations dropped. This was also the time for the growth of religious institutions, which had been fighting a losing battle against the influence of the community federations during the 1950s. It was the synagogue, not the federation or community organization that now began to represent Judaism for the Jews. Reform congregations, like other Jewish religious movements, moved to the suburbs, composed predominantly by unaffiliated second and third generation American Jews largely unaware of the long history of the Reform movement.[62] In effect, "the new expansion was transforming Reform Judaism from a movement dominated by second- and third-generation Reform Jews into a body composed mainly of new adherents whose parents or grandparents were Orthodox or who had at least grown up in observant homes."[63] This post-World War II generation witnessed American Reform Judaism's greatest expansion in numbers and in programming. Well over 1,000 synagogues and temples were built or rebuilt through the mid-1960s, and there was a dramatic expansion of Jewish education with a corresponding increase in Jewish religious school enrollment.[64] This Jewish revival was also fueled by an increase in adult Jewish learning, including Bible study, and the publications of new editions of Bible translations.

> "It saw new theological ferment within its ranks, unprecedented social activism, a yet fuller appreciation of tradition, and the first appearance of women in positions of spiritual leadership. But there were also some years of nagging self-doubt…Beset by unrelenting forces that sapped its vitality and threatened to rip it apart, Reform Judaism passed into the late seventies seeking to throw off its malaise, heal internal division, and regain its earlier confidence."[65]

The Reform movement, especially as expressed in the Pittsburgh and Columbus Platforms, was a liberal attempt to adjust Judaism to the surrounding culture. As the neo-Orthodox (modernistic faction of German Orthodoxy aimed at creating a correlation of traditional orthodoxy and modern German culture[66]) set out to adjust the philosophic and religious changes of the times to the Jewish tradition, the Conservative Movement, with a strong desire to conserve the historical religious tradition as faithfully as possible, aimed at answering the needs of those Jews who were not at home in either neo-Orthodoxy or Reform and who could not disregard current scientific thought and intellectual achievements.[67] In a general sense, each group chose one of the three-fold elements of Judaism for major emphasis. Reform gave priority to God, Conservatism to the community of Israel, and Orthodoxy to Torah. Although subject to potential questions, the implication was that Reform Jews were concerned primarily with the theological issues raised by modern culture; Orthodoxy devoted itself to the preservation of rites and practices in the face of secular demands; while Conservative Judaism placed Israel, peoplehood, at the center.[68] The Reformers attempted to meet the challenges of the nineteenth and twentieth centuries by giving the Jews in their new world an honest formula for addressing the demands of modernity. Olan linked the basic liberal function of Reform Judaism to keeping alive and fresh the experience of the people in their struggle with destiny. "The liberal spirit seeks to keep clear the relationship of form to essence, while at the same time to give man's new experience an opportunity to extend the faith of the fathers. Reform Judaism is part of this liberal tradition,"[69] a tradition steeped in freedom, rationalism, and reason.

Before concluding, it should be noted that "American Reform has in recent decades restored some of the traditional observances and doctrines previously abandoned. It is worth noting that many of the ideas and practices that were violently opposed as being against tradition a century and a half ago, or less, have been introduced in congregations purporting to be traditional. These are simply the vagaries of time."[70] In the late twentieth and early twenty-first centuries many of the ideological and theological differences between early Reform and Conservative Judaism had been mitigated. As a result, the most recent 1999 Pittsburgh platform has been labelled "Conservative lite,"[71] a move by the Reform Movement that originally began with the Columbus Platform. In contrast, Dr. Byron Sherwin also points to the Conservative Movement's shift in many ways toward Reform.[72] Although other examples can be provided, the most obvious is the acceptance of women rabbis and cantors within the Conservative Movement.

Rabbi Levi A. Olan

In conclusion, the vision of the German and European reformers was the genesis for what became the distinctive characteristic of the American Reform Movement. This was thought to be a healthy liberalism seeking the best of all truths rather than a set of beliefs or a fixed theology of an established orthodoxy wholeheartedly attached to tradition. As demonstrated in the following chapter, Levi Olan professed this religious liberal inclination which continued to be prominent among Reform Jews throughout the postwar generation through the 1950s, 1960s, and 1970s.

CHAPTER 3

An Untired Liberal

Introduction

While the Pittsburgh and Columbus Platforms were the Reform Movement's liberal effort to modify Judaism to the surrounding environment, the term "liberalism" does not necessarily lend itself to a meaning that is satisfactory to everyone. It has been explained as: a belief in tolerance and gradual reform in moral, religious, or political matters; highlighting an individualism that rejects authority while defending personal freedoms; an economic theory favoring free competition and minimal governmental regulation; and designating a theological program that emphasizes intellectual freedom and the moral content of a specific religious movement over traditional theological doctrines.[1] The common theme in this explanation represents some sort of freedom or liberation from bondage and servitude, a connotation that characterized Olan's over all view of liberalism. "Where one man serves another against his will, he is not free and must be helped toward liberation."[2] This would include: political bondage, where man is a slave to Pharaohs and Czars, and to the likes of Hitler and Stalin; economic slavery where man is in bondage to old-fashioned aristocrats or oppressive employers, as well as mental and religious bondage where one is bound to inflexible rituals and traditions.[3] Programs written into the law covering social security, health care, job opportunities, and other governmental social programs may be viewed as a secular liberalism that favors authority, but these specific welfare programs and benefits target a particular social reform or political platform, none of which were strangers in Olan's liberal discourses.

In his 1949 essay, "Rethinking the Liberal Faith," Olan presented explanations of "liberalism" from both adversaries and friendly critics. Referring to the lifelong opposition to religious liberalism of John Henry Cardinal Newman (1801-1890) in his *Apologia,* Olan wrote that liberalism (in the critical view of Cardinal Newman) was meant as an "anti-dogmatic principle and its development;" while a more conflicting explanation revealed liberalism as "negativeness and vagueness," supporting the charge by some scholars that it is inadequate for the bitter realities of life.[4] Additionally, Olan presents the term liberalism as described by Professor Edwin A. Burtt of Cornell, an admitted liberal philosophic thinker, as a "rupture with established orthodoxy. It gives no positive clue to the novel conditions by which the orthodox position is modified or replaced."[5] But Olan provided what might have been his most acceptable formulation, insisting "that liberalism is a method, not a creed ("denying its followers the warm comfort and security of a dogmatic faith"[6]); that liberals are unified by their approach to truth, not by their conclusions."[7] This latter interpretation places significance on the journey, thereby allowing the liberal the possibility of arriving at multiple options.

Prophetic Reformation

Although religious liberalism was a dominant theme of the Jews arising from the European Enlightenment of the eighteenth century, in the history of the development of the religion of Israel its origin can be traced as far back as the prophets. As the moral conscience of ancient Israel, the Hebrew prophets called for the elimination of social ills and oppression, and as the founders of ethical monotheism their prophetic proclamations were a "progressive step" in religious evolution that fueled "the Prophetic Reformation."[8] This reformation, in Olan's view, represented a prophetic liberalism that challenged acceptable standards of biblical society.

> "Look for a moment at the period of Hebrew history when the prophets appeared. They were real liberals who came to free their people from all sorts of bondage. They brought new truths about God, about man, about justice, about mercy and love. They challenged the institutions of the priests, of the kings, of the owning slaveholders. There was a fresh breath of life in the prophetic movement."[9]

Olan believed the prophets were "severe critics of the orthodoxies of their day; the Pharisees were the champions of freedom from fixed and unchangeable dogma…and the Reformers of the nineteenth century broke sharply from the established institutions of their time."[10]

Religious Liberalism

Like the prophets of the Hebrew Bible and the scholars of the Enlightenment, the significance of liberalism shaped Olan's philosophy, not only religiously, but also secularly, and the propensity to discuss this issue was demonstrated by his comment in a 1970 essay: "A review of my writings and lectures during the almost half century in which they occurred discloses the intriguing statistic that my most common title was 'The Faith of an Untired Liberal.'"[11]

For Olan, the principles of liberalism were incomplete without a theistic foundation, and he is remembered as an eloquent champion of "religious liberalism,"[12] a liberalism that was a recurrent theme in his commentaries and monographs, Sunday morning radio sermons, addresses, and lectures to the Central Conference of American Rabbis. Two of his noteworthy addresses, "Liberal Judaism in a Reactionary World (From the Point of View of Philosophy)" (reprinted in *Reform Judaism, a Historical Perspective*, 1973, edited by Joseph L. Blau) and "New Resources for a Liberal Faith" (reprinted in *Contemporary Reform Jewish Thought*, 1968, edited by Bernard Martin), were presented to the Fifty-third and Seventy-third annual conventions of the Central Conference of American Rabbis in 1942 and 1962, respectively. Additional essays and monographs, with emphasis on religious liberalism and conveyed in numerous venues, included "Rethinking the Liberal Faith" (1949), "The Faith of an Untired Liberal" (1949), "An Unrepentant Liberal Jew" (undated), "The Attack on Reason" (1954), "Theological Foundations for Guiding Principles for Reform Judaism" (undated), "A Theology of Jewish Liberation" (1978), "Jewish Liberation Theology" (undated but 1976 or later), "The New Liberalism — An Interpretation of the Scientific Revolution" (undated), "Liberal Religion Faces the Post-Liberal World" (undated), and "Reform Judaism in a Post-Modern World" (1981).

It was common for Olan's liberal writings and sermons to be infused with politics, capitalism and industry, and social justice issues. He cautioned members of the Reform Movement against the inclination to resist change as he continually sought to revamp and reaffirm core liberal values that he believed essential to both Reform Judaism and the general community. For this liberal rabbi religious ideas had to be fashioned in harmony with current knowledge and living conditions, along with being receptive to scientific development and reason rather than bound to a doctrine and tradition believed no longer reasonable or relevant to the times. "Being a Liberal movement we must be open to all insights into the nature of life and the universe no matter where they come from," calling for liberal Jews to examine all of the existing varieties of theological doctrines in seeking the ultimate truth.[13]

In his 1942 presentation at the fifty-third annual convention of the CCAR, Olan suggested four general characteristics as a possible basis for definition and formulation of principles for a philosophy of liberal religion. First was the affirmation of faith in the competency of human intelligence — the theory of knowledge formed out of reason and experience. "Liberalism was born out of the discovery that one could progressively know more and more of God and the universe."[14] Secondly, the epistemology of liberalism must be "eclectic,"[15] coming from the best of various sources. "Knowledge about the ultimate nature and character of the spiritual must be sought in mind, in experience and in nature."[16]

Theism comprises the third characteristic as Olan advocated that "liberal religion is meaningless without an affirmation of the validity of the objective reality that is God."[17] Although the nature of God cannot be definitely defined, characteristic differences are subject to further research and analysis. "Lastly, the ethical beliefs both personal and social should be established on the first three principles. Religious ethics as distinguished from humanitarian ideals must rest upon the reality of basic laws in the universe. These are to be sought by all the methods at man's disposal and should be held eternally possible of discovery."[18]

Olan stressed that the above principles are not proposed as new dogmas for liberal religion, but are, at best, suggested minimal standards for giving shape to a liberal movement. These principles provide the general character of liberal thinking as an intellectual approach, "an attitude of mind,"[19] favoring self-determination and intellect instead of an authoritative body. With this approach, liberalism seeks "to liberate man from all that enslaves him, whether in mind or in society" and "comes nearer to being a philosophy whose distinction is its rejection of a closed system of thought fenced in by fixed, unchanging dogma."[20] This meant that well-founded reason, experience, freedom, individualism, and progress were applicable to any claim of liberals seeking absolute truth. All truths, Olan added, secular and religious, and all institutions, political, social or ecclesiastical, are subject to critical examination.[21] Fundamentally, in Olan's view, unchanging dogma and liberalism were contradictory to each other, identifying dogma with authority and intelligence with liberalism.

From the standpoint of authority, in his 1949 essay entitled "Rethinking the Liberal Faith," liberalism was understood as the freedom to accept or reject authority on the basis of reason and experience.[22] Olan provided two approaches to the matter of authority.[23] In one group, there is the literal interpretation by the traditionalists who accept the Torah as divinely revealed. Authority, therefore, is supernatural and leads to ideas and practices that can be neither discarded nor changed. The second group looks upon the custom as the record of the community's experience with God in history, written by men who preserved it and interpreted it for their own times. Reading it with the critical approach, this second group takes the liberty of selecting the essential and discarding the rest. The traditionalists are champions of the first approach and the liberals adhere to the second. By one's own designation, a liberal subjects his mind to the bewildering spectacle of a rapidly changing scene.[24]

The intellectual approach, or "attitude of the mind," reflected Olan's conception of the core tenets of liberalism: freedom, reason, and progress. "The major components of liberalism have been fairly stated. Its theory of knowledge is based upon a broad foundation of reason and experience; its theory of values centers about the concept of freedom and the infinite worth of the individual; its view of nature is basically optimistic and full of promise. Upon these pillars the liberal built his structure for a better life."[25] Fundamentally, the liberal desired to free man from repressive forces — political, economic, mental, and spiritual. In this regard life was recognized as a process involving intellectual freedom, intelligence (reason and experience), and progress, all subject to change while affirming man's motivation to achieve his own ideals.

Intellectual Freedom

As a fundamental tenet of liberal Judaism, Olan's assertion of intellectual freedom was the foundation for understanding man's ability and desire to improve their lives. "The idea of freedom, the benevolent conception of man's nature, and the faith in progress were not novel to Judaism. Indeed, these pillars of the liberal faith were part of Jewish thought long before they received formulation at the hands of moderns."[26] The unique concept of individual freedom, allowing the individual to thrive through the economic, political, and religious opportunities available in American society, helped shape the pattern of American Jewish life, where, as a free society, everything is subject to conjecture or enquiry. For the liberal, freedom permits every doctrine, every philosophy or economic theory, every political or social idea to be subject to investigation, criticism, and the principles of logic and reason.[27] "Nothing is true merely because it appears in a book, was said by his forefathers, or is dictated by a state or a church."[28] "The commands of a king or the revelation of a Bible bear authority only as the free intelligence of man accepts them...Religious liberals are free to question the truth of all the contents of the Bible. They are not beyond challenge merely because they are found in the Bible...The validity even of the highest authority must be examined. Indeed, man is free only to the extent that he employs his rational faculties in evaluating the experiences of nature and life."[29]

Prior to the scientific revolution, it was believed that nature, fate, or God determined the outcome of events or conditions. Man's freedom was limited either by natural law or by divine power. But the scientific revolution extended man's freedom to a situation wherein he must choose the means for arriving at desired results. Man is basically an evaluating being, Olan said, whose nature enables him to do what no other object in the universe can achieve. His freedom lies in his ability to select from alternative possible goals and alternative possible means. Where there are no alternatives, there is no freedom, contrary to the pre-modern view that gave man no choice in the selection of goals.[30] If man is not free to choose his goals and cannot direct his energies toward them, then he cannot be blamed when nothing is done about solving his problems. He is free today to change not only nature, but himself, and he faces the responsibility to utilize his freedom for the good of society.[31]

Reason

The progress of life has been enhanced through forces brought about by the development of abundant scientific programs resulting in man's ability to control his destiny. Olan explains this as the ability to control one's destiny beginning with the movement departing from "a state of unconsciously nurtured fantasy to one of consciously forced reason."[32] Humanity is related to the animal kingdom, but has evolved from it and has emerged with the unique capacity to create culture rather than be its creature. He is endowed with ability for conceptual thought to accomplish his predetermined goals. Olan believed that a sensible attitude challenges modern man to do with human nature what he has already done with physical nature. Man can actively begin to organize the principles governing the discovery and discharge of his potentialities. In this regard, "man responds to the world with a limited amount of instinct and high degree of observation, reflection, and learning from experience. It is his capacity to reason which permits him to learn the ways of nature, to adjust to them, and to use them to meet his needs. His senses give him an encounter with nature, his reason enables him to interpret what he discovers."[33]

Philosophically, reason is understood as the ability to think logically as the basis for obtaining knowledge, as distinct from experience and emotions. The writings of the medieval Jewish philosophers were instrumental in promoting the importance of reason. Maimonides and Gersonides gave reason preeminence and the universality of reason validated the later departure from traditional Jewish faith.[34] For Olan, reason was an intellectual formula that enabled man to "penetrate from appearances to reality, where it is found that the real is rational and the rational real."[35] Liberalism affirmed reason based on faith, and its theory of knowledge is formed primarily out of reason and experience.[36] However, for Olan, religious beliefs could not be justified solely by experience, for he believed in the rational aspects of human nature and by upholding reason as liberalism's standard for truth and faith. "Reasonable faith" he said, "demands rational answers to…basic questions of religious life."[37]

Believing that Judaism had always upheld the authority of reason in formulating religious beliefs, Olan claimed that reason gained broader acceptance as a theological standard in the modern world because of its universality. Modern science and thinking has shown that human beings have the power and intelligence to reason, and a religion that upheld reasonable truths would prosper in the modern world. "The scientific method became authoritative in man's understanding of nature, and reason the guide to knowledge of man and morals."[38]

Human beings, Olan said, are "endowed by nature or by God with a faculty to test all evidence for its rationality. Since reason was common to all men, it was seen as the uniting element in mankind which would lead to human brotherhood. Reason became the instrument man must use continually in his search after larger truths, acknowledging always that the truth he now declares is not an absolute."[39] A religion based on reason was consistent with the intellectual climate of modernity, and for Judaism, reason made it receptive to innovation and new scientific discoveries. "Impulse and desire play an important role in conduct, but they do not provide the principle of organization. Only reason can provide that, and important a tool as it is, it is the only tool we have to guide us. To reject it is to wander in a hopeless jungle."[40]

To be sure reason can be deceiving, for what may be valid for one person may not be true for another. However, Olan rejected discarding the use of reason, turning everything over to the 'grace of God,' for how is one certain that it will not be the devil instead of God who will take over?[41] It is incumbent upon man to maintain a positive attitude regarding the state of his intellect. "The picture of man as a cringing creature, afraid of his intelligence, and appealing for some irrational salvation, can lead only to some form of authoritarianism, whether to the left or to the right...A mind which forfeits the right to analyze and criticize, to test by fact and by reason will soon fill itself with new devils when the old ones are cast out."[42] Reason, from time to time, may lead us to imprudent decisions and behavior, "but anything else as a guide is confusion compounded by chaos."[43] Olan believed that the major theological trends revealed the need for a more popular and effective exposition of the basic Jewish faith, as much of the new theology revealed a 'failure of nerve' and a break away from rationalism to irrationalism and vagueness. He affirmed his faith in reason, as follows:

> "The time is propitious for Judaism to affirm its faith in reason as a divine instrument, in God who is near and far but concerned with man's daily struggle, in the possibilities of good in human nature, and the reality of God's kingdom in historic time. The theological insights of Judaism have a unique and a positive relevancy for our time."[44]

Progress

Another essential principle of liberalism concerns the nature of man and his value as an individual. The optimism of the liberal gives him the capacity to grow, develop, and determine his future and destiny. Darwin's theory of evolution provided evidence for the belief that progress is an essential ingredient of life. This idea of progress is integral to the whole liberal tradition, for society's progress is tied to advancements in scientific development, the creation of new instruments to satisfy the material needs of the community, the introduction of more democratic political systems, and the general increase in popular movements. "New discoveries in the fields of philosophy and science played havoc with the established dogmas of religion, politics, economics, psychology, and indeed every aspect of man's conscience and unconscious existence."[45]

> "The whole trend of the nineteenth century up to the First World War gave incontrovertible testimony to the idea of ceaseless progress along all lines. The final conquest of evil was an article of every liberal faith. Poverty, war, bigotry, indeed, all the ills which once were looked upon as the visitations of an irrational force, was now on the road to being mastered. Social movements, cooperating with scientific achievement, held before man the early attainment of the complete good life on this earth. God was definitely in His heaven, and if all was not well on earth, it soon would be."[46]

Nineteenth and twentieth century immigrant reformers were very much at home in the new world. Their optimistic outlook of the condition of man corresponded with the Jewish doctrine that the person has freedom to choose between good and evil. "Progress was founded on the faith that man has the capacity to move freely from the evil to the good until the great day in the end of time. The philosophy of Reform Judaism was hopeful, suffused with a glowing confidence that fulfillment was at hand. It not only supported the democratic patterns of the period, it staked its whole future on the early achievement of that pattern."[47]

"If there is one thesis upon which all liberals agree, it is in the definition of history as a process. What we are today is the consequence of what men did yesterday."[48] Liberals have an appreciation for democratic pluralism, and, like history, they accept the principle of change and view life as a process. "Nothing is sacred merely because it has been: conversely, nothing is better merely because it is new. All institutions and all customs are subject to re-evaluation and change. A liberal is not afraid of change, although he avoids change for its own sake."[49] Liberals, in contrast with orthodoxy, are continually in an eternal search for new truths, for new evidence, and for new discoveries. In essence, the liberal desired to free man from repressive forces — political, economic, mental, and spiritual. Life was accepted as a process subject to change while affirming man's motivation to achieve his own ideals.

Olan's belief in progress resulted from his optimistic view of nature. The unified status of body and mind, an essential quality which Judaism gave to man's nature, placed him in a unique status in relationship to other creatures and to God. This inborn feature provided human beings with the ability and freedom to reason with intelligence while improving their status of life.

> "Though related to all the other creatures of the earth, man possesses the unique gift of self-conscious reason which in its intellectual faculties, its creative and originative power, enables him to develop and make progress in arts, in sciences, and in civilization generally. It is this which gives him the power to rise superior to the impulse of the senses, and enables him to subdue and transform them. It is this unique human quality, the self-consciousness of reason that man finds the capacity to apprehend general principles, and to conceive of intellectual and moral ideals. It is this that gives him the power to pass beyond himself into a relationship of sympathy for his fell-men, and thus endows him with the faculty to distinguish between right and wrong. Indeed, this basic Jewish idea of man made in the image of God is the corner stone upon which rests man's moral destiny upon earth."[50]

Throughout his numerous commentaries and essays, Olan presented evidence of continuing progress in many fields of endeavor, including social and physical sciences, technology, medicine and birth control, nutrition, business and economics, and the arts. "New experiences and new discoveries become transformed in man, ever changing him into a new human being. We are not at the end of new discoveries and not, therefore, at the finish line of human development."[51]

Synopsis

The increasing development of intellectual and moral faculties over many generations allows society to control its own destiny to a greater extent than was previously possible. The contributions of science and technology have assisted human nature in a continuous process of change. "After all, man himself is the result of a mutation in the process of evolution. His introduction was a change."[52] This gives man the ability to intellectually define objectives and set goals for further achievements. "If we add some perspective to our view of the development of life, we are forced to the realization that man's control of destiny is just beginning and that the movement is from a state of 'unconsciously nurtured phantasy to one of consciously forced reason.'"[53] The evolution of man in the universe and the realization of his uniqueness formed the liberal foundation that radically altered his view of the universe and his place in it.[54]

Religious Liberalism Criticized

But somehow and somewhere, liberalism went wrong. Since the latter part of the nineteenth century, liberalism had been under attack and accustomed to continued assault by those opposed to social and religious changes. And in the early part of the twentieth century, the First World War, testing the strength of liberalism, shook the foundations of everyone's faith as the proponents of liberalism found disapproval from certain segments that defended the established order of society and religion before the war. The technological revolution and scientific advances introduced rapid changes in the conditions of life; greater wealth, larger cities, better methods of transportation and communication, improved medical procedures and facilities, and an enormous display of new conveniences. Instead of bringing paradise to many people, liberalism appeared to have led to a supreme crisis in history.

The transition in what appeared to be an "orderly and regular pattern" from yesterday's way of life to the way of life in the twentieth century left much to be desired. Society, Olan said, was "violently torn loose from the world we knew and set adrift in an alien place."[55] With change came crisis and uncertainty, and man sensed he was on the verge of despair. Society was in a revolutionary period, Olan said, not so much because of violence, but because of the loss of confidence in reasonable and rational man and in his ability to overcome the terror confronting him. Olan believed the liberals' faith in science, reason, man's perfectibility, freedom, and in progress ended with the barbarism of Hitler and the madness of Stalin and misguided enthusiasts of Communism. We were at the brink of despair as man stands paralyzed before the very weapon his mind fashioned.[56]

In the eyes of the critics, the fallacy of liberalism was embedded in the very structure of the liberal philosophy. The selection of goals, Olan explained, was largely based on yesterday's knowledge which soon became outdated. "When, and if, its ideal program is achieved, it is already obsolete because the evolution of the interrelations of man and culture has created a new situation. Liberalism needs the prophetic or poetic imagination to envision the organization of life that is potential in the environment and in men."[57] Philosophically, the categories by which the liberal tried to understand history, science and reason, were not suited to the experiences of the people. According to the opponents of liberalism, the liberals neglected the fact of man's limitations to his intellect and his imperfectability. Reason was confined to "unconscious wishes, to passions, to the 'vague, veiled chaos of the human soul.'"[58] In his discussion of Olan's "Judaism and Modern Theology," Ephraim Fischoff dissented from Olan's views regarding the acceptability of reason and rationalization of liberalism. "Already before the end of the Nineteenth Century and increasingly into the Twentieth, liberalism had to learn that it had been too optimistic in its conceptions of man's rationality and innate virtue. Hazardous indeed was the neglect of the non-rational factors in belief and conduct, a weakness of liberalism due in part to a defective psychology which regarded man's rationalistic potentialities alone as worthy of study."[59]

Another critic of Olan's liberalism was Karl Barth (1886-1968), a prominent twentieth century Christian theologian and vigorous opponent of theological liberalism and modernism. According to Barth, religious liberalism was idolatrous, subordinating God's word to human beliefs. He alleged that liberals had produced a compromised, apologetic theology which had lost its power to redeem. "God and man, revelation and reason, faith and religion, theology and philosophy are *qualitatively* distinct and ought to be kept apart."[60]

Many opponents of liberalism believed the liberals failed to consider deeper implications of freedom that society revealed. "Too often," Olan explained, "in the house of liberalism, freedom was divorced from duty, and denied the check of reason. Freedom too often was characterized by indifference and known chiefly for its independence from the basic factors of mind and nature. Liberals failed to grasp the limitations of freedom."[61] This resulted in an economic individualism in which the desire for more became a primary objective with liberals. Freedom's limitations, Olan continued, are imposed by reason, by society and by the environment in which man resides. He affirmed the belief that "freedom is still the foundation for all concepts of morality, in that it is opposed to chance or random choice. The basic need to choose the good has not been removed, in fact, it needs reemphasis. Liberals will do justice to their faith by bringing the idea up to date."[62] Olan warned the liberal Jew to use his freedom reverently and cautiously, selecting, discarding, and innovating only when he is convinced that he will not weaken the foundation upon which the covenant and the people stand.[63] This entails a more severe demand of one's own integrity and represents the basis of authority since its practice is the result of a voluntary commitment.

The liberal Jew must impose upon himself those disciplines which will preserve, keep alive, and give life to the people, its covenant, and its mission.[64] In addition to Ephraim Fischoff and Karl Barth, numerous other critics of the liberalism of American Reform Judaism appeared outside the liberal camp. For purposes of brevity the comments of two additional critics are included in the following paragraphs.

Two Jewish critics of liberalism and contemporaries of Olan were Arnold Jacob Wolf (1924-2008), prominent American Reform rabbi and teacher, and Olan's *Talmud* study partner, Rabbi William Braude (Chapter 1). Although both wrote and taught extensively, one essay in particular of each rabbi accompanies those of Olan's in two separate textual venues. In one collection, Joseph L. Blau, recognizing Braude's views compared to Olan, wrote: "It is hard to conceive of two more different approaches than those presented by Levi A. Olan and William G. Braude to the question of the road ahead for Liberal Judaism in a world grown increasingly reactionary."[65] This was a concern raised before the CCAR Fifty-Third Annual Convention in 1942. Essays by both Olan and Braude appeared before that convention and published in the 1942 CCAR Yearbook. Although both essays were titled "Liberal Judaism in a Reactionary World," Olan's was from the point of view of philosophy while Braude focused on the point of view of history. Olan began his essay by introducing the French philosopher and mathematician Descartes (1596-1650) as "the first modern philosopher to affirm without equivocation the supremacy of reason" and the basis for rationalism.[66] Throughout his essay, Olan critiques the reactionary forces of anti-liberalism and anti-intellectualism in contradistinction with the basic principles of liberal thought — human intelligence, intellectual freedom, and progress. The timing of these essays is noteworthy as the events surrounding Hitler's success in Germany and America's entrance into World War II contrasted totalitarianism with the liberalism best characterized by the overthrow of authoritarianism.

While Olan's paper deals with concepts of religious liberalism, Braude's paper was concerned with religious beliefs.[67] Advocating a traditional Judaism and representing only a small minority in the Reform rabbinate,[68] Braude declared Olan's liberalism to have been proven bankrupt by the recent events of the First World War and the weaknesses and internal developments in liberal Judaism.[69] Braude denounced the spiritual emptiness of Liberal Judaism and noted the failure of Jewish nationalism to fill the spiritual void.[70] We have stopped believing, he said, and Liberal Judaism became a burden without a meaning. "In a world where cruelty is recrudescent and men's regard for truth has declined, in a world shaken in its optimism, dubious of progress, suddenly aware that the Messiah will not be ushered in through pulpit oratory, in brief, in a reactionary world, what of Liberal Judaism?"[71] The concluding paragraphs of Braude's essay paints the liberals as having paid "lip service to the permanent values of Judaism," and outgoing preoccupation having destroyed the "art of contemplative study."[72] He called for a resumption of sacramental study, a new learning centering on holiness, while refocusing on the more traditional Jewish practices and customs.

In a second collection, Bernard Martin positioned Wolf's essay, "On God and Theology," and one presented by Olan, "New Resources for a Liberal Faith," in *Contemporary Reform Jewish Thought*, a collection of essays edited by him and published in cooperation with the CCAR. At the end of his essay, Martin contrasted Wolf's pessimism with Olan's optimism. While Olan affirmed human rationality and reason, he was aware of their limitations and dangers, but there was no substitute for reason, even though reason may lead to error.[73] Wolf, on the other hand, declared that "reason tests and systematically discloses false assumptions. God's truths are the hidden and the unreachable. Man longs for light, but God remains nonetheless impenetrable dark."[74] Wolf confirmed his opposition to reason, and what might be termed unwarranted faith in man's control of human nature, by arguing that rationality presented far more dangers than irrationality. "It is not certain that more atrocities have been committed in the name of unreason than in the name of reason. If I understand the greatest atrocities -the concentration camp and the atomic bomb — they were very rational. Perhaps one could even say that evil is scientific. Or, to put it in a slightly different way, there is no escape from the problem of evil, neither with reason nor with unreason."[75] Wolf's pessimism and his rebuff of reason and trust in human nature was demonstrated by his own admission. "I am told that I elucidate a dooming theology. But I understand the meaning of death to include more than the threat of extinction for my personality. I understand it to signify the extinction of my idea system, the utter transiency of my reason, and the utter doom of everything I create…If you read the great scientists, the great artists, you find a mood of doom hanging over everything they write."[76] Although Wolf was critical of those claiming to trust in the core tenets of liberal Judaism, Olan's optimism and reliance on reason and faith in progress were not singled out by him.

In Defense of Liberalism

The forces which had rocked the entire liberal world had not left Judaism untouched. The real menace, Olan pronounced, was the new school which employed the language of the modern intellectual disciplines that called in evidence the failure of the liberal world to achieve its goals.

> "It is the philosophy of Rosenzweig and Buber that truly disturbs the self-confidence of Reform Jewish thinkers. The introduction of the 'existential' philosophy into the modern Jewish scene has profound implications…Reform Judaism must therefore reexamine its basic principles: its theory of knowledge, its concept of human freedom and the nature of man, its messianic theory of progress. There have been great contributions from science, psychology, and philosophy which make the nineteenth century formulation inadequate."[77]

Olan cautioned against the substitution of ecclesiastical authority for reason, and he believed the rise of irrational schools of thought in philosophy was disconcerting to liberals as social theory coated in a nineteenth century shell would contribute nothing to the future.

Although no specific evidence was found in which Olan directly addressed the various detractors, he wanted to neutralize those programs antagonistic to liberal religion by calling for a reexamination and rethinking of the whole liberal position. "The chief failure of liberalism" he said, "is that it tended to congeal into unchangeable formula… it closed its doors to truths that came through other sources."[78] In referring to those groups antagonistic to the liberal tradition, he contended that by placing narrow limits on the use of reason and experience, and confining themselves solely to the traditions of the past, they ceased to accept their own basic faith. He continued to criticize groups centered on anti-intellectual and anti-rational messages. The essence of Jewish epistemology, Olan insisted, rests upon the continued use of the intellect. The basis of this belief stems from divine revelation along with natural theology. "The religious truth contained in Scripture is understood as emanating from God, but it cannot be in direct contradiction to the human intellect which is itself of divine origin."[79]

Believing the main structure of liberalism was still sound, Olan called for the urgent need to bring it up to date.

> "There is a great need for a revival of the liberal faith, for emphasis upon reason, experience, freedom, individualism and progress. Whether mankind sinks into another era of mental and spiritual darkness or rises again into light depends in great measure upon the liberals. They must stop reshuffling the doctrines of their predecessors and with confidence continue the search for truth not yet fully revealed. The essence of liberalism is the search."[80]

Olan called for a new liberalism, informed by scientific advances and an awareness of the fantastic growth of knowledge. "The real tragedy of modern man is that he does not use what he knows to resolve his seemingly unresolvable problems and to enhance the joy and fruitfulness of his life. Liberals today are encapsulated in the shell of the nineteenth century, unaware that new goals, undreamed before, are now possible. Man is now free not only to devise means to achieve ends set for him by God or nature, he is at liberty to choose his objectives and direct his course."[81] With the exception of death, Olan believed that no human problem can be designated as inherently ineligible for solution by scientific thought and reason. Unlike previous generations, this was a period in which man had at his disposal the opportunities and the means to attain his fondest dreams. The new scientific revolution provided the means for man to achieve his goals, and he is at liberty to select what he wants as he develops the tools to attain them. Man's future is unlimited if he uses his intelligence to experiment with programs based on new knowledge. The proposals for a new Liberalism, Olan said, must go beyond anything then existing. They must call for the kind of social planning which dares to exploit not only what we already know but what we are rapidly learning about the cosmos and about the nature of man. "The task of a new Liberalism is to rise above its own small and momentary world and to move with imagination into the vision of the shining hour now made possible. This calls for a reshaping of the educational curriculum so that students may get a chance to sense the real potential for the future. The new Liberal will go beyond the resolution of the immediate causes of war, hate, poverty, and disease. He will confront our age with the radical potential for a new hope for man as man."[82] Like Judaism, liberalism is a faith that articulates realistic hope when rooted in basic assertions.[83]

For Olan, the liberal faith was more valid than ever before in human history. The belief in human improvement is supported by organized intelligence reinforced by a new understanding of science, nature, and man. "The smashing of the atom has shattered forever the materialistic interpretation of the universe. The old dualism of matter and force must give way to a unitary principle. They now constitute different forms of energy revealing the universe as an organism, not a machine."[84]

In connection with their concern for the future of Liberal Judaism, the program committee of the CCAR posed the question: "What does this mean for the Liberal Jews?" The heart of Olan's methodology rested on the universalistic tradition of liberal thought. He saw the various antagonistic forms of reaction as belated attempts to restore a medieval authoritarianism, destructive of the freedom of the human mind and spirit. He regarded the future of Liberal Judaism as inherently bound to the future of liberalism in general. Consequently he advocated a continuing pressure on the "fighting faith" of liberalism as the best guarantee of a future for Liberal Judaism.[85] "The need is for liberals who will not grow tired in the search, who will be fearless and courageous in the march, and who will resist the pull of the Garden of Eden and the flesh-pots of Egypt. The hour calls for men who can hear and follow the voice of God as He proclaims, 'Tell the children of Israel that they go forward.'"[86]

The fact is, of course, that we cannot really go back, nor can we remain in the present moment of history longer than an instant. As human beings, we are obligated to courageously face the changing manifestation of humanity and challenges of life. A new theology was emerging in which religion was not only a matter of personal faith, but also involved in many other aspects of life within the secular community. In this connection, the next chapter demonstrates Olan's liberal religious and secular philosophy addressing life's challenges and the shifting winds of religious, civic, and political society.

CHAPTER 4

Religion and the Social Problem

Introduction

As an "Untired Liberal," Olan's rabbinic career spanned an innovative period in which many old and established institutions and customs were being fundamentally challenged. We are well aware that change is the very essence of life, and as previous chapters have demonstrated strict compliance and observance of religious traditions of previous generations were being significantly modified. The developing theology which was rapidly taking its preferential place was a "liberation theology" that replaced the "traditional messianic promise" with secular programs of liberation.[1] This was a political and social liberation theology with an integrationist agenda that reduced the richness of Jewish religious tradition while the Jewish community assimilated into American society. Rather than emphasize religious formalism of the past, Olan placed significance on a religion of faith in the meaning of life and one's purpose in the universe, a process that should be hastened to bring religion in thought and practice into conformity with the truth revealed by modern science and philosophy. With this vision, he preached that religion encompassed more than a matter of personal faith; it had to be involved in other aspects of life, taking a stand on the side of justice and equality towards the correction of evils in the economic, political, and social lives of society.[2]

Olan presented the roles of religion in his "Religion and Social Crisis" radio address of March 24, 1968. In general, he said, religion plays two roles in society. Initially, religion performs a priestly function in its roles in worship, prayer, teaching, liturgy, and pastoral service in life cycle events. In these capacities religion functions as the spokesperson for the community during religious holidays and such sacred life-cycle events as birth, marriage, and death. "Man's search for peace of mind, his concern with death, and his need for a living God is ministered to by the theology of his faith."[3]

Moreover, Olan continued, religion in its prophetic role seeks God as the judge of one's actions in society and among nations. It was the Hebrew prophets who created the faith of Israel which proclaimed ethical monotheism to the world. They revealed that God's relation to man was one of moral demands to join Him in building a kingdom where "men shall beat their swords into plowshares...and none shall make them afraid."[4] The prophets rejected the demands of the majority who found comfort in a program of ritual and ceremony that was unrelated to the demands of justice.[5] Ritual practices became unimportant next to the ethical demands that God imposes on the people: the obligation of doing right, showing mercy, punishing evil, and doing justice. It was in this prophetic role that Olan called for the injustices of society to be interpreted from the perspective of God's concern for mankind, challenging the religious community from his pulpit to respond to God's demands.[6] This was not pious sentiment, but rather a dynamic social standard of moral living that denounced greed, selfishness, and social abuse in direct, clear, and understandable terms.[7] For religion to be successful in fulfilling its purpose, both priestly and prophetic roles had to be exercised with equal passion. These dual roles were explained by Olan as follows:

> "Man needs the experience of worship, the confrontation with God who becomes real. He needs help for his loneliness, his sufferings, his inevitable death. A church or a synagogue which

fails to help men find God has failed both men and God…The spokesman for religion must demand of men that they do justice and act mercifully. They must require sacrifices, sharing, and acts of love. They should disturb men's smugness; condemn their false piety and their unbearable self-righteousness. Their job is not only to bring peace and comfort. They must make men uncomfortable in an unjust world, uncomfortable enough to begin to do justice, to love mercy, and to walk humbly before God."[8]

But Olan's understanding of the priestly and prophetic functions of religion included all aspects of society in the pursuit of justice and equality. "No religion is worthy of its name which does not concern itself with the social, political, economic and international problems of its time; likewise no religion can be acceptable which does not give men and women a philosophy of life for unsteady and uncertain times."[9] These were the dominant themes during Olan's rabbinate, and the concern of religion, he stressed, was not with the nation but with the person individually and with mankind as a whole. The dominion of religion encompasses the world of human needs and, therefore has no boundaries as it extends beyond race and creed.[10]

The theological idea pervading the Hebrew Bible, as interpreted by Olan and most Jewish theologians, is that God is the Father and all of the people are God's children. This is to say that the prophetic faith conceived society as being one human family with God as the Father, and frequently alluded to as the Fatherhood of God and the Brotherhood of man. And we know that in our family environment, a father does not disregard the less gifted or laziest child, or refuse to care for those less blessed with other gifts. In fact, most fathers go out of their way to help the weaker or less fortunate child. But when we step out of the family environment, the attitude seems to change from one of family to one of contention or denunciation, concerned more with our own selfishness than the needs of less fortunate members of society. "Me-ism dominates our culture"[11] and society readily accepted as normal those actions that conflicted with the teachings of the prophets.

> "We feel little or no responsibility for other members of our family, for our brothers, if you will, who go hungry and naked. To believe in God means to care for, to share with, all other children of God what, for reasons unknown, has by grace been given to us. There is no escape for the religious man from the fact that 'I am my brother's keeper.'...To affirm God the Father and God the Creator is to bind oneself to all of His children in bonds of family loyalty and love."[12]

Furthermore, the first moral law revealed by religion reflects man as sacrosanct, being made in the image of God. As such, man and God are co-workers in the pursuit of justice in God's world. "Whatever disagreement there may be among us about the nature of God, there is unanimous acceptance of *kadosh hachaim* (the sacred being). From the opening chapter of the Bible to the latest word of any Jewish theologian, the one certainty is the belief that man, made in the image of God, is a sacred being. The entire value system of Judaism, whether personal or social, is determined by the answer to the question: Is man regarded, treated, respected, and loved as one who is fashioned in the image of God?...It is crucial that the answers be sought by men who begin with the belief that human life is significant in a universe which is friendly to his ideals and values."[13]

Religion allows us to change the nature of man. Being in the image of God, we are born with the capacity to grow, to develop, and learn how to overcome evil. Olan recalled the story of Joseph: boastful, brash, and irritating in his youth, being sold by his brothers into slavery, betrayed by a deceitful woman, Potiphar's wife, imprisoned and then deceived by the people he saved. Yet, Joseph ultimately became the prime minister of Egypt and controlled the world's greatest food supply.[14] With the help of God, Olan suggested we can resolve the issues of the day. "Great religion teaches that man and God are co-workers on earth; that if man does his part, lives by the moral law and in brotherhood with other men, God will assure him that his ship will safely reach port."[15] The time was ripe for society to begin to speak for the God whose kingdom men must build.[16] It was time for the people to obtain the same spirit of love outside the home as we experience inside the home. We either voluntarily bring harmony or order to our lives or someone else (an apparent reference to non-democratic governments) will force order upon us.[17]

Olan's relentless attacks against the ills of the social order concerned numerous aspects of life and human rights including such topics as racism and discrimination, philanthropy, poverty, the elderly, capitalism and industry, and war. The following pages of this chapter briefly summarize Olan's more noteworthy viewpoints on these specific topics.

Racism and Discrimination

America has experienced crucial racism and discrimination throughout its history. This xenophobia was about slavery and slaves and connected to the violation of human rights. Olan's career embraced the civil rights movement which, from a religious point of view, reflected that first moral law revealed by religion: "And God created man in His image, in the image of God He created him; male and female He created them."[18] An understanding of this verse suggests that the human being, made different from all things and other creatures, has a greater inherent value than animals and, as such, provides him with the potential to overcome immoral and unjust actions and improve the plight of mankind.

Race relations were one of the dominant themes permeating the social consciousness of Reform Jews after the end of World War II. Beginning with the CCAR comprehensive statement entitled "Judaism and Race Relations" in 1946, Reform Jews called for an end to the inferior economic conditions of the Negro (currently considered African-Americans), and to the persistent blight of multiple lynching, segregation in the military, and discrimination in the professions. But the civil rights takeoff point for Reform Jews began with the 1954 landmark decision outlawing segregation in public schools and subsequent civil rights legislation, where the distinct issues of desegregation and integration remained at the forefront of society for years. Though one may consider the essence of the two issues as similar, they are in fact different. Desegregation originates from governmental laws affecting the rights of certain people while integration is a matter of an unwritten moral code affecting equality within a given society. Olan advanced the following:

> "There is a difference between desegregation and integration. In one case (desegregation) it is the preservation of the rights of the individual. This is a matter of laws and their proper enforcement. Integration, however, is more than a matter of the removal of prejudice as well as discrimination. It is more than just desegregation. It calls for an attitudinal change, removal of the fears, hatreds, suspicions, stereotypes, and superstitions."[19]

> "Integration is not only a matter of the law of the land, or of State Rights — it is a moral issue in which the souls of men are in danger."[20]

Racism was more than a sociological or a humanitarian concern for Olan. "The process of civil rights legislation is impressive and warrants all of our support for more and more of it. Like poverty, racism is also a symptom of the basic violation of the sanctity of man…The roots of the disease reach to the deep-seated evil which denigrates a person without regard to the quality of his life…The sin of racism, as of poverty, is its violation of…sanctification of the Holy Name."[21] Bad laws foster civil disobedience, and as such they "must be protested, even to the extent of arrest and jail. Human rights are from God, they are natural to men, and no society which flaunts them can endure."[22]

Housing and race relations resonated within the Dallas community at the time of Olan's arrival to the City of Dallas in 1949. Olan believed the city was having a "black-white" problem, which to him was due to an original violation of a moral law — slavery.[23] His arguments continually addressed the community's moral and ethical responsibilities to rethink its positions on these issues.

> "More important than anything else in the world today is the recognition, the acceptance, and the living by the basic natural fact that humanity is one. To flaunt it is not only going against nature, it is the height of immorality. It is too late to argue that you have the right to sell or rent your house to whomever you

please. If all men qualify financially, morally, and responsibly, then it is not your right to deprive him of the right to buy your house or rent your apartment because his skin is black. This is to perpetuate a prejudice which is both immoral and blasphemous."[24]

One of the two forces shaping life in America was the ever present consciousness of group discrimination which taxed the faith of American democracy.[25] The great sin of the times, Olan stressed, was "our tendency to generalize from the particular. We take the shortcomings of an individual and ascribe it to an entire group, thus condemning the many for the sins of the few…This is the terrible sin of our society, this generalization. Its essential sinfulness lies in its emphasis on our superficial differences and its neglect of our common unity."[26] He explained that it is one of the strange aspects of our life that the things that divide, or conversely unite, human beings are these accidents of life; the superficial and artificial aspects of our being. This dilemma was elucidated in his February 20, 1949 radio address ("The Religious Basis for Brotherhood") during the beginning of Brotherhood Week. Olan emphasized that we are divided by three superficial things or characteristics that one may label as the three "C's:" color, creed, and cash. All of these are accidents of birth or station. One is born black not of his own choosing, yet the world sets him apart, exploits him and abuses him merely for the crime of having been born of a different color. Yet, for Olan, the color of skin is superficial and accidental, and tells us nothing about the individual's character, hopes, and dreams. From the aspect of creed, when one is born a Jew, it is not a matter of choice. He or she could become a member of any religious denomination and not be subjected to any suffering. However, one born a Jew is set apart just as the millions of Jews persecuted because of their religion. From the standpoint of money or cash, that is purely an accident of life. Many individuals inherit it by accident of birth, and consequently are set apart from those who have no money. In effect, they become a separate class, a privileged class. Although one's wealth tells us nothing about the person, our financial standing determines our social environment. However, we divide and clash on the basis of this accidental superficial aspect of our lives. Many people condone the unfortunate circumstances that separate them because of the three C's. "We rationalize it, even while we may recognize that it is wrong. But from a religious point of view, there can be no compromise and no rationalization. Either we believe in the Fatherhood of God and the Brotherhood of man, or we do not."[27] This is no pious piece of liturgy that can be pleasantly chanted on the Sabbath, Olan, said, but rather a radical idea dealing with the basic nature of God and men.[28]

There is no evidence, Olan continued, "to validate any theory that race, blood, nationality, class, or any other distinction among men makes one group superior to another."[29] Some are born disadvantaged because they are deprived; but this happens to whites as well as non-whites, to Chinese as well as Americans.[30] "We must remember it says man, not white man, rich man, American, Baptist or Jewish."[31] The fact remained, Olan preached, that humanity was indivisible. Although distinctions may exist among individuals within racial groups, there are groups within all races that are more or less advanced than others.[32] Given the same opportunities, all groups respond similarly. It is man's common humanity that unites all men, and to deny that fact is both immoral and blasphemous.[33] This meant that we are all part of one family with God as our father, regardless of race, religious preference, economic status, physical characteristics, and political leanings, a concept imparted by most religious leaders.

The death of Martin Luther King, Jr. awakened American society to a truth that many people would rather have avoided. Olan attributed the agony of the nation in large measure to the failure of good people.[34] The angry black community resented the white liberals who attempted to assist their people to become free, while the white community bristled at the black resistance and grew angry in return due to the seemingly lack of gratitude for their well-intentioned efforts.[35] What the whites did not understand was that their good intentions only aggravated the misery. Actually, the whites really did not share in the misery and suffering of the Negro. "We give more or less to the cause, we may even march and demonstrate against the evil which oppresses, some even go to jail for a day of two. But we return to our community of privilege while the Negro remains in his prison house of deprivation and misery."[36] For Olan, this was a bankrupt moral code that treated its minorities so brutally, and needed to be replaced by a new morality.[37]

Perhaps the most controversial racial issue addressed by Olan demonstrated not only his integrity but also the truthfulness of his commitment to leadership and the social order. Though interracial marriages and unions are more common in the twenty first century, society in general frowned upon such unions during the first seventy-five years of the 1900s. Yet, Olan's progressive vision and perceptive nature placed him well in advance of most of his colleagues in addressing this controversial issue. He believed that in a free society, "no home, no church, and no State has the right to interfere on the basis of class or religion or of race" for the freedom to love and to marry is an inalienable right from God, rather than man, and that two people whose love is genuine have the right to unite that love in marriage.[38] Speaking of racism as a symptom of the basic violation of the sanctity of man, Olan said: "the overt or the covert resistance to the marriage of a man and a woman because they are racially different is the crux of the matter."[39]

> "One of the most sensitive areas of human relations is marriage. Two people who are mature and love each other have a right to marry each other. No church, no State, and not even parents have any prior rights to their love. We will just have to face the fact that two people of different color skins have a right to love one another, marry each other, and raise a family together. That they may face problems in our society is only part of the problem of any marriage. They face problems only because our prejudices have become so hardened that they are seemingly impenetrable. But the cold fact is that there are no exceptions to the unity of the human species."[40]

Democratization of ethnic groups since our country's founding was and still continues to be an integral feature of our society. Olan recognized the importance of maintaining a group's ethnic culture, as he campaigned that it was in our national interest to work for the final termination of African-American segregation. "In the national interest, it is important to work for the final liquidation of Negro separation in all areas of life — economic, social, cultural and residential. At the same time, the new mood of ethnic identity emphasizes Negro separation."[41] This new mood reflected the African-American's desire for full acceptance within the community without any discrimination while concurrently seeking to preserve the racial heritage and structural separation of that community.

From the standpoint of discrimination, no groups have been repressed more than gays, lesbians, bisexuals, and transsexuals. Though not an issue of race, it is discrimination and falls within the purview of Olan's social justice advocacy. The Reform Movement became an advocate of gay and lesbian rights in 1965, near the close of Olan's pulpit years, when the Women of Reform Judaism (WRJ) passed their first resolutions calling for the end of discrimination of homosexuals.[42] In 1977, the Union of Reform Judaism (URJ) and the CCAR passed resolutions dealing with this issue, calling for human rights for homosexuals. Since then, the URJ, CCAR, WRJ, and other Reform Movement affiliates have passed resolutions dealing with issues specific to Reform Judaism, such as inclusion of gays and lesbians in the rabbinate and as cantors, as well as national issues supporting civil rights for gay men and lesbians, including civil marriage, elimination of discrimination within the armed services, and the support for explicit workplace non-discrimination and civil rights legislation. In addition, in March 2000, the CCAR made history by becoming the first major group of North American clergy to give support to their rabbinic members choosing to perform same-gender ceremonies.[43] And in March 2015 the CCAR installed it first openly gay president, marking an historical moment for the governing body of American Reform rabbis. Even though the above resolutions supporting gay and lesbian rights occurred well after Olan's pulpit years, this writer emphasizes that discrimination against any person from indifference, insensitivity, ignorance, fear, or hatred would not be consistent with Olan's fundamental beliefs and preaching's regarding social justice issues and practices. Evidence of Olan's views regarding discrimination is presented in an August 22, 1974 interview by Joseph Rosenstein with Judge Irving L. Goldberg, former president (1955-1957) of Temple Emanu-El. During his tenure as president of the congregation, Judge Goldberg was concerned because of an application of a "black man" seeking membership in the congregation. Though some fear was exhibited because of racial demonstrations around the country, Olan's forceful opinion prompted, in the end, unanimous acceptance of the man by the board of trustees.

Philanthropy

Olan was greatly motivated by the Hebraic understanding of charity, clarifying the meaning of the Hebrew word "TZADAKAH" as justice or righteousness.[44] In this tradition, he said, charity is a matter of justice.[45] Charity was a demand upon mankind as a condition of existence, and projecting the conviction that society is understood in terms of family life, Olan stated: "When I speak of the Fatherhood of God and the Brotherhood of Man as a basic doctrine of my faith, I project the foundation upon which my philosophy of philanthropy is established."[46] Explaining that theologians had been troubled for centuries by the injustice of life in a world where a good God is the Creator, the Hebrew tradition is more concerned with the demands of life rather than the theological paradox. Therefore, by accepting injustice as part of existence, it requires of those "who are blessed with wealth to provide for the poor, the strong to help the weak, the talented to share with the less endowed."[47] With these views, one can comprehend charity to be a demand upon mankind as a condition of its existence. "Man was born to do justice."[48]

Upon obtaining his first rabbinic position, Olan immediately began soliciting funds for the needy. His philanthropic understanding encompassed the three basic doctrines of his faith — the family of man, the call to justice, and the dignity of the human personality (respect for human rights).[49] He became President of the United Jewish Charities (in New

England) attempting to solicit additional funds for the poor since the Charity itself was not able to provide sufficient funds.[50] While in Texas, he believed the failure of members of the community to care decently for the poor was disgraceful. Yet he understood his role as both a teacher and solicitor placed limitations upon him. "When I accepted the pulpit, it was with the understanding that laymen raised the money and I was the religious teacher."[51] Over the years, the role of the congressional rabbi has significantly expanded, and, as a practical matter, a central responsibility of the rabbi today, rightfully or wrongfully, involves the seeking of funds for the congregation as well as providing philanthropic benefits for the needy. This would allow compliance with Olan's conviction that each person deserves the opportunity to fulfill his best self.

Poverty

Poverty in America was another essential theme of Olan's addresses. In recalling the early days of America, he believed that Ben Franklin would shudder in disbelief at the existing poverty and refer to us as lunatics after learning of the many miracles of the twentieth century. In Franklin's mind it would be a dawning of the golden era: no more want, no more starvation, no more oppressive poverty, no more slums, no more bare feet and naked bodies supporting bellies gnawed by hunger pain.[52] And if this line of thinking were correct, there would be plenty of food and worldly goods for everyone, as well as the disappearance of most evils and diseases that follow in the train of poverty. There is certainly no secret that crime, lawlessness, immorality, and prostitution can be influenced by poverty.[53] With poverty erased and the needs of everyone fulfilled, it would seem that the miraculous golden age of society would be experienced by everyone. But with an abundance of resources, a plethora of power, and swollen storehouses of grain and clothing, the line of the poor apparently continues to grow.

As it continues to exist today, poverty in our country during the latter part of the twentieth century was on a scale which was shocking. The U.S. Census Bureau indicated that approximately twenty-five to thirty million people (approximately 15% of the population) lived below the poverty line in 1970. Although the percentage is slightly lower (approximating 14%), over forty-six million Americans lived below the poverty line in 2012.[54] Describing those many millions of Americans below the poverty line and living on the brink of starvation, Olan found the lack of reasonable financial support objectionable and personally frustrating as funds required to alleviate poverty were being redirected to other venues.

> "We are sickened by the present callous decision of our national legislature to let the poor pay for the war in Vietnam. We are justly outraged at the heartless use of the economic scalpel upon programs which aim to relieve in a small measure the terrible suffering of the poor. We must and we certainly shall declare ourselves unequivocally against such moral obtuseness. This we do in concert with all men who are sensitive to the pain of the poor."[55]

In his 1976 address just prior to the dedication of Thanksgiving Square in Dallas, Olan said: "But from the view point of justice, the strong must help the weak, the rich care for the poor, the talented support the simple. That is justice; it is also the essence of giving thanks. God blessed some of His children so that they may help others who need it."[56] However, there was a more fundamental source of the plight of the suffering of the poor.

> "The agony of the poor…is experienced in a condition of unprecedented affluence. Some children go hungry while others are fretting over where to keep the third car. In a day when profits are soaring, dividends climbing, 'luxury living' the new slogan of merchants and their advertising geniuses, low wages, slums, and all the degenerating effects of poverty live as a festering sore alongside the ivory couches. This is more than inhumane, unjust, and immoral. It is downright blasphemy. It is desecration of God's name, it is (in Hebrew letters) defamation of God…The disease (of poverty) grows out of a rejection of (Hebrew letters) sanctification of the Holy Name."[57]

"A world in which millions (of people) die of hunger amidst vulgar display of luxury and affluence needs to hear the prophetic call for distributive justice, and something more than the charity which the Internal Revenue Service allows as a non-taxable deduction."[58] Poverty continues to remain a fundamental issue within religion and our society even after the passing of more than forty years since Olan's retirement from the pulpit. One must inquire as to whether any real substantive progress has been made over the years in resolving the issue of poverty in our affluent society. Olan would certainly respond to this inquiry in the negative.

The Elderly

In many respects the test of our civilization may be shown by the manner in which we treat the aged. An attitude seeking a decline in importance of the elderly and their ensuing financial liability to society is looked upon with condescension by most Americans. The Biblical view toward the elderly is very explicit. Olan cited the Psalmist who expressed the plea that arises in all people: "And even until old age and hoariness (extremely old or ancient), O God, forsake me not; until I proclaim Your strength to the generation, Your might to all who will yet come."[59] With this view, old age affords one the opportunity to transmit one's knowledge of God accumulated throughout a lifetime. Olan recognized the importance of caring for the elderly and presented references to biblical and prophetic teachings. The duty of the young is to care for the old, as they said to Ruth when her son was born: "He will renew your life and sustain your old age."[60] The Bible also cautions us that if we want to live, we had better care for the Aged. "Honor thy father and thy mother that thy days may be long upon the land."[61] The Prophets went further, Olan said, as they declared that any time people show disrespect to the elderly it is a sign of evil days. And Isaiah, describing the confusion that comes from sin and the evil days which will bring God's judgment upon the people, declared: "The child shall behave insolently against the aged."[62] These references represent the basis for Olan's declaration that the foundation of Western civilization is founded on the biblical principle that a society that abandons the elderly is not worth saving.[63]

With the growth of American society the care of the elderly began to shift from the private sector of religious institutions and private charities to government programs. Like other social needs such as philanthropy, hospitals and schools, the number of elderly grew too large for the capacity of the private sector to properly provide for that segment of the social order. State and Federal programs were instituted through legislation providing Medicaid, Medicare and social security benefits. This was evidence of social responsibility on the part of the state and nation and an official declaration that the elderly must be cared for as a right of life. "In this connection, it is important for us to recognize that the Social Security Program of our government was the greatest move toward social responsibility in our history. It was an affirmation of faith in the worth of the person."[64] Yet, Olan continued to question whether these programs were sufficient to properly care for the aged to keep them from dying or adequate enough to allow them to live. Over time, with the changes within the structures of budgets and the trend to divert funds to other programs, not to mention the increasing number of elderly, these programs have not resolved the financial burdens that severely damaged the economic status, morale, and health of millions of older Americans. Several statistics were presented by Olan that, in his view, appeared to indicate condemnation of our treatment of the aged during the third quarter of the twentieth century. While the United States spent 3% of its national income upon social security for the aged, Denmark, Italy, New Zealand, Sweden, Switzerland, and West Germany spent 5.3%, 5.1%, 4.4%, 4.6%, 4.7%, and 8%, respectively.[65] "The richest nation in the world with the highest standard of living spends less than all other nations upon its older people."[66] Furthermore, and certainly much closer to home, Olan pointed to the State of Texas as the 43rd state in the nation in welfare spending.

Olan alleged that the treatment in America and Texas of its older people to be miserable. "It is shameful! It is Blasphemy. It reveals a breakdown of our value structure."[67] Although many older people retain abilities and strength to remain productive members of society, many are neglected as they are hidden away in poverty, sickness, loneliness, and boredom. Though it is certainly easier to blame others for the deficiencies in the care of the elderly, we are all guilty, Olan stressed, as we live in semi-comfort while the aged next door dwell in poverty. "There is something indecent and immoral with news accounts of fabulous parties, of millions of dollars spent on sports events, of high-priced furs and automobiles, while to the old people we say 'we must cut back even on the miserable little you now get to maintain you below the poverty level.' Sometimes we must in conscious ask ourselves, how any of us can swallow a bite knowing that there is an old person who has nothing...No nation can survive, nor should they survive with values that blaspheme against those created in the image of God."[68]

Though the plight of the elderly was a continuing concern for Olan, progress has been made in elderly care over the years. Mention must be made of both the significant growth in total and elderly population statistics from the time of Olan's retirement to the present. In addition, and considering progress in various government programs, there has also been a substantial increase in the number of private nursing and assisted living facilities for the elderly while, at the same time, providing improved medical and quality of life benefits. Yet millions of elderly Americans continue to suffer. Olan would certainly approve of the progress transpiring in the past forty years although much still needs to be accomplished.

Capitalism and Industry

The foundation of Olan's attacks on the evils of the social order began early in his career with the Great Depression of 1929, coincident with his rabbinic ordination when America experienced devastating economic adversity and human suffering. Beginning with the industrial revolution of the nineteenth century, and continuing through the scientific-technical revolution during the twentieth century, the rapid growth in industrial technology made steady inroads into the commercial culture affecting the internal structure of business organizations and the larger society. The worker, or as Olan more fittingly called the producer, was being replaced by the machine, with consistent improvements in costs and efficiency. The machine was in the hands of a commercial world whose interest was private gains and not social welfare.[69] The importance of the product took precedence over the welfare of the worker. Olan's primary concern was for the worker, placing the enterprise in a secondary position. "Far more important than what we produce are the people who produce it."[70]

Olan believed the industrial world was overbuilding its capacity. That is to say that there were more manufacturing facilities, more mines, more machines, and more agricultural farms and fields than could be economically utilized. Not only was the resultant production almost always in excess of purchasing power, it frequently was in excess of consumption requirements. Olan's message was that excess plant capacity without articulating supply to demand would eventually lead to a financial drain for the factories as well as related employment reductions.

Olan also believed that an overproduction of goods and services gave rise to an under consumption of goods and services by the public. People lacked the purchasing power to consume to the extent of produced goods and services. This is a failure of the modern economic and industrial world and the greed and selfishness upon which they were built. He pointed to the profit motive as being the central purpose of business — buying cheap and selling high. "Instead of building private fortunes if we had built a sensible social economic structure with a more equitable distribution, we would today have an outlet for our goods. What do you expect from an economic structure where the buying power has been put at its lowest and the producing power at its highest? Business cannot eat its cake and have it!"[71]

Though possibly an oversimplification of America's economic situation during his early rabbinate, Olan attributed the fundamental causes of the depression to the technological unemployment fostered by the uncontrolled advance of the machine, the excess production of goods under free competition, and the sad state of the under-consumption of such goods. Olan suggested a revision of the industrial structure from its present selfish-profit seeking basis to a more humane and sensible social foundation. He called for a change in direction and an entire reorganization and reformation of the commercial world with emphasis not on profit or private gain (the social egoism of capitalism[72]) but rather on social welfare.[73] "The justification for any economic system, Olan said, is not whether it produces the most goods or the greatest prosperity, but whether it serves to dignify the person who works, and gives him an opportunity to fulfill his basic needs. A political order is good not because it is efficient and powerful, but when it makes room for the expression and achievement of every person as a free and dignified child of God."[74] Simply stated, industrial strife in Olan's view was not only a matter of economics or prosperity; the issue was the worth of man who is a child of God.[75]

Olan focused his concern on the individual workers rather than the corporate enterprise and its physical assets. He emphasized the strain put on the workforces as they struggled to live decently from an average wage that many members of society would not dare to live on.

> "From the viewpoint of God it is difficult to justify poverty amidst luxury, Hovels surrounded by mansions. It is not surprising that millions of decent, hardworking people have turned not to God, but to their own labor organizations, and by their concerted effort have endeavored to get justice for themselves. That there have been excesses in this labor struggle, and that there will continue to be violence and the threat of economic paralysis, is due not so much to power greedy labor leaders, or to communists, as it is our own fault for having failed to build on the moral law, where each human being is treated as a child of God. From the point of view of religion, human beings come before profit. A man who works honestly is entitled to a decent standard of living for his family; he is entitled to some security, some recreation, and a normal education for his children."[76]

An emphasis upon racial, religious, or national background instead of competence and training as a basis for competition in an industrialized society is self-defeating."[77] For Olan, man cannot be valued based on what they can bring to the market place; and likewise, man made in the image of God cannot be discarded like an old piece of clothing.

Olan recognized that free enterprise sanctioned by capitalism quite often allows the powerful to disinherit the weak, while bestowing blessings upon the profit motive and competitive incentive.[78] He did, however, concede that in the early years of the Industrial Revolution, during a time of scarcity, the capitalist system succeeded in producing sufficient quantities of goods for society. He considered capitalism a dying system, due to its immorality and sanctification of egoism, suggesting that capitalism deviated from the social message of the Hebrew prophets, which, according to him, had more in common with Marxism than with capitalism. "Both hold in common important values, and not the least of these is the conviction that social solidarity is better than egoism. Both reject individualistic self-seeking, just as both affirm that man's supreme worth is not the single individual but his integral part in a social unity which can be understood in relational terms."[79] This Marxism, of course, was meant by Olan to be more of a religious socialism and revolutionary view of social change required by society in reducing economic oppression under capitalism. History has shown that capitalism not only did not die, it has expanded well beyond the imagination of Olan's generation. With the growth of multi-national and international organizations and the related industrial expansion beyond our national borders, the profit motive continues to be paramount among commercial ownership, management, and investors. However, over the past fifty years there also has been significant expansion in the growth of not-for-profit and labor related organizations whose target beneficiaries are employees of commercial enterprises and other less fortunate members of society. One can also point to various federal and state governmental agencies or departments whose current functions include protection, oversight, and restitution involving specific societal issues involving labor and management.[80] Referring to our capitalistic society and industry's desire for profit, Olan said: "To use a man for one's own profit, to exploit him, to treat him as a commodity, to cast him off when he is no longer useful is a far more serious offense than being inhumane or unjust. To so treat a man is blasphemy."[81] "If man is endowed with worth and significance because he is an integral part of a meaningful universe, then we blaspheme against God when we buy him cheaply for our own pleasure and profit."[82]

Olan was a member of the Texas State Committee of the National Development Program of the Sam Rayburn Foundation. Its purpose was to encourage young persons of exceptional ability to seek careers in political science and government. The Foundation was to award scholarships, fellowships, and grants-in-aid to deserving students, as well as awards to be given to encourage educational institutions at all levels to strengthen and improve their courses of study in political science and government.[83] He was also invited by Vice President Lyndon B. Johnson to participate in a one-day conference at the Ambassador Hotel in Los Angeles, California on November 14, 1963 sponsored by the President's Committee on Equal Employment Opportunity.[84] The purpose of the meeting was to obtain information and counsel from community leaders in the states of Arizona, California, Colorado, New Mexico, and Texas concerning courses of community action which might be undertaken to make equal employment opportunities available without regard to irrelevant considerations of ancestry.[85] Although Olan was honored to be considered, his schedule was so burdened that he was not able to attend and participate.[86]

War

Olan's views of military conflict cover the spectrum of his rabbinate from his time in Worcester through retirement in Dallas. From an early sermon entitled "Disarm!" presented sometime during 1933 or 1934 (approximately 15 years after World War I), Olan spoke out about the danger to peace stemming from a rise in the production of military armaments. He attributed a nation's failure to disarm to the minds of men that are set in firm traditions and hesitant with doubts about the future. There are problems in misconception and thought, and of self-interest that must be removed before real progress towards disarmament can be made. Olan outlined the obstacles for peace, beginning with the sincere conviction present in the minds of most people that preparedness for war is the only sane and sure method of maintaining the peace. Although this represents an old idea, Olan disputed its validity and reminded his community of the fact that men have been arming themselves and fighting since the beginning of time. "It is not unreasonable to argue that there is some vital connection between these two facts (arming and fighting) of human experience."[87] Furthermore, and addressing the preparedness of the armies of France, Germany, Russia, Italy, and Great Britain prior to the beginning of World War I, he said that "preparedness for war never had preserved the peace of the nations. It simply widens and soothes and thus makes easy the road to war."[88]

A second obstacle alluded to by Olan in the way of disarmament was the plea for security, grounded on the idea that so long as war is probable or even possible, we must arm ourselves in order to protect the nation from possible invasion. These armaments are thus described as a form of insurance against damage inherent in sudden war. On the basis of the cost for this kind of insurance, Olan thought it costly in proportion to the actual security perceived as gained. The presence of arms is in itself provocative not of security but of insecurity, because when one nation builds new armor a rival nation builds more and improved armor.[89] Safety is achieved only by disarming, Olan said, pointing to Holland and its lack of an army and navy to protect that country. Being disarmed Holland posed no threat to any country anywhere. He also pointed to the border separating Canada and the U. S. where, at that time, no military presence existed over the 3,000 mile border.

Olan recognized a third obstacle to disarmament in the impressive fact that our military establishment represents a vested interest for business and economic concerns, upon which large segments of our population depend. "Armaments are a survival out of an age when men were barbarians; and are sustained in our day by the stupidities and terrors of a barbarism which still endures among us…If our civilization would live we must get rid of armaments."[90] Olan summarized these chief reasons why nations do not disarm: preparedness as a means of preserving peace; preparedness as means for security; and preparedness for selfish interests. All of these factors represent a compound of superstition, ignorance, and self-interest.[91]

But unfortunately world conflict did not and does not appear to be avoidable in modern culture. A few months prior to the bombing of Pearl Harbor, and in connection with his opposition to supporting the buildup of arms, Olan wrote: "I look upon the present tendency of my country in its rapid steps towards war as a great tragedy of our time. It seems to me that we are missing a rare opportunity of being peace-makers in the world."[92] And responding to a report of the Committee on International Peace for the Central Conference of American Rabbis, Olan objected to the wholehearted support given to the defense program of the U. S. administration. Indicating that the report appeared to relate to the post-war world, it did not reflect the immediate concern or conflict. "Peace is something that is immediate and not post-war. There is grave danger in a religious body assuming that man must go on in helpless destruction, exhausting his energies, feeding his hate, and emphasizing destruction. Is there not room for a more powerful weapon to defeat evil than evil itself?"[93] As a religious body, Olan believed the CCAR should call upon the President and the administration to use as much of their wisdom to stop mass-murder as, in his opinion, they were towards extending it. The religious background of Judaism requires reliance as much on love as we do on force, and while addressing those complications arising from malevolent actions of others, Olan said: "As a religious body there ought to be loftier and at the same time more dynamic an attitude towards the problem of evil in our day."[94] Again, preaching from the prophetic tradition, Olan said: "the prophets viewed war as the supreme violation of the sanctity of man. They urged men to live righteously so that the swords may be turned into plowshares and spears into pruning hooks… The Prophetic religion brings to man peace of mind when he confronts him with God who demands of him that he be himself, his real self, his best self."[95]

As a humanitarian, Olan acknowledged the duty of the Central Conference of American Rabbis towards the immediate problem of the starving millions on the other side.[96] He supported the U. S. Senate Resolution calling for the relief of the millions of hungry and sick in the small democracies of Europe. "I cannot see how we honestly can avoid the issue inherent in this resolution. I would urgently suggest that the report of the Peace Commission take a positive attitude in this matter."[97] In concluding his radio address of October 3, 1943 ("The High Cost of Peace") Olan preached that a lasting and durable peace may be futile and empty unless we are resolved to pay for peace at least what we paid for war. "The challenge to us now is to recognize something higher than obeying the law. We must begin to hear an inner voice that drives us on toward great and noble living, no matter what the cost."[98]

When comparing the issues of victory for democracy with the defeat of oppression, Olan's sincere ethical and religious beliefs are displayed. As a member of the National Committee on Food for the Five Small Democracies, he expressed his concern of the future of religion when many religious leaders were opposed to sending food to "innocent victims of the world upheaval."[99] He was willing to place his faith that "love is greater than hate, that kindness is more powerful than cruelty.[100] "My religious convictions mean as much in times of crisis as they do in times of normal living. It is because the Hoover plan (the plan of the National Committee on Food for the Small Democracies to supply food to those starving communities during the Nazi blitz through Europe) at least attempts to meet these beliefs in practical form that I propose to continue my support of that program…I shall raise my voice wherever I can in behalf of the project of feeding the starving people of Europe."[101]

In connection with World War II, Olan proposed that Hitler's actions widened the gap of understanding between Christianity and Judaism. "The failure of Christians, with few exceptions, to comprehend the meaning of Jewish survival and the theological significance of the creation in our time of the State of Israel renders dialogue difficult, perhaps impossible. Auschwitz burned not only six million Jews; it burned the bridge of dialogue between Christianity and Judaism."[102] "The Hitler savagery upon six million Jews was not directed by Christian leaders; but it cannot be denied that it was the culmination of almost two thousand years of persecution by the church of Jews who were charged with deicide and with rejecting the messiah."[103]

The advent of the Cold War era in the 1950s resulted in the desire of the U. S. government to prevent the spread of communism at home and abroad. The United States began sending financial aid and military advisors to South Vietnam in the 1950s, hoping to thwart a takeover by the communist North Vietnamese led by Ho Chi Minh. As troop levels and casualties escalated throughout the 1960s, the war became increasingly unpopular at home, inciting large-scale protests, profoundly affecting popular culture and fomenting mutual distrust between the public and its leaders. Olan was outspoken in his opposition to the war for he believed this war was a moral issue rather than a war against communism, referring to both by saying that "we are carrying on a dance in a cemetery."[104] Olan believed this to be a senseless and cruel war[105] and one of the most tragic pages in American history. "The bitter part of it all is that it is a futile, useless massacre in which not even the Administration of the U. S. believes."[106]

In October 1965, 100 clergy members met in New York to discuss what they could do to challenge U.S. policy on Vietnam. Believing that a multi-faith organization could lend credible support to an anti-war movement often labeled as Communist, they created a group which became known as the National Emergency Committee of Clergy and Laymen Concerned about Vietnam (CALCAV). In his letter of August 8, 1968, to Dr. John C. Bennett, Co-chair of CALCAV, Olan consented to the use of his name in the organization's literature against America's policy in Vietnam. Martin Luther King, Jr. was one of the few black members and the only member from the South. After the group opened its membership to laypeople, King used the organization's platform in April 1967 for his widely acclaimed "Beyond Vietnam" speech that condemned the war in Vietnam. And during a 1966 organizing meeting of the CALCAV Abraham Joshua Heschel was asked if representatives were located in Dallas. Heschel responded that he spoke with Rabbi Olan and when Heschel said "I hear you're the only clergyman in town who is willing to speak out against the war," Olan replied, "come to think of it, that's both true and not funny."[107]

America's intrusion in Vietnam was not viewed by Olan as an invitation of the Vietnamese people; the decision came from our leaders' desire to combat communism. In essence, the concern involved the risk of their people choosing a way of life not approved by our government in opposition to the moral issue of killing and destroying innocent lives.[108] Speaking out of the prophetic tradition he had no choice but to confront his own country with the moral demands of God: "To kill men rather than let them choose a false God, as we see it, is arrogant and immoral."[109] He saw the war in Vietnam as a corruption in the moral character of American society which was manifest in the other wars of the twentieth century.

> "We are witness to a callous enjoyment of prosperity, a bacchanalian (Roman festival) revelry of luxurious living and sumptuous partying while children are burned with napalm, boys are killed and wounded in the hundreds of thousands, homes are reduced to dust, and millions are made homeless. This is a blasphemy of which every American who is not in the battle itself is guilty...It is bitterly ironic that man's death and destruction produces high profits and high wages (referring to domestic financial gains resulting from production of essential war materials) of war."[110]

Olan also questioned the United Nations' ability to resolve the crisis of the day. He saw the United Nations to be a very limited organization in which the "bully can veto any action against himself." It is not based on law, he continued, but upon the consent of the lawbreaker to be judged, "as if a policeman were to get the consent of the criminal before he could perform his duty." Olan's way out of this dilemma called for the prophetic faith — the acceptance of a higher law than the law of the State. "The view that law is a basic requirement for order among men is the essence of the Hebraic prophetic tradition."[111] "If we are to be saved at all, it is only by organizing ourselves as an international community of law with the power of courts and the police. We must take nuclear missiles out of the hands of individual nations and entrust them to the authority of a common community of nations. If we would live, we must accept the reign of law." He insisted that man must take over and commit to a world of law, while persuading other nations to go along with us; to submit to law, judges, and police to lessen the threat of the bully. As a society of laws rather than of men, the time had come for law, rather than men, to control world crisis.

Olan continued to be vocal throughout his rabbinate on the issues of war. "War is not only costly and destructive; it is an affront to the divine quality stamped upon the brow of man. It is an evil because it besmirches the image of God…Anxiety and loneliness, guilt and inferiority are not only psychological phenomena; they are alienations from the divine source of being."[112] War is immoral, Olan said, even when it is fought for supposedly principled reasons. "It is immoral because it uses man as things, expendable things to be exploited so that others may be free, enjoy, and live safely."[113] He questioned whether America was better, greater, and more powerful; are we free of race prejudice; and do we push our imperialism on others? Using Communist Russia as an example, he directed attention to our discrimination, our poverty, and our privileged classes. Olan continually alluded to the prophetic tradition that challenged accepted leadership of their time in the name of God, the source of righteousness. The prophets insisted that foreign and domestic issues could be solved successfully not in terms of practical politics but only in the light of the moral law imbedded in the universe by the Creator. Their philosophy of government was expressed in the Biblical declaration: "Righteousness exalts a nation, but sin is reproach to any people."[114]

Olan was skeptical about humanity's ability to limit or prevent conflicts among countries. Nations refuse to sacrifice power and glory; just as in the problem of poverty those who have the financial means selfishly refuse in numerous instances to pay the price of assistance.[115] The solution lies in developing the same attitude towards war and poverty that we have developed towards disease.[116] If a plague broke out in our city, Olan said, we would employ every means at our disposal to stop its spread and destroy it. "We would isolate the sick; condemn the goods of the diseased, as we would not stop at anything in our struggle. We need only the will to stop the plagues of war and poverty. The fact that we have achieved so much yesterday encourages the belief that a better world is possible tomorrow if we will do it."[117]

Wars and conflicts among nations and peoples have been a fact of life throughout history and Olan pointed to many religious believers who rejected an absolute pacifist approach on grounds that some evils are greater than the evil of war itself. He referred to those people who had subscribed to the pacifist view before the rise of Adolph Hitler, reversing their thinking when it became clear that failure to resist his "barbaric and satanic power" was a greater evil than to fight a war against him.[118] "Some evils must be resisted," Olan preached, "one cannot turn the other cheek to Hitler. Life at any price is not morally acceptable."[119] "Can you, or dare you, turn the cheek to a madman with a gun in his hand? Is it moral to stand by while the murdering of innocent people goes on, and trust that love will ultimately triumph?"[120] Olan explained the Hebraic tradition that sanctions two kinds of wars — the commanded and the permissive. Equating the Nazis to the Amalekites, Olan saw this as a commanded war against the Nazis, whose basic barbarism was a threat to life itself; and to refuse to fight against them was terribly immoral.[121] On the other hand, permitted wars are to be decided by a majority who represent the best in intelligence and morality of the people. In this case we have a rejection of the pacifist or absolutist position and the recognition that a community must be free to choose war as a moral necessity.[122] With this in mind Olan professed the war against Hitler as a just war, a war in which the cause is worth the bitter price that must be paid by society.

And in the Middle East, following the 1967 Six-Day War in which the Arab states attempted to eliminate the State of Israel, Olan cited the "awful bankruptcy of international morality."[123] Alluding to groundless accusations accusing Israel of aggression and Hitlerism, the sessions of the General Assembly of the United Nations demonstrated the real sickness of men and nations. "No one, yes no one, not even the representatives of the United States arose…The moral degeneration of our age revealed itself in the silent acceptance of the 'big lie' as a policy of international relations. More than the war in Viet Nam, the loneliness of Israel in its mortal distress pleads for a world of nations governed by law and not by man."[124]

Finally, and except for Olan's beliefs concerning permitted and commanded conflicts, one can surmise that fundamentally Rabbi Olan was a pacifist when confronted with the issue of international military confrontation. In his August 6, 1969 letter to the local board of the Selective Service System, supporting his son's claim for exemption from military service on grounds of conscientious objection, Olan wrote: "In the present struggle, I have expressed my conscientious opposition to the participation of the United States. My position has been stated on television and radio."[125]

Conclusion

The struggle for equality in issues of social justice extends well beyond Olan's years in the rabbinate. Human rights as stated in the Declaration of Independence and the Bill of Rights continue to be addressed and challenged by various members of society. Though not as prolific as in the time of Olan's rabbinate, second class citizens still exist in America because of race, national origin, and often creed, barring the realization of the sanctity of the human personality. Unfortunately, Olan's commentary remains appropriate today:

> "The paradox which puzzles us is that our greatest success is the cause of our most eminent failure. Scientific technology today enables us to create abundance, to produce enough food, clothing, and shelter to provide adequately for the needs of every man, woman, and child in the world. Yet hunger and starvation decimate millions of lives."[126]

And we all know that Judaism is not alien to the tragedy of human existence. Referring to the first Jews settling on American shores, Olan said "the Jew has been in the center of the struggle to make real the destiny of the nation."[127] The achievement of the Jews in America in the struggle for human freedom is comparable in value and significance to those of previous generations and other lands. "The Prophetic period was creative of our basic faith; the Talmudic era concretized our idealism; the Golden Age of Spain was rich in poets and philosophers; the ghetto of Eastern Europe exhibited the power to endure in the face of constant oppression. These are glorious pages in a long history of Jewish creativity…What, after all, is the aim and purpose of prophetic Judaism, if not the creation of a world in which man may pursue life, liberty and happiness"[128] With the beginning of the fourth century of Jewish life in America, the role of American Jewry has been identified and strengthened. With its primary concern being enveloped in humanity, the real meaning of Judaism derives from one's positive contribution to continuous creation. Religion must concern itself with the social, political, economic, and international problems of its time. Likewise, no religion can be acceptable which does not give men and women a philosophy of life for unsteady and uncertain times. Yet, life must be faced as it is and not as we wish it to be.[129]

> "We are the bearers of the message of moral consciousness unto all mankind, and we dare not cease our efforts in its behalf until man universal has acknowledged its validity and has made it an essential factor in his life…Our religion will center not upon lifting man to some ethereal world of the imagination, nor upon fitting men for life beyond the grave. It will take up rather the fight against poverty, bad conditions of labor, low wages and long hours, indecent tenements and noise…commercialized vice, rotten politics, selfish business, inequitable taxation and war. It will once again sound the great spiritual note that all men may hear it and take heed."[130]

Social justice is not just about the elimination of racism or caring for the elderly. In American society social justice and civil liberties enable everyone an opportunity of free expression and achievement as a free and dignified child of God. It involves the actions of one individual to another and one community to another. "In the Jewish tradition what is immoral is basically a blasphemy...a profanation in the name of God. Race prejudice, economic injustice, and war are condemned under the judgment of God's purpose in creation because they deny the innate worth of man. By the same token what a man owes to his fellowman, he must ask for himself and he must give to himself. Hillel was speaking for the tradition when he said, 'If I am not for myself, who is for me.' It implies that a person must respect himself, for he too is formed in the image. Indeed this basic Jewish idea of man is the corner stone upon which rests man's moral destiny on earth."[131] In the final analysis, social justice is commanded by God in precisely the same way that Shabbat observance and Torah study are God-mandated: "For I the Lord act with kindness, justice, and equity in the world; for in these I delight."[132] Throughout Jewish history the tradition emphasizes healing the sick, clothing the naked, assisting the poor, pursuing peace, and loving the neighbor, all of which are attributes of God. "Never before in human history has slavery been so universally condemned by moral sensitivity, and never before has human suffering on a worldwide scale been so much the concern of sympathetic people everywhere."[133] In spite of the countless calamities experienced by humanity, society has moved more and more toward liberty, equality, and community. What seems to go unnoticed, Olan said, is that the very crisis which terrifies us is the painful experience accompanying man's higher expectations. "Men are not satisfied to die young, to accept hunger as a natural condition, and to submit themselves meekly to powerful men and nations who seek to exploit them."[134] Olan's words and actions were indistinguishable; he did not just preach about racism, poverty, and other injustices of society, he worked to eliminate them. He did not just speak about the errors of capitalism and industry; he sought their shift to social welfare. He did not just speak about the elderly; he worked to improve their lot in society. "We should take heart from our sad history," Olan preached, "to unite our forces against the social evils of our time against war, poverty, racism, and violence. We should recapture that spirit from the Enlightenment which emphasized the idea that the love of God means the love of man."[135] Olan would most certainly agree with the words of Abraham Joshua Heschel: "God is hiding in the world. Our task is to let the divine emerge from our deeds."[136] As succeeding pages illustrate, the significance of our deeds are contingent upon their authenticity and our sincerity.

*Bishop Thomas Ambrose Tschope, Minister Albert Cook Outler, and Levi A. Olan.
Thanksgiving square Groundbreaking
April 16, 1973*

Religion and the Social Problem

H. Rhett James, Levi A. Olan, J.A. Sanfield, and Martin Luther King.

CHAPTER 5

The State of Israel

The 1885 Pittsburgh Platform refused to recognize the nationalistic nature of Judaism. "We consider ourselves no longer a nation, but a religious community, and therefore expect neither a return to Palestine, nor a sacrificial worship under the administration of the sons of Aaron, nor the restoration of any of the laws concerning the Jewish state."[1] This statement removed the American Reform Movement from the centuries' old yearning of the Jewish people to return to their homeland and the resumption of Jewish sovereignty in the Land of Israel. It was the foundation for the majority of early American Reform Jews not supporting Zionism[2] or the establishment of the State of Israel. With the issue of Zionism gaining support, Pittsburgh, in some measure, was also a response to the Eastern European movement of the 1880s known as "Lovers of Zion" that represented a firm expression of nationalistic sentiment and an effort to translate the idea into a program of action.[3] While a small number of Reform rabbis [e.g., Bernard Felsenthal (1822-1908), Gustav Gottheil (1827-1903), and Maximilian Heller (1860-1929)] embraced the Zionist cause, the majority opposed it. Isaac M. Wise, "the great architect of Reform Judaism,"[4] believed Zionism clashed with his philosophy of Judaism as a universal religion and denounced it as a "nationality swindle," explaining that "we are Jews by religion only."[5] Within this framework and in the eyes of the Pittsburgh reformers, Judaism could not be linked to any particular form of nation building. In America, Wise saw the "embodiment of the Messianic ideal which was to usher in an era of brotherhood and equality. To him, as to most Reform Jews of his day, America was Zion and Washington was Jerusalem."[6]

With changing sociological conditions and international developments in the early decades of the 1900s, transformation of American Reform ideology began to take place. These conditions included the rise of anti-Semitism, the decline in immigration, the declining economy, the crisis facing European Jewry from the escalation of Nazism and Fascism, and the changing social composition of American Reform. With the continued growth in the number of people supporting Zionism, Jewish nationalism became a vibrant and debatable issue pitting anti-Zionist reformers against pro-Zionist forces that ultimately resulted in the aspiration of a Jewish homeland. The growing numbers of Zionist supporters hoped that Jewish cultural and spiritual creativity in Zion would vitalize Jewish life everywhere, including America.[7] All of these factors were instrumental in convincing Reform leaders that American Reform had been too radical, and therefore needed to be more flexible in considering its doctrines and practices. At the 1937 conference of Reform rabbis, held in Columbus, Ohio, a new platform was adopted that repudiated many of the fundamental principles of Reform Judaism previously included in the Pittsburgh Platform fifty years earlier. The 1937 Columbus declaration of guiding principles for Reform Judaism took a positive stand in the issue of a Jewish homeland, calling for "the rehabilitation of Palestine" and affirming the "obligation of all Jewry to aid in its upbuilding as a Jewish homeland by endeavoring to make it not only a haven of refuge for the oppressed but also a center of Jewish culture and spiritual life."[8] This revised perspective reflected not only a change in the foundation of Reform, but also the different social environment in which it functioned. While the Columbus Platform represented the substance of Olan's rabbinate, he saw the State of Israel in both political and theological terms, viewing the State as the secular home for Jews in the wake of the Holocaust as well as the center of Jewish culture and religious life.

The creation of the State of Israel in 1948 was the most significant date in the Jewish calendar since the year 70 CE when the Second Temple was destroyed and Jerusalem fell to the Roman Empire. For most Jews around the world the establishment of the State of Israel was a divine event and decisive moment in history "that turned a long, involuntary exile into a diaspora where the Jew became free to choose. Some are now free to choose to be Jews…outside of Israel, and others to live as Jews…in the land of Israel."[9] For Jews outside the land of Israel, what was once an exile — the forced separation from a homeland — had now become the diaspora. The declaration of Israel's independence restored a necessary sense of balance between time and space in Jewish life, as Olan described in his address to the Rabbinical Assembly Convention in 1969: "While in exile, the Jew lived in the eternal, only in time with no dimension of space to his existence, no piece of ground upon which to begin building the kingdom."[10] Olan believed that all Jews, wherever they may be or how much they may differ, are bound by a mystic bond which neither time nor space can sever.

The creation of the State of Israel might be considered a physical redemption of the Jewish people to their homeland marking the beginning of the process of restoration of autonomous Jewish life to some degree of normality and healthy balance. With the establishment of the State, the emphasis of Zionism shifted from its original conception of returning to the land to a movement for the development and protection of the Jewish people in a Jewish nation.

With the conclusion of the Six-Day War in 1967, realization of the State of Israel had risen to a higher level throughout both the Jewish world and non-Jewish world. The reality of the peoplehood of Israel was never as visible as in those six crucial days of June. The conscience of the world, with few exceptions, seemed prepared to witness placidly the destruction of Israel and the Jewish people, even as they did during the 1930s and 1940s in the gas chambers of Poland and Germany. The difference in 1967 was the determination by Israel to fight for its life.

What resulted was a "spiritual miracle," the will of the people against a world which sought its destruction.[11] The willpower for survival, Olan preached, must receive our most sacrificial support both in money and in the unwavering assurance that we are bound to their destiny by an unbreakable bond regardless of the cost.[12] In his address to the 1969 Rabbinical Assembly Convention of the Conservative Movement and the President's Messages in the 79th and 80th annual conventions of the CCAR in Boston and Houston, Olan stressed the importance of American Jewry declaring an unyielding commitment to the survival of the State of Israel.[13] And in 1968, for the first time, the World Union of Progressive Judaism changed their planned biennial conference from Amsterdam to Jerusalem, where they proceeded with only one motive:

> "Visibly to demonstrate our unity with them and our unswerving support to them in this hour of their agony...We have come here to affirm our unity with our brothers in Israel, to confirm it, and to pledge to them our hearts, our souls, and our might."[14]

This was the period of time when American Jewish community leaders placed an urgent and inescapable call upon the financial resources of Jews everywhere to meet the needs and pressing demands of Jewish physical survival in the land of Israel. The significance of the diaspora's call for assistance to Israel was presented in a number of venues by Olan, including presentations to the annual conventions of the American rabbinical conferences.

> "Our fellow Jews in Israel must know now with certainty that we will not let them stand alone. There must be a sacrificial outpouring of the resources of the American Jew to help guarantee that when the desperate hour strikes, Israel will be strong and confident...The lesson of the Nazi program of obliteration of the Jew should not be lost...The resolute, unwavering commitment of American Jewry to the survival of the State of Israel must be declared now and made manifest by deeds of extraordinary dimension. The one unalterable fact is the right

of the Jewish people to live and work in the land of Israel. This is not negotiable."[15]

With few exceptions, one being the United States, Israel stood alone in the international community of nations following the Six-Day War. The moral failure of the international community was made evident to everyone as they watched their representatives in the United Nations debate the issues of the Six-Day War. Even many of our own American representatives, lacking moral purpose, failed to dispute the charges against Israel. "Israel stood alone in the battle, alone in the assembly of nations, and she is now, and will be alone for months and probably years to come."[16] The assertion of Israel's isolation continues to the present day when analyzing the news media stemming from political events and resultant accusations of many leaders throughout most of the world.

Olan described the crisis in Israel following the Six-Day War as a tragedy of cosmic proportions. Reflecting the whole as being characterized by its parts, he compared the well-being of the world to the existing experience of Israel. "As the macrocosm is known through the microcosm, the ocean in one drop of its water, so is the moral health of the world often revealed in the experience of Israel?"[17] In other words, the moral compass of world leaders is reflected by their concern for Israel, and few leaders in the vastness of the world cared about the survival of a tiny Israel. "The international sensitivity to the demands of justice and mercy was poignantly revealed by the total collapse of all moral considerations when the Middle East exploded in June of 1967."[18] For Olan, the moral deterioration of the period and corruption of modern society were symbolized by the silent, and often vocal, acceptance of anti-Israeli actions that threatened the survival of the country. What was needed, Olan said, was harmony among governments and adherence to obligatory international sanctioned agreements. "The loneliness of Israel in its distress pleads for a world of nations governed by laws and not by men."[19]

International immorality was certainly on display then, and in many areas of the world continues to present times. It is in the Middle East that the appalling collapse of international principles was revealed, and again continues through the twentieth century and well into the twenty first century. Concerning the aftermath of the Six-Day War, Olan said: "The sessions of the General Assembly of the United Nations which followed the six-day war in June, seen and heard all over the world by radio and television, demonstrated the real sickness of men and nations. A year later, it now seems wholly unbelievable that representative men of the nations of the world listened as Russian and Arab spokesmen, and their satellites, accused Israel of aggression and of Hitlerism, and that no one, yes no one, not even the representatives of the United States arose to point out that the king did not have on a shirt."[20]

Another distressing fact brought about by the crisis in Israel following the Six-Day War was that dialogue with the Christian world had been a dismal failure. With Judaism being portrayed by many Christian theologians as a disembodied theology and a faith without people, it became very clear that the church in its organized structure was at best neutral, and at worst antagonistic to the struggle for Israel's survival. Olan called it frustrating to hear atrocity stories from the Christians as they exploited the problem of the Arab Refugees to bolster their stance on neutrality. Without entering into the field of theological polemics, Olan said we cannot avoid facing once again in our time the church doctrine that Israel's successful existence is a Christian heresy. Olan projected Christian feelings as follows: "The people that reject Jesus the savior must fail and suffer so that their sinfulness will be proved."[21] Fortunately, Christian sentiment, especially in America, supporting American Jews and the State of Israel has improved during the balance of the twentieth century and well into the twenty-first century.

The creation of the State of Israel might be characterized as a dualism existing among those living in the State of Israel and the Diaspora. They are both charged with indisputable responsibilities. Olan recognized the need to forge a unity among all Jews in America to declare with passion an unyielding commitment to the survival of the State of Israel.

> "We must get beyond the existent organizational structures which function adequately for normal times. We need to reach the masses of Jews and involve them directly in this fierce struggle. The affirmative response which followed the Six-Days in June must now be fashioned into an instrument of popular will. Our heroic and beleaguered kin in Israel must know with certainty that their destiny is ours too. The world at large must be made aware that when it comes to the existence of Israel there are no divisions among us."[22]

He suggested that the Reform movement take the initiative and assume the leadership in calling for an American Jewish Conference whose sole purpose was to devise programs of large-scale support of money and spirit to the State of Israel. "We must move beyond the existent Jewish establishment and bring every man, woman, and child into a dedicated *kehilah* in support of Israel's will to live."[23]

But the responsibility of sustaining Jewish living and culture was not a one way street. Those living in the land of Israel must understand the essential and authentic place of Diaspora Jewry in the historic situation of the times. Olan projected the importance of their understanding for a strong and dynamic Diaspora for their material support as well as moral loyalty in time of need. Furthermore, for the Jews in the diaspora, without the State of Israel there would be a disparity. "The Jew in the Diaspora is in imbalance unless there are Jews on the land who are engaged in translating the prophetic vision into a living reality. Without a vital State of Israel, the Diaspora Jew will find himself in that euphoric condition in which a man experiences reality only in the dreams that come during sleep. Without the land, Judaism in the Diaspora is too heavenly to be meaningful on earth."[24]

"Jewish survival calls for Jews who will freely choose to live in the land of Israel as well as Jews who in freedom choose to live in the Diaspora."[25] Olan called the establishment of the State of Israel "a genuine miracle. It will take a miracle to bring order out of chaos in the world.

The first miracle has already taken place. The next, the bigger miracle, cannot be far behind."[26] "It is indeed good news," Olan said, "when we can announce that for the first time in two millennia, we are again one normal people united in body and soul."[27]

While American Reform was officially anti-Zionist until about 1948, reform Jews as a group were not. In connection with this, Olan did not recognize any conflict between Reform Judaism and Zionism. Reflecting on the idea that Reform Judaism is, in effect, one of several "American Judaisms," Olan professed that "Reform Judaism is by its very nature neither Zionist nor anti-Zionist. It arose as an answer to the intellectual problems of our age. Its union is among those whose needs must be free from the authoritarianism of revelation and whose religious faith can rest only on freedom of thought."[28] In fact, considering that Zionism represents a significant strategy for continuity of the Jewish tradition and Jewish survival, Olan believed that Jewish life needs both Zionism and Reform Judaism. The crisis, he said, arises because of the attempt to merge one with the other.

Though not a Zionist in the original understanding of the Jewish people returning to their homeland and their resumption of Jewish sovereignty in the land of Israel, Olan's views represent a paradigm shift in the thinking of the Reform rabbinate. By supporting Israel, he saw the State as an answer to a political challenge that gave hope for those viewing nationalism as the only salvation for the people of Israel. "It was and is a union of those who believe in Jewish nationalism, regardless of their philosophic approach to religion."[29] Olan advocated for a place for Jews to live and he encouraged the creation of an independent homeland in Palestine. He viewed Zionism essentially as the belief that the Jews comprise "a nation whose normal life is possible only by the acquisition of the three essentials, of a land, a language and a people."[30]

The Jewish people advanced the political idea for a way of survival and salvation with the establishment of the Jewish state. They also had a leading role in the drama of human history and its survival is crucial to man's destiny. Some are born into this covenanted community and maintain their loyalty and commitment. Others may choose to join themselves to it and give witness to its faith. Their faith may develop, and indeed for many it has, secular characteristics that are political, social, and cultural. These are significant only as they strengthen the ability of the Jewish people to survive and give testimony to their mission in the world. And yet, the importance of the State of Israel must of necessity be linked to the significance of Jews elsewhere. Although the security and growth of the State of Israel is important to the survival of the larger community of Israel, "it is, however, no more and no less important than communities of Jews in other lands. Israel, the covenanted people, must survive no matter how or where, in order that God's Kingdom may be brought near."[31]

Thirty-nine years after the 1937 Columbus declaration, in the 1976 Centenary Perspective and the 1999 Pittsburgh Principles, Jewish nationalism and the State of Israel were no longer matters of conversation. The Reform Movement became committed to the full democratization of the Jewish community by making Reform Judaism available to everyone, and considered the State of Israel vital to its objectives and the welfare of Judaism: "We are bound to that land and to the newly reborn State of Israel by innumerable religious and ethnic ties…We have both a stake and a responsibility in building the State of Israel, assuring its security and defining its Jewish character."[32] And in the 1999 Pittsburgh Principles, the Reform movement reaffirmed its commitment to the State of Israel, encouraging immigration (*aliyah*) to Israel, while asserting the continuance of "vibrant interdependent communities" in both Israel and the Diaspora.[33]

With the State of Israel, the Jewish people have now achieved a homeland that provides autonomy in their government and security of peoples' lives within their borders. With most of Israel's assistance from the outside coming from the United States, Jews in America maintain a sense of pride in their distant homeland. In 1973, after his retirement from the pulpit, Olan wrote: "The Jew has come home to find rest from his seemingly endless wanderings. What has been a prayer of hope…of yesterday is today a fulfillment and a cause for thanksgiving and rejoicing…The presence of the Jew in Jerusalem today is, as the Midrash informs us, only the first sound of the footsteps of the Messiah. It is a visible testimony that the *Malkhut Shamayyim,* the Kingdom of God, is a little nearer to realization. The establishment of the State of Israel in our time is only a partial fulfillment of the covenant."[34] And although the State of Israel represents a homeland for Jews, it has yet to achieve true security or know lasting peace.

CHAPTER 6

Judaism and Modern Theology

Introduction

While the preceding four chapters present a comprehensive view of Reform Judaism and religious liberalism, Olan's understanding of the relationship of Reform Judaism to society, and his views of Zionism and Israel, this chapter concentrates on the development of modern theology and its role in Judaism. In the literal sense, the term "theology" may be interpreted as a "discourse about God." The expression developed from the Greek words *"theos"* meaning God and *"logos"* meaning discourse to form *"theologia"* — more specifically meaning the "study of divine things."[1] As its origin stems from Greek philosophy, the term "theology" was used by Plato and Aristotle to denote the knowledge concerning God and things godly, by which they meant the branch of philosophy later called metaphysics.[2] In the main "theology" has also been defined as: the study of religious faith, practice, and experience, especially the study of God's relation to the world; a religious theory, school of thought, or system of belief; and a course of specialized religious training, especially one that leads the student to a career in the church or synagogue.[3] From these descriptions, the fundamental meaning of "theology" may be understood as a dedicated system of belief and dialogue involving the divine relationship of God to man and the world. This leads to viewing theology "as thinking God's thoughts after Him," and thusly portrayed as "walking in God's footsteps" with the theologian being the one "who walks in the footprints of God;" the real subject being "not God, per se, but the human relationship with the divine, and the nature and implications of religious faith."[4] In Olan's view, the theologian is a thinker whose roots are in a specific historic tradition or one who deliberately puts himself in that tradition by an act of faith.[5] In other words, the theologian "works within a particular faith commitment, community, and tradition which he takes as authoritative. While hoping that his message will have universal significance, he writes primarily for the fellow members of his circle of faith."[6]

When one speaks of being Jewish, he or she obviously is identifying with the Jewish religion, those individuals practicing Judaism, and those individuals belonging to or relating to a people descended from the ancient Hebrews of the Bible.[7] But some distinction must be made when using the terms "Judaism" and "Jewish theology." The expression "Judaism" was first used by Greek speaking Jews of the first century of the Common Era, and, as the religion of the Jews, had its foundation in the Bible and Talmud. Following Jewish religious practices, traditions, customs, and culture, "Judaism is both a way of thinking, as well as a way of living."[8]

In a general sense, Jewish theology in its common use for the Jew means "a rational interpretation of religious faith, practice, and experience;"[9] or more specifically, "an attempt to think through consistently the implications of the Jewish religion."[10] It is a Jewish way of thinking about Jewish faith and understanding more fully the significance of the Jewish religion as it draws on the particular insights of the Jewish teachers of the past.[11] Olan clearly distinguished theology from faith, religious experience, and philosophy. While religious experience and the faith which succeeds it may be common to man, theology is an intellectual undertaking by professionals and explicit for each respective system of belief.

> "Theology is a by-product, an exercise of the intellect in which we abstract from living religions those experiences which are reducible to some self-conscious system. It is for the expert, the professional religionist, and rarely the concern of laymen.

The Hebrew prophets and poets spoke the language of the people. It was religion they spoke, not theology."[12]

Olan continued by describing the significant difference between philosophy of religion and theology. "Philosophy is a cognitive approach in which reality as such is the object. It deals with structures, categories, and concepts and is by its nature general and abstract. It aims at a universal free inquiry, and strives after knowledge for its own sake. Theology is specific and concrete and is the presentation of one particular system of faith."[13]

Because it is neither faith nor religious experience, theology fulfills different roles within different religious groups. Christianity, for example, was described by Olan as "primarily a theological religion in which an article of belief is a condition of salvation and one who denies the dogmas of the church ceases to be a Christian. At the heart of it is mystical experience of the Incarnation, the Trinity, and the realty of a supernatural Resurrection which alone purifies and redeems from eternal destruction. Its claim upon the allegiance of men is that the logos became flesh — 'Jesus the Christ.' In Christianity dogma is primary and creed is of the essence. The vital and often excited interest of its theologians in the articles of its faith is in character with its theological nature."[14] In Judaism, unlike Christianity, "there is no man who is God, no three that is one, no incarnation, or miraculous birth to explain."[15]

The Role of Theology in Judaism

A primary task of Jewish theology is to formulate and express in contemporary language those categories of covenantal theology that would be directly relevant to modern man's search for his place in God's world. Abraham Joshua Heschel provided a practical description of Jewish theology in his book *Moral Grandeur and Spiritual Audacity*: "Day and night we spoke only about 'prayer' and *kavanah* (undivided concentration, particularly in prayer) and about *Hakodesh Boruch Hu* (the Holy One, blessed be He), and about *mesirat nefesh* (extreme devotion; literally, 'giving over one's soul'). What is this? It is Jewish theology."[16] And Louis Jacobs stated that "at the center of any Jewish theology is the doctrine of God."[17] Simply stated, Jewish theology represents the means by which the individual attempts to know God. In this respect man's primary concern is to discover what God requires of him and to devise a program to assist in the fulfillment of the divine commandments.

The people's attention in the early 1940s was devoted to the Second World War and what little theology there was resulted from the revival of Protestant theology.[18] Yet, the essential characteristics of our faith are better understood, and our ability to discuss our faith and beliefs among ourselves and with those outside the Jewish religion are enhanced through the study of Jewish theology. Contemporaneously, the study of Jewish theology became essential for an understanding of the differences that exist among the various modern Jewish religious movements. The study of Jewish theology, providing us with the understanding and knowledge to think and act in Jewish terms, is charged with the following mission:

> "to establish the nature and the parameters of Jewish religious thought, to articulate coherently authentic views of Judaism, and to demonstrate how the wisdom of the Jewish religious teachings of the past can address the perplexities of contemporary Jewish existence in a manner that is compatible with the thought and life of the Jewish faith community at a given juncture in time and space. The four criteria that characterize a valid Jewish theology are identical to those of any valid theology. They are: authenticity (the nature and use of sacred literary sources consulted); coherence (cohesion, clarity and communicability of a formulated theological perspective); contemporaneity (applications of past traditions to present situations); and, communal acceptance (ratification of a theological posture by committed members of a specific faith community)."[19]

The above mission may be described as two-fold: "first, to define our relation to B'nai Yisrael to the sons and daughters of the covenant who experienced God in history as reflected in the writings of the Torah and rabbinic tradition; and, secondly, it is our task to formulate and express in contemporary idiom those categories of covenantal theology which are directly relevant to modern man's quest for a place in God's world."[20] For the contemporary Jewish theologian, the task must attempt to accomplish for his age what the great medieval theologians wanted to do for their age by presenting a coherent picture of what Jews can believe without "subterfuge and with intellectual honesty."[21] With this in mind, detail topics which should be a concern of Jewish theology, as well as Judaism as a religion, are: the Jewish approach to God; the relationship between God and man; the meaning and significance of prayer and worship; the doctrines of revelation, the Messiah, resurrection and immortality, free will, sin and repentance, and the problem of evil; the idea of the Chosen People and the theological implications for the State of Israel; the question of divine providence and miracles; the authority of Torah and halakhah; in short, all of those topics which have to do with Jewish beliefs in contradistinction to Jewish practice.[22] In its strictest sense the ultimate aim of Jewish theology is the establishment of an era in which God becomes the focus of human thought and practice.[23]

Jewish Theology through the Ages

Throughout Jewish history until the middle of the twentieth century the study of Jewish theology had not been significant for an understanding of Judaism. And in America during the first half of the twentieth century, there scarcely existed anything that one could call Jewish theology. "Before 1945, a strong anti-theological bias existed within the American rabbinate and the Jewish intellectual community. The rabbi-theologians who studied in the rabbinic seminaries during the period of the 1940s objected to the type of theology that was taught, with considerable concern about the lack of Jewish philosophy and theology included in the rabbinic curriculum. In their opinion, theology taught at the institutions was limited by obsolete methods of thinking (primarily nineteenth century German idealism) and did not take into account the new trends in European thought. In essence, teaching methods and content failed to respond to the issues of the day which included the horrors of war, anti-Semitism, the problem of evil and immorality, the problem of self-transcendence and Jewish identity. "According to most observers of the religious situation in America, the achievement of Jewish theology prior to 1945 was not commensurate with its potential."[24] Few original theological thinkers existed in American Jewry, and there were no attempts to develop comprehensive systems of thought in the manner of earlier scholars to serve as a guide to the current generation.[25]

Jewish theology was condemned as dogmatic and un-Jewish. The religious writing that did exist was designated "Jewish philosophy" or Jewish thought."[26] Milton Steinberg, Olan's life-long friend and prominent liberal rabbi of Conservative Judaism, was instrumental in the initial quest for solution to a "shallow humanitarianism" insensitive to the spiritual needs of a religious liberalism.[27] Steinberg was driven by his philosophical search for truth and began to re-examine the fundamentals of religious liberalism in the light of existing trends in American philosophy and theology. This revival was further sparked by articles by Will Herberg, Emil Fackenheim, Abraham Joshua Heschel, and Martin Buber in important journals, and bolstered by the revival of Protestant theology influenced by the writings of Kierkegard, Barth, Tillich, Reinhold Niebuhr and H. Richard Niebuhr.

"The emergence of the modern era has often been interpreted as a victory of modernism over medievalism, a victory of the ideals of human freedom, reason, and autonomy over those of religious authoritarianism, divine revelation, and heteronomy. Modernity, therefore, marked a reversal of priorities, replacing supernaturalism with naturalism (or phenomenalism), theoretical or metaphysical reason with practical, functional reason, and, as a result, theology and metaphysics with science and technology."[28] The major religious movements in American Judaism believed they had discovered methods in which to reconcile tradition with modernity; especially important to the first and second generation Jews for whom becoming modern appeared to be synonymous with acceptance and success in their desire to become truly American. "From the viewpoint of the argument from modernity, Jewish theology did not gain a foothold prior to 1945 because, for most modern Jews and Christians, theology was associated with a pre-modern world of church dogmatism and religious supernaturalism."[29] In actuality, the word 'theology' was unpopular, and sounded too narrow and medieval, when compared to such more reputable and suitable terms as 'religious philosophy' and 'religious thought'.[30]

Revival of Jewish Theology

The revival of Jewish theology can be explained from the diverse environment within both the secular and religious communities which, in fact, are interconnected with each other. From the religious point of view and from a study of the literature available during the period, Robert G. Goldy revealed five reasons generally given for this revival of Jewish theology and the form that it took.[31] Briefly stated, they are: the emergence of a radically new religious consciousness; the coming of age of a third generation of American Jewish intellectuals who, imbued with this new consciousness, emerged to write and read a new theology; the establishment of a number of significant Jewish journals which played host to the new theology; the introduction of European trends in philosophy and theology by means of refugee intellectuals living in America; and the revival of Protestant theology in America.

The conception of man and God by the "postwar generation" was theocentric, having God as the central interest and ultimate concern. The question facing man had become, 'What shall we acknowledge as absolute — some man-made God…or the God beyond the abyss, the God who is Lord of all."[32] "The postwar consciousness was not only God-centered and theological; it was also people-oriented and survivalist. While a segment of the Jewish community was concerned primarily with the need for greater theological self-expression, a much larger part of it was devoted to projects that would assure the continued physical and spiritual existence of world Jewry."[33]

The quest for the renewal of Jewish theology marked a fundamental break with existing circumstances in American Jewish thought. The request for renewal included an attempt to justify the theological initiative itself, a demonstration of the relevancy of Jewish theology to the immediate postwar situation, and an argument for a new way of doing theology that was contrary to the prevailing outlook in religion. "The call for a new theology revealed a generation gap that existed within the rabbinate. Convinced that the events of the Second World War had shown religious liberalism to be bankrupt, many of the younger generation (i.e., the "third generation" immigrants to America) responded positively to the call for a theology which would show the way back to a more traditional picture of God, man, and the world. The older (i.e., "second") generation, on the other hand, tended in large part to oppose any talk of a theology which took as its starting point the rejection of religious liberalism."[34]

The emergence of "third generation" American Jews was a significant sociological condition for the development of Jewish theology in America after the Second World War. Will Herberg believed they were the revolutionary vanguard of the new era with the task of creating a radical, prophetic theology which would inspire and lead the generation of their era.[35] Although previous American generations had produced little original religious thought, what did exist was not theology in the strictest sense of the word. "The 'third generation' produced both theologians and an audience for theology…The war's influence was twofold: it helped create among Jewish intellectuals a strong dissatisfaction with established forms of American Jewish thought, and it was responsible for the presence in North America of refuge scholars and theologians who represented new ways of thinking in religion."[36] This "third generation" American Jews displayed a more traditional attitude or viewpoint; secure as modern Americans and, therefore, more critical of modernity and more appreciative of tradition than previous generations. It was pointed out that in immigrant societies, the children (the 'third generation') wish to remember what the parents (the 'second generation') wish to forget, namely, the traditional religious and ethnic heritage of the grandparents (the 'first generation').[37] "As anti-Semitism declined during the postwar decades, the religion of American Jews gained widespread recognition as America's 'third faith' alongside Protestantism and Catholicism."[38]

While American Jewish theology was mostly limited to scholarship among and within differing religious denominations before the 1950s, American Jewish theologians after World War II began to develop new approaches to understanding the particular character of the various Jewish religious movements comprising American Judaism. The maturing of a new generation of Reform, Conservative, and Orthodox rabbi-theologians resulted in the establishment of Jewish journals that would generate theological discussion and debate. "These journals provided the forum necessary for theologians to test their ideas and exchange their views. They also provided a way for theologians to reach beyond the narrow denominational and professional orientation of the established rabbinical journals."[39] "Among the best are the quarterly *Judaism*, sponsored by the American Jewish Congress, *Tradition*, issued under Orthodox auspices, *Conservative Judaism*, published by the Conservative Rabbinical Assembly, and the *Journal of the Central Conference of American Rabbis*, sponsored by the Reform rabbinate."[40] The 1950s began with a barrage of works on Jewish theology from such prominent scholars and authors as Abraham Joshua Heschel (1907-1972), Will Herberg (1901-1977), J. B. Soloveitchik (1903-1993), Mordecai Kaplan (1881-1983), and Louis Jacobs (1920-2006).[41] The period also included liberal theologian Rabbi Levi A. Olan among those individuals providing existing and prospective Jewish theological points of view relating to American Judaism in general and Reform Judaism in particular.

Olan's interest in theology originated from his deep seeded concerns for social justice and his pessimistic view of the nature of man. "Modern man is in search of a faith that is resourceful enough to give meaning to chaos, and reliable enough to encourage hope for the future."[42] Olan attributed the revived interest in theological matters of the 1950s to crises resulting from the instability and state of affairs existing in the world. In other words, he believed that all was not well with the world. The crises were ascribed to multiple factors, including: the continuing threat of war and the chaos among nations; the diminution of confidence in business resulting from the impersonal power of technological advancements; and the instability of our social ties as people became less permanent in their communal environments. The ideological struggle between democracy and Communism, known as the Cold War, began shortly after the end of World War II and fueled painful anxieties and apprehension of hostility and persecution through much of the second half of the twentieth century. There was an atmosphere of intimidation driven by the ongoing anti-communist hearings held by Joseph McCarthy's Senate Committee on Government Operations and the House Committee on Un-American Activities. Industrial technology brought significant changes to a pattern of life, the impact of which had yet to be fully confronted by the people. Citizens of the nation had become more mobile with an ever increasing assimilation, resulting in the more temporary character of communal social ties and ghetto living. "Western man in our time is characterized by such psychological terms as anxiety, loneliness, and hollowness...We join many groups but belong really to none and the family which once nourished us is losing its significance and its influence."[43] In essence, the twentieth century produced the "maladjusted man:" "the man who had been disembodied from the roots of family, church, and community; the man who had been isolated like the atom from the neutrons of his culture which, before this isolation, had provided a generic substance, a significance and a meaning to his ways and to the end purposes of his life."[44] As the individual gained more freedom, he or she had moved from a position of order in a defined community to a place in an unknown and lonely gathering of many communities. It was essential that the theologians fashion a faith that could give meaning to the swift and dynamic changes occurring in western culture.

Olan believed the period of the mid 1950s was an age of revolution and the product of radical change in every aspect of American culture. There was a vast emptiness in the world making human life an insignificant experience. Man was represented as a "creature of conflicts in the depths of his unconscious which determine his conscious behavior and the rational systems he fashions to guide his course. Life has become a matter of adjustment, instead of a matter of right."[45] The individualism of the twentieth century, responsible for numerous blessings such as religious freedom, political democracy, and the growth in the production of goods, was, for Olan, also responsible for a threatened family life. This possible revolution resulted from an emphasis upon personal rights and a cultural disunity where people failed to understand each other. Moral patterns were changing, questioning the presence of a divine moral law based on the knowledge of reality and reasoning. Olan understood many individuals were seeking theological ideas in a state of hysteria or were moved to failure of nerve because they believed that all was over for man's hopes on earth.

Fundamentally, many Jewish intellectuals came to believe that modern American Jewish thought was not compatible with the reality of the era and the realities of what war had taught them about man's relationship with God. "They found it difficult to accept…what they understood to be liberal Jewish notions concerning the absolute perfectibility of human nature and the inevitable progress of human history toward the Rational and the Good. American Judaism, they argued, did not deal adequately with the problem of evil; nor had it room for belief in the living and redeeming, Supernatural God of Jewish tradition…"[46]

The new Jewish theologians of the 1950s and 1960s concentrated on two concurrent levels. On the one hand, they attempted to clarify their understanding of a genuine Jewish theology in a polemical context, attempting to persuade the uninitiated that theological reflection was important for both Jewish life and Jewish leadership. They attempted to defend themselves against the opponents of a theology that rejected the notion of a living, personal God. On the other hand, these theologians met with each other, probing their theological commitments together, posing problems, exploring difficulties, and debating the content of an authentic Jewish theology.[47]

In the past, and as it continues today, Judaism's theology is expressed through its unique experiences among God, man and destiny, but as Olan stressed, it is not a theological religion.[48] Unlike Christianity which has to explain the mysteries of a man-God, miraculous birth, and supernatural resurrection, Judaism does not require an elaborate and highly imaginative theological organization to explain man's relationship to God.[49] There is no formula of confession or divine grace, and even an unbelieving or nonobservant Jew remains a member of the community and is expected to advance the religious truths that the historic experiences of the people have selected for survival.[50] The fundamental truths of Judaism, Olan continued, are not formulated into an authoritative or dogmatic assertion of ideas, and even though Judaism possesses no inviolable system of belief it is certainly rooted in a group of ideas fundamental to its faith. Olan understood that Judaism was the ideal religion because its basic principles were in harmony with the demands of reason, which is universal and accessible to everyone regardless of their particular historic experiences.[51] If Judaism were reduced to a narrow code of legislative observances, it makes a sham of the long history of Jewish survival among numerous cultures under circumstances of suffering and the threat of extermination.[52] Although never officially formulated into an authoritative code, Judaism, in common with all historic religions, possesses a theology. It existed then, as it does now, in a large collection of sayings, laws, and historic textual material. Olan deferred to Solomon Schechter: "the old rabbis seem to have thought that the true health of a religion is to have a theology without being aware of it."[53] "Rabbinic literature reveals a continuous emphasis on belief climaxed by their attributing the greatest historic event of the people, Exodus, to the doctrine 'and the people believed.'"[54]

It is the constant resistance against an authoritative formulation of theology that one must look for evidence explaining the distinctive nature of Judaism. Olan attributed numerous factors responsible for this resistant attitude. Being a historical religion, one in which the events in the life of the people revealed the nature of divinity and the purpose of human destiny, is certainly crucial to the situation. The content of its religion was always under the challenge of new experiences which kept it from becoming a rigid conception. From their continuous struggles for spiritual existence spanning many centuries, Judaism came into contact with a variety of ideas and it had to constantly test its own unique identity. Olan attributed the Jew's intellectual ability to their successful survival throughout history. "As a minority without the confidence of power it was ever under the necessity of scrutinizing its basic beliefs and had to have the freedom to grow and make changes if it was to survive. Thus one finds a variety of ideas, and even a certain wavering, in the history of Jewish religious thought, but this is the price it paid for continued existence. A formalized creed in Judaism would have spelled certain doom for its survival."[55] And Louis Jacobs, a prominent Jewish theologian during the time of Olan's career, wrote: "Historical investigations into the nature of Judaism have revealed that it is a developing faith, influenced at every step in its growth by ideas and cultural patterns of the various civilisations (sic) with which Jews came into contact."[56]

Jewish resistance to a formal theology rested in the unique relationship of faith to law as interpreted by the prophets and rabbis. The prophets were men who certainly stressed the element of belief in God as a prerequisite to salvation but they insisted upon its expression in concrete ethical terms. Although the prophets were not theologians, they were specific and demanding upon what the people must do; they were nonspecific, though equally demanding, upon what they must believe. The rabbis, sympathetic to a large variety of ideas about God and man, were thorough on the matter of Jewish law. The principles of the Torah for the rabbis were proper conduct which is personified in "concrete norms and behavior;" and in relation to religious doctrines, they allowed a freedom which alleviated the need for final and exacting conclusions.[57] "Where the church found its unity in dogma, the synagogue achieved it by an insistence upon obedience to commandments which are obligatory for all. Judaism cannot be conceived of other than an 'active faith.'"[58] This strong emphasis on the value of the good deed was a deterrent to a fixed theology and performance of the mitzvoth assured God's loving kindness. "It is more religious to serve the good without knowing God than to know God without serving His will."[59] Olan emphasized that in the long history of the Jewish people there was no instance when acquiescence to a fixed body of beliefs was sufficient to qualify an individual as a member of the religious community.[60]

Among the organized movements in American Judaism, Reform appeared to be more interested in and more receptive to theology than the other traditional Jewish movements. Yet even in Reform circles, especially among rabbis, theological discussion was marginal and controversial. "The announcement of the March 1950 convening of the Institute on Reform Jewish Theology at the Hebrew Union College in Cincinnati was received with the keenest attention, being taken as evidence of a reawakening of interest in the spiritual problem of the day."[61] The purpose of the conference was to formulate a declaration of belief and fashion a faith that would give meaning to the rapid and dynamic revolution in western culture, and, at the same time, create a base for confidence in a real and assuring future.[62] The general as well as the Jewish press carried stories declaring this to be its aim, although in the end it can be fairly said that "this institute was a success — perhaps just because it did not proclaim a credo." Although the event was of some significance, "it exposed the lack of theological sensibility and orientation among even the most interested and committed Reform rabbis. It also showed their ignorance of theological literature and strategies."[63] Issues presented for discussion included God and man's relationship to God, history and action, revelation and conduct, authority and self-determination.

The above issues and the petition for theological erudition had their effects. Certain essays were presented in 1951 at the convention of the CCAR, and in the CCAR 1953 convention a Jewish theology symposium was held with papers submitted by Samuel Cohon, Abraham Joshua Heschel, and David Polish. Then, in 1956 the CCAR established its Commission on Jewish Theology whose members were Jakob Petuchowski, Emil Fackenheim, Eugene Borowitz, Lou Silberman, Steven Schwarzschild, Levi Olan, Henry Slominsky, Balfour Brickner, and Samuel Cohon. By 1958 it was clear that the Commission was given little support and less financial resources by the CCAR. Nonetheless, limited success did ensue with the founding of the CCAR Journal in 1953, which frequently published articles in Jewish theology through the years, as well as other articles dealing in theological and philosophical topics, such as autonomy, authority, Reform practice, naturalism, existentialism, Jewish survival, God, *halakhah*, Israel, and the mission of Israel.[64]

The theological market place in the 1950s was alive with enthusiastic activity, including a wide range of ideas in the collection of texts comprising classical Jewish literature. The products offered were abundant and, as Olan described, consisted "of some precious antiques, some refurbished and redesigned old pieces, and a very few genuinely new creations."[65] There were many patrons with varied backgrounds and interests, including some who previously rejected the suggestion of shopping for theological items and were somewhat ashamed at being caught doing it. The only characteristic common to all potential consumers was that they were primarily 'western man,' with relatively few shoppers from the east, subject to the pressure of decision making.[66] The multiplicity of ideas and classical Jewish writing may be compared to a "smorgasbord" offering a variety of foods and dishes.

> "The assortment of dishes served is vast, though limited. As each individual attending the repast takes an empty plate and proceeds along the table, he or she creates a combination of foods particular to his or her taste and appetite. Choices can only be made from those dishes that are on the table. Similarly, the Jewish theologian constructs his or her own collage of Judaism or of a particular issue or problem of Jewish theology, ethics, or law from the menu at hand. The menu derives from the smorgasbord of ideas and statements contained in classical Jewish literature."[67]

With the lack of a central theological authority like the Catholic Church, the wide boundaries presented by Jewish religious literature provide the means for an assortment of inventory items in the development of an authentic Jewish theology. "Just as the Jewish dietary laws permit a wide variety of foods to be eaten and proscribe that certain foods may not be eaten, the ideas that comprise an authentic Jewish theology and the texts that may be utilized in its formation are diverse, but not without limits."[68] The authenticity of theological development outside the broad boundaries of the "smorgasbord" would surely be challenged and most likely rejected.

For Olan, the challenge of the period was crucial and confronted all theologies with unusually new demands. Pointing to the many crises of past generations, Olan maintained a sense of history and perspective.

Referring to the Prophets of Israel and their adjusted religious insight during periods of upheaval, Olan wrote that to offer modern man, who is inundated with enormous problems and blinding confusion, a theology required out of a mood of despair, is to throw him only deeper into the gloom out of which we propose to save him.[69] But responsible Jewish scholars were challenged by no more urgent demand than the examination of Jewish theology and its relevancy upon modern man. Doubting that any theological statement would satisfy all religious Jews, or even those of the Reform movement, Olan believed that it was not incumbent upon these scholars to complete the task but they were not free from beginning the work.[70]

In examining the theological items on display, Olan believed it was essential that a sane attitude toward the cultural situation be maintained along with the awareness of the nature of the literary material under consideration. In his mind, the time was overdue for a rethinking and a re-examination of the Jewish liberal religious program of faith. "The call to re-examine the theology of Reform Judaism is always in order. Being a liberal movement we must be open to all insights into the nature of life and the universe no matter where they come from…There are many winds of theological doctrine today and a liberal Jew must examine all in his search for the ultimate truth."[71] He suggested there were many important intellectual forces within the decades following World War I that challenged the theological ideas of the late 1800s and first half of the 1900s. The prevailing influences in which Judaism must confront included the emergence of Darwinism, higher biblical criticism, comparative religion, the followers of Karl Barth (1886-1968) who represented Judaism as a complete caricature and falsification of Jewish reality, the anti-rationalists, the anti-humanists, and the anti-historicists.[72] The whole structure of the liberal faith appeared to be under attack. "Every time has its own perplexities and therefore needs its own guide."[73]

Olan cautioned the leaders of Reform Judaism to beware of the danger that troubled previous liberal movements, its tendency to transform at some future time into a new fixed program resisting all change. With the challenges confronting Reform Judaism Olan turned to the advice of

Kaufmann Kohler who summed up his own formulation of ideas with the suggestion: "We too must do as Maimonides did — as Jews have always done — point out anew the really fundamental doctrines and discard those which have lost their hold upon the modern Jew or which conflict directly with his religious consciousness. If Judaism is to retain its paramount position among the powers of thought, and to be clearly understood by the modern world, it must again reshape its religious truths in harmony with the dominant ideas of the age."[74] This presented the necessity for a process of change in Reform Judaism and Jewish theology adapting to the current political and social environment. The results would bring about a true liberalism and the heart of Reform Judaism.

Before Olan examined the new items in the theological market place he desired to place them in their proper perspective in the Jewish household. Addressing those Jewish thinkers about the "deplorable state of theology among American Jews," Olan spoke of their anxiety about man's burden of guilt and agony of his fears, stressing their concern more about man's fate than his duty. In Judaism, Olan wrote, the beginning of wisdom is the fear of the Lord, not one's individual destiny. Burdens are removed when the individual performs God's will on earth, having little or no concern with his own fate… The truly religious man, he says, asks, "What is my role, my task, my duty?"[75]

Judaism is a religion that is more concerned with the individual's acceptance to the way of life demanded by God, emphasizing the commandments rather than religious sacraments and the supernatural. It is a moral religion rooted in basic convictions about God and man, nature and history. Olan believed the moral demands are without authority unless they are preceded by "I am the Lord thy God." "To cleave unto the Lord" is interpreted by Olan as doing God's will. Jewish mystics, who sought union with God, centered their thoughts upon the commandments and gave religious experiences of fulfilling the law a cosmic significance.[76] In this manner, cleaving to God implied "living a godlike life, and emulating through one's deeds the moral attributes that characterize God."[77] Quoting from the *Sefer Ha-Yashar* (*The Book of Righteousness*) Olan said: "The foundation of religious activity lies in belief…Neither can you find belief save in religious activity."[78] "It is this interaction and indivisibility of faith and action which is unique with Judaism and which conditions its interest in theological matters. It must concern itself with basic aspects of faith if it is to avoid the pitfall of secularism, and it must be wary of an overemphasis upon theology lest it destroy its unique reason for survival."[79]

Conclusion

A significant development in religious thought among American Reform Jews in the 1960s and 1970s was a developing new theology characterized especially by its attention to the biblical concept of 'covenant,' manifesting the mutuality in the relationship between God and the people of Israel. Covenant theology set the Jewish people apart and bound it together as a "covenant community."[80] In essence, this implied an ongoing relationship between man and God and formed the basis for the historical and open-ended dialogue between God and the people of Israel.[81] This relationship was not limited to that Biblical generation that literally stood at Sinai, for every Jew in every generation was deemed to have stood at Sinai and obligated to renew and to uphold the covenant. As liberals, however, Reform Jews were granted the freedom on the basis of their own selective interpretation of the texts, to renegotiate within limits their own covenantal obligation, their search for religious truth, and their interpretation of God and sin. This was an intellectual methodology devoted to the relationship of God and man, and man's interpretation of the theological concepts of grace, sin, revelation, redemption, covenant, resurrection, and immortality. With this in mind, the following four chapters reveal Olan's search for religious truth, his conceptions of God and sin, the nature of man and his relationship to God, and his review of Judaism's evolutionary aspects of life after death.

CHAPTER 7

Religious Truth

Introduction

In Judaism, truth is primarily an ethical concept describing not what is but what ought to be. This perception, supported by Olan's belief that the whole framework for theology was to find a rationality behind creation, can be demonstrated in the many verses in the Bible articulating expressions of God as "the God of truth."[1] For example: "The Lord God...abundant in goodness and truth" (Exodus 34:6); "He is the Rock...a God of truth and without inequity" (Deuteronomy 32:4); "But the Lord is the true God" (Jeremiah 10:10); and "You have redeemed me, O Lord, God of truth" (Psalms 31:6). This similarity is also present throughout the Talmud in such propositions as: "The seal of the Holy One, blessed be He, is emeth (truth)" (Shabbat 55a); and "the learned men study Torah and give true judgment for the sake of the truth" (Eiruvin 54b).[2] Similar notions are found in medieval Jewish philosophy: "He," the Lord, "judges a true statement to its absolute truth;"[3] while in rabbinic theology "truth" is one of Maimonides' thirteen attributes of God.[4]

The major focus is not "truth" in terms of creedal principles, but authenticity and sincerity in the management of one's personal existence and experience. In the words of Abraham Joshua Heschel: "The meaning of living was found in commitment to truth as the infallible standard for all decisions."[5] Credence to the values of a commitment to truth originates in copious verses in the Bible where truth is connected with: peace ("Speak the truth with one another; and in your gates judge with truth, justice and peace"[6]); righteousness ("The teaching of truth was in his mouth, and injustice was not found on his lips; he walked with Me in peace and with fairness, and turned many away from iniquity"[7]); grace ("And now, if you intend to do kindness and truth with my master, tell me…and I will turn to the right"[8]); justice ("Thus said the Lord of Hosts: Execute true justice, deal loyally and compassionately with one another"[9]); and salvation ("Lead me in Your truth and teach me, for You are the God of my salvation"[10]). And in the Mishnah (Avot 1:18) truth is one of three things, along with justice and peace, on which the world endures. These illustrations represent moral principles or values governing the conduct of individuals and communal groups; and in Judaism "truth" becomes primarily an ethical concept describing not what to believe; but how to live according to the law. The commitment to truth as an infallible standard parallels the sincerity of one's existence and experience, as well as one's conformity to moral principles and values.

The Essence of Liberalism

In American Reform Judaism the essence of all liberalism was a dedication to the recurrent search for truth with an open mind to the philosophic currents of the times, resulting in a "refusal to congeal into a changeless absolute."[11] This was especially true since the strength of liberalism, with its right to disagree, was apparent through its continued resistance to dogmatic principles and creedal dogma. "Liberalism emphasizes the continual search after larger truths acknowledging that the truth we now hold is not one of them, it is not absolute. There may be, and for some there is, one eternal truth, the absolute. But what we now know is not it."[12] The real dilemma confronting the theologians of the period was how to transform a faith that could provide meaning to the rapid and dynamic changes within western culture, while simultaneously creating a base for confidence in a genuine and realistic future. The intellectual foundation for newly reported concepts in natural sciences was, in Olan's view, destroying the philosophical underpinnings of a fixed concept of nature and life; and the rapid progress in social sciences (e.g., psychology and anthropology) questioned current thinking about the nature of man.[13] With this chapter's emphasis on obtaining the truth, the fundamental question that requires attention concerns the method in which one achieves knowledge of "religious truth," or what might otherwise be called "ultimate reality."

Any suggested system of religious thought is sanctioned by the principal prerequisite of epistemological legitimacy — how one considers the origin, nature, methods, and limits of human knowledge. In response to the fundamental question of how does one achieve knowledge of religious truth (also interpreted as how does one know the truth, or reality, or God?), Olan focused on three major epistemological systems or approaches for acquiring religious truth: fundamentalism (fundamentalist supernaturalism and at times called orthodoxy or traditionalism); liberalism (super naturalistic liberalism); and neo-orthodoxy (liberal naturalism). "The fact is," Olan wrote, "that no one of these or all of them together can ever bring us to 'the Truth.' Wisdom, it would seem, would encourage us to avail ourselves of all roads that lead toward the final truth."[14]

Fundamentalism

The oldest method, dominant in history through the Middle Ages, was that of supernatural revelation to a specific person or in a sacred Scripture.[15] This method, currently known as "fundamentalist supernaturalism," continues to be operative today in Orthodoxy and fundamentalism. Some form of truth or knowledge is revealed or disclosed through communication with a deity or other supernatural entity. "It denies the presence of a human element in the revelatory event and in sacred texts that represent the record of such events."[16] The chief feature of this method is its resistance to all changes in basic beliefs, even though minor changes in form and practice are acceptable.[17] Cautioning the community of the growing secularism of the times, the fundamentalists appealed for the return to the forms and practices of yesterday's religion.

Olan believed it significant that the majority of religious people in the world supported this school of thought; and they were united in opposition to all modern philosophies and cultural criticism which challenged the tenets of their respective faiths. He explained that the common trait or theme binding these fundamentalists together was their acceptance of supernatural revelation as a method of apprehending the nature of God and God's will for men. Following this thought process fundamentalist religious leaders understood that Judaism was a self contained system which was supernaturally revealed and must be the standard by which all truth was to be measured in the future. "All fundamentalists point to some event in history where God revealed Himself and His way of life for the welfare of all earthly creatures. This revelation was recorded in a book and interpreted by chosen servants who were entrusted with a special mission of making clear the word of God."[18] Olan viewed the fundamentalists' primary strength in the theory of revelation as "an immovable rock amidst the changing scenes of time" and "a steadiness in an unsteady world."[19] The fundamentalists and those following Orthodoxy, absent the ability of an authoritative body to allow changes of traditional concepts to conform to modern culture, found no urgent need to recognize the demands of a changing Judaism. Olan believed the future of fundamentalist Judaism and Orthodoxy to be problematic as he could not foresee their resurgence in the last decades of the twentieth century and beyond.

> "Orthodox Judaism appears to have lost all power to change because it has no confidence in its ability to issue new interpretations. It feels inadequate to continue the creative process of Halachic development. There can, of course, be no new legislation as there was in the past because there is no authoritative body within Judaism acceptable to all Orthodox Jewry. The tree of the Torah tradition has been deprived of the living waters of growth in Orthodox Judaism and is destined to

wither and die. Orthodox Judaism today rejects the demands of a changing world and like the Sadducees of Talmudic days it repulses all effort to give life to the tradition by interpretation and responsible innovation."[20]

The above perspective was evidently borne from those fundamentalists who agreed to remain untouched by the realities of cultural changes and it would appear their effectiveness would be limited in coming to terms with modern scientific changes, transformation in current social structure, and lessening of restraints in personal morality. One example is the present thinking in Jewish Orthodoxy that limits the role of women in certain religious practices of worship. With commercial systems and organizations invariably undergoing transformation, governments growing powerful only to collapse, and ever changing scientific theories giving way to new principles, every aspect of man's culture is constantly changing, except for God and His will which remains unchanged.[21] However, social changes were not confined to Olan's rabbinic era as humanity continually experiences endless changes within its environment and culture. Although the above described rigid doctrine would originate from fundamentalist groups such as the Orthodox, Reform theologians were not ready to abandon the view that Judaism is a process and a constantly growing and evolving system of beliefs and practices.

It should be noted, however, that some Jewish orthodox groups agree with the view that Judaism is a constantly changing process. Modern Orthodoxy, for example, in its attempt to bridge Orthodox Judaism and modernity, was borne out of the context that it was possible for Jews to maintain Jewish law, ritual observance and customs while exposing themselves to secular society, science, and modern ideas. Furthermore, the current state of Orthodox Judaism in 2015 is not as dire as Olan predicted. The anticipated demise of Orthodox Judaism has not occurred, and there have been numerous positive developments within the Modern and ultra-Orthodox communities since Olan's rabbinic years. According to the October 2013 Pew Research Center survey of U.S. Jews, approximately ten percent of the nearly six million Jews in America identify themselves as Orthodox or Modern Orthodox.[22]

Liberalism

Olan's second method of acquiring religious truth is known as liberalism, also referred to as supernaturalistic liberalism that considers revelation and its resulting condition to constitute a combination of the divine and the human. This method, which Olan also called the Modernist approach, was characterized by its rejection of supernatural revelation, yet retaining faith in Scriptural inspiration, and acceptance of the scientific and rational categories of investigation.[23] This approach illustrates the initial displacement of divine revelation with human intelligence. The common bonds for scholars following this supernaturalistic liberalism, were the "spirit" rather than the "literal meaning" of revelation; their acceptance of reason, experience, and experiment as the primary sources of knowledge of the nature of the universe and of life; and, their acceptance of Scriptural interpretation in a manner that supported the conclusions derived from those sources.[24] This is an intellectual method that relied on the rational and empirical (verification by observation and experience) criterion as tests for any idea or value;[25] and it was a distinguishing characteristic of most liberal religions including Reform Judaism. "If we recognize that an absolute objective reality is not available to us, and accept the proposition that by the methods of empirical research and rational interpretation, we can arrive at the best basis for action, we can avoid much of the hopelessness which pervades our modern culture."[26] This enables man's creative capacity to provide him with the means for developing and understanding the sciences, philosophies, and arts.

But questions arose among scholars within this Modernist approach inquiring whether the legitimate source of truth stemmed from reason or experience. While certain modernists accepted the views of reason or experience, Olan believed the dominant view to be reason for it was a divine gift with the Jew and a principal method in determining God's way.[27] Viewing the Reform movement as liberals, they are committed to examine all truths, to relate them to Reform Judaism's purpose in history, and to push forward the frontiers of the knowledge of God.[28] One of the significant attributes of liberalism is its use of the historical method of evaluating the importance of the body of beliefs that have come down through the ages. This historical evaluation attempts to recapture the human experience from which doctrines arose. "It employs the tools of a historical critical method to capture the real significance of the faith of our fathers. Its positive contribution arises from the attempt that liberalism makes to restate the ancient problem in terms of modern experience."[29] In this manner, a person is provided the freedom to accept or reject a belief or an authority and this places him in the prominent role as a final judge of truth leading to a strong emphasis on individualism.

Neo-Orthodoxy

The third general theological approach competing for the modern mind was described by Olan as "neo-orthodoxy." Neo-orthodoxy is a comprehensive term mostly used in the sense of modern contemporary theology or liberal theology. It denies the strict orthodox approach of infallibility and Divine influence of the Bible. This method was also referred to at various times as the theology of crises, dialectical theology, existential theology, or neo-supernaturalism; and in more recent times, liberal naturalism.[30] Olan considered this third and newest epistemological system in religious thought as being critical both of the pre-modern emphasis on revelation and the modernistic scientific and rational approaches for the verification of religious truth.[31]

Neo-Orthodoxy represented a late 19th-century development under the leadership of Samson Raphael Hirsch, and sanctioned modern dress, the use of the vernacular in sermons, and a more positive view of modern culture. This signified a break from the traditional Judaism of Eastern European Jews who followed the literal interpretation of the Bible. Following the rabbinic tradition, neo-orthodoxy cautioned against the tendency to find theology in the Bible instead of attempting to understand the writing within the framework of its natural setting. "This is not orthodoxy or fundamentalism in the historic sense, for this system is in sympathy with all critical exegetical investigation though it considers such labor irrelevant to the main concern of faith."[32]

Olan described the proponents of "neo-orthodoxy" as former liberals who have lost faith in the rationalism of the philosophers, the methods of the scientists, the reliance upon the natural phenomenon, and the confidence in progress. Not able to return to the supernatural revelation of the traditionalists as expressed in one moment of history and recorded in some sacred book, this school of theological belief turned its back upon the two aforementioned significant religious methods of fundamentalism and liberalism, and began to fashion a set of religious concepts that involved both the past and something entirely new. In essence, neo-orthodoxy represented a post-modern return to a traditional faith, one which superseded orthodoxy and liberalism, traditionalism and modernism. This method attacked the liberal methodology of modernism, calling into question the objective capacity of man's mind. This confrontation, Olan wrote, was based on the neo-orthodox view that the rational consciousness had been infringed by the irrational unconscious, labeling man's ability to reason as contaminated and therefore ineffective.

> "The major tendency of our age appears to be anti-intellectualist; the mind of man is not to be trusted to apprehend the truth that matters. The failure of the modern age to fulfill its promise of peace and order among men is attributed to the empirical-rational spirit of its philosophers who engendered a shallow optimism among liberals and social reformers."[33]

Olan admitted that although there was disagreement between theologians of this anti-intellectual view, they were convinced that the mind of man was not capable of achieving a saving truth. The important objective for them was deliverance, not truth, and that lay beyond any rational system.[34] Karl Barth (the only truth being the incarnation) and Reinhold Niebuhr (there is reason in all things but concludes that the intellect is not able to discover the core for itself or validate after it) were presented by Olan as examples of theologians convinced that the mind of man was not capable of achieving a saving truth.[35] He opined their attack was valid protest against man's confidence in the absolute power of logic. Although reason had been criticized, there is a difference between the limitations placed on the mind of man and quite something else to invalidate completely the mind's usefulness in comprehending the reality of God or the meaning of value judgments.[36] In this regard, belief, for which there is no evidence, is often an accessory to evidential truth; and faith is a means of obtaining evidence, "the thought being father to the fact, as the wish was father to the thought."[37] Therefore, in order to achieve knowledge of religious truth one must exhibit the initiative to obtain evidence through faith and belief. This approach was anti-intellectual as it avoided the premises upon which faith rested. A criterion for faith, Olan wrote, is indispensable in order to avoid the loss of principles for a belief in God.[38] In other words, faith is essential for one to believe in God.

Much of the anti-intellectualism of the third and newest epistemological system in religious thought was attributed by Olan to the distinctive Christian doctrine rooted in the mystery of the Trinity (Father, Son, and Holy Spirit) and the spirit becoming flesh (no incarnation or miraculous birth to explain). "The Resurrection is advanced as transcending the limits of the conceivable and is a consummation beyond history."[39] Olan affirmed that faith transcends reason, a view that has been acceptable to religious thinkers throughout the ages; and the notion that reason is a "scandal," a "stumbling block," is alien to most religious thinkers including those in Judaism.[40] The essence of Jewish epistemology is the covenant of Law which must be studied, understood and obeyed, actions for which require the continued application of one's intelligence.[41] With the traditional recognition by Jews of the authenticity of divine revelation with natural theology, religious truth contained in the Bible "is understood as emanating from God, but it cannot be in direct contradiction to the human intellect which is in itself of divine origin."[42] This is compared by Olan to the prophets who were men especially accustomed to divine revelation but with a faith fashioned on the basis of reason through experience and thought. "We can never know God in all His ways, we must seek to know His will with all the powers we have, and reason is a gifted instrument in our search."[43] Olan understood that some modern Jewish thinkers had been tempted away from their traditional origins by their submission to the concern of Christian theologians. "Their condemnation of the modern rational-empirical philosophy as being the cause of modern man's crises, has led them away from a balanced and sensible view."[44]

In alluding to the three primary approaches of attaining truth, Olan suggested there is value in each of them and finality in no one of them. Promoting the values and weaknesses of scientists and also disparaging the theologian, Olan wrote:

> "It is probably true that absolute truth is beyond our human grasp. Science unfolds a good measure of the natural world, but not all of it. Reason lights up some of the dark areas of life, but unquestionably not all of them. The mystic by his individual intuitional sense has hold of some aspect of reality but surely not all of it. In this regard the scientist and philosopher often display the weakness of the theologian. All of them are tempted to claim an absolute and exclusive patent on truth. Wisdom would argue for a more humble spirit upon all who seek to find the ultimate. It is probably beyond all of us, and certainly out of reach of any one of us."[45]

Balancing Faith and Reason

For Olan the position of Reform Judaism had little to gain in the area of religious knowledge from those theologians critical of both pre-modern revelation and the modernist scientific and rational methods for the verification of religious truth. Faith and reason, he concluded, are essential to a liberal epistemology: "faith to lay the first postulates, to arouse a passionate commitment; and reason to evaluate the possibilities of ultimate concern and always to guard against a blind irrationalism by which we may never know whether we are worshipping God or the devil."[46] Alluding to government leaders that began thinking with their "blood instead of their minds," an obvious reference to the existing global political environment that witnessed two World Wars, Nazism, Fascism, communism, the Korean War, and the early stages of the Vietnam War, Olan suggested the time was not favorable to forsake the Reform Movement's trust in reason, or for a faith beyond comprehension. "This is the road to a hopeless outlook on life and destiny as is evidenced by the almost complete rejection of man's possibilities on earth by the neo-Orthodox theologians."[47]

Theologians are faced with the concern of whether faith and reason are opposing approaches in the formula for obtaining truth. Although both represent different approaches to truth, faith and reason are not mutually exclusive. In Olan's view, reason disclosed one aspect of reality while faith revealed another. The issue, he said, is how we shall know that God is and what He is. In order to comprehend this dilemma, one must rely on all aspects of individual experience, faith, and reason in grasping religious truth.

> "Here the role of the existentialist and the rational-naturalist is not an either/or. The fact is that both are necessary and complementary. One without the other is inadequate and can be misleading. The existential experience alone suffers from the fact that it is purely individual and personal. It may reveal God or the devil, and history records both. The rational truth alone may reveal God who is a force in nature, or a logical syllogism. It will not disclose the God whom we need for worship and commitment…Faith must lay postulates, draw upon a truth revealed by personal experience. Reason must guard us against irresponsible and capricious irrelevancies. Both existentialism and naturalism are sound as protests against the exclusive rights of each other. Each by itself, however, is not adequate as a program for the apprehension of religious truth."[48]

The major concern here was with the degree of significance for those fundamental skills (reason, faith, rationalization) that are necessary in determining religious truth. We are reminded by Olan that Jewish philosophers were religious men, and the Hebrew prophets preached a faith that was rational and reasonable. To be sure, if there is an authentic attribute of the Judaic spirit which is obvious and clearly identifiable, it is its rational nature.[49] Olan pursued an extreme Jewish rationalism based on science, nature, and logic. Recognizing the faith element even in his scientific version of Reform Judaism, he saw the task of the Reform theologian as one of purging Judaism of supernaturalism and of replacing it with the immanentist (in dwelling of God) findings of science.[50] Man, it is believed, is a rational creature, though not always reasonable, and he possesses the faculty of challenging all evidence for its rationality. Olan alluded to the following philosophers who welcomed the opportunity to clarify Jewish faith by categories of reason: Maimonides (a supreme rationalist and an intellectual elite, who, using reason, can understand by means of demonstrative arguments[51]); Hermann Cohen (reality is rooted in God, man's reason itself originating in God[52]); and Philo (passions of man controlled by reason[53]).

> "The prophets were, of course, sensitive to the mysterious confrontation with God in revelation, but they conveyed these visions by an appeal to experience and to logic. Faith by its very nature involves affirmations beyond the rational and the Hebraic spirit is not characterized by a rigid syllogistic encasement. But it did not look upon reason as diseased (referring to Reinhold Niebuhr's contention that reason is an incurable disease)."[54]

"In point of fact," Olan continued, "reason is energetically used to purify man's faith of its impurities...It is employed as a corrective, freeing the intuitive truth of its primitive corruptions, deepening it and permeating it."[55] By itself, reason is never the source of truth, yet it is an integral ingredient of truth. Man's rational capacity in Judaism follows inevitably from the Jewish belief in a rationally just order of creation which man understands through reason.[56]

In essence, rationalism represents a balancing act between faith and reason, all of which maintain significant roles in the search for truth. For strict rationalists, "reason is a source of knowledge in itself, superior to and independent of sense perception."[57] Olan's views regarding the complimentary aspects of both faith and reason in the search for truth mirror those of Rabbi Roland B. Gittelsohn, successor (1969 to 1971) to Olan's CCAR presidency. Gittelsohn explained the resemblance as follows: "The fact is that a religion of rationalism, a religion of tension between faith and reason in which neither is by definition always and in every confrontation superior to the other — such a religion has been and continues in our day to be an authentic alternative within the Jewish Tradition."[58] Gittelsohn expanded his affirmation of reason and faith by referring to Milton Steinberg:

> "From my point of view, religious truth is properly achieved not by reason alone — because reason alone is unavailing. Religious truth, however, is not discovered by faith alone — certainly not in our time…we are equipped with reason, we know the power of reason, and it is our most potent possession as human beings. Reason cannot be repudiated or denied. It cannot be stifled or put asunder…The real dialect of the religious life is not a plunge into faith or a descent into inwardness, leaving the intellect behind. The real movement of personality is a continuous alternation between faith and reason."[59]

The significance of rationalism is further demonstrated by Alfred North Whitehead, the father of process thought (see Chapter 8) and a significant influence on Olan. He wrote: "Rationalism never shakes off its status of an experimental adventure…Rationalism is an adventure in the clarification of thought, progressive and never final. But it is an adventure in which even partial success has importance."[60]

Noteworthy commentary affirms faith and reason as companions on the road to achieving religious truth. This is noted further by another Olan colleague during the seventy-fourth annual convention of the Central Conference of American Rabbis: "Reason, in a sense, prepares the path on which faith can walk. Reason clears the path once faith has begun to walk it and writes an intelligible record of the distance covered. And when faith has reached its destination reason embraces faith, and the two companions unite in the kiss of the Messiah."[61]

Normative Judaism

Olan believed Judaism to be life-giving with an intuitive ability to allow one to grasp the inner nature of new concepts provided they fall within specific boundaries. He believed in a normal Judaism, or what he called "normative Judaism." "There is such a thing as normative Judaism…New ideas and ideals, new values or insights are acceptable if they are in harmony with the basic Jewish outlook. If a new idea or value is validated by reason and science but is not at home in the unique Jewish view, one cannot deny it or reject it on that ground. But we must recognize it as a departure from the norm."[62] Olan's meaning of basic Jewish outlook refers to traditional Jewish thinking where, in the present instance, it represents an omniscient and omnipotent God. This understanding is perhaps rooted in the Jewish belief in a rationally just order of creation which one can understand through reason. As an example, Olan provided the idea of a limited God which for some theologians, including himself, had intellectual legitimacy and religious merit. But he believed it would be disingenuous to force it into the frame of normative Judaism. As tradition understands it, the God of normative Judaism is omnipotent and omniscient. On the other hand, Olan explained, if tradition is incorrect, we must admit such and not spread the impression that Judaism vanishes into an uninspired and worthless complex of concepts.

Faith

With the stamp of the divine upon man that he is created in the image of God, to the *imitation Dei*, he is placed in a unique position in relation to other earthly creatures and to God. Upon this doctrine rests the whole structure of Jewish ethics for it makes man supreme in the animal kingdom by providing him with an intense awareness and potential for unlimited personal fulfillment. Yet man is still limited and requires assistance in fulfilling his numerous objectives in an imperfect world. We are constantly assailed with egocentric thoughts and actions placing us in position of not recognizing our own shortcomings. Man's confidence in his own capacity to resolve his problems is his greatest sin—hubris—the sin of pride.[63]

> "The tragedy of modern man is that he is too proud to see his own limitations and to acknowledge that he needs help. The first step towards a meaningful religious faith is for a man to know that he is human and not God, which he cannot alone and by his own strength handle the complex business of living. Faith is born when a man speaks the truth in his heart."[64]

During the course of Jewish history, faith has been paramount in the successful struggle for survival. The life of the Jew is nourished on faith: faith in man, the dignity of man, and the divine potential within humanity. The moment the Jew accepts fatalism his history ends. The faith is woven into the whole history which he has written in letters of pain and suffering.[65] "Faith is like sun and rain to the earth. It permeates whatever is healthy in us to grow and blossom and bear fruit...Life demands that we believe in ourselves that we believe in the possibility of achieving our aims. Healthy living demands faith, for that is creative. That the Jew still maintains his faith in the value and meaning of life may well be accounted as one of the miracles of our day."[66] However, many obstacles need to be overcome by man in order to perfect a wholesome meaning of life. "World wars, a cataclysmic depression, Nazism, Fascism, and communism, and a mad race toward a final self extinction on the part of man are hardly the soil for faith in inevitable progress."[67]

Conclusion

This chapter, focusing on the methodology of obtaining religious truth and ultimate reality, comes to a conclusion by referring to Olan's radio sermon of March 27, 1949 captioned "Religion is One — Religions are Many." In the first place, Olan suggested that although religion began out of wonder, need, and fear, the concepts of different religions are essentially the same. They all believe in God, in a moral law, in freedom of the human will, that life has a purpose, and that the grave is not the end. The interpretations of these ideas vary, and the forms of worship may be different, but the essential truth is the same for all of them. Olan asserted that although the languages may differ and the rituals alien to one another, every religion is basically true for they all seek the same thing — blessings for comfort, strength, and hope. The need for our time and the essence of all religions is a belief that there is meaning and purpose to life, a sentiment that has been offered by numerous religious leaders over the course of history. "Too many of us have paid too much attention to the forms (of the differing religious faiths) making a fetish out of the symbols and externals of our faith, but neglecting the basic truths that are common to every religion…People who are truly religious will find unity in their diversity."[68]

The difficulty of humanity is the ability of the individual to determine that which is expected of him by God. Principles differ among the minds of humankind and it requires the intellectual capacity of faith and reason in the search for God in order to know His will. Although the mind of man may have definite limits, he had better use it before his future is placed in the hands of others. Faith is not commanded in Mosaic Law, for there is not one command that states 'thou shalt believe' or 'not believe.' "Where the question is of eternal truth, there is nothing said of believing, but *understanding* and *knowing*."[69] Olan believed that for religion to continue to be relevant, it must examine its faith, its "commitment to God"[70] and "affirmation that life is a fulfillment of God's kingdom"[71] by acceptable standards of reason. This simply meant that it takes faith to know God, but it takes reason to know the will of God.[72] "Failure to accept reason as an essential of man will sound the death knell of the church. The fact is that religion must present itself in the court of reason as does every aspect of life."[73] Olan continually described himself as a religious liberal, a rationalist who stressed the role of reason and experience in the search for truth. Since reason was common to all men, it was seen as the uniting element in mankind which would lead to brotherhood. Reason became the instrument man must use continually in his search after larger truths, acknowledging always that the truth he now declares is not an absolute."[74] Yet, as Olan knew, and surely we all agree, the world possessed by man is not perfect. To announce that man has grasped the absolute truth is to attribute perfection to his own image. "Man, a creature less than God, must constantly use his mind to search nature and himself in the hope that he will reach a point nearer the absolute."[75] This search for truth appears to be a never ending task of rational thinking borne from intelligent reason and faith. And as Olan succinctly phrased it: "religious faith cannot successfully avoid the ceaseless search (for truth)."[76]

As mentioned earlier in Shabbat 55a, truth in Hebrew is Emeth and it is spelled with the first (alef), middle (mem), and last letter (tav) of the Hebrew alef-bet (alphabet). Since it is considered to embrace the whole Hebrew alphabet, the sages concluded that God made truth the beginning, the center, and the end of the world.[77] Corresponding Talmudic commentary (Shabbat 55a) interprets the "seal of the Holy One…is emeth (truth)" as another name for God. Kabbalah notes that Emeth is the power to realize one's own deepest potential, which is in fact the ability of the soul to bring about the ultimate experience of God. Therefore, from a Jewish perspective, one can conclude that the search for truth entails one's concept and understanding of God and His omnipotence and omniscience. The next chapter illustrates how this concept and understanding plays out in modern theology and the Reform Movement and Olan's concept of God and the meaning of sin.

CHAPTER 8

A Polarity of Thought — God and Sin

Introduction

In an April 1962 sermon to the congregation of the Unity Church, Olan searched for an answer to the primary religious question of modern man reflected by the title of his sermon: "Is There Really a God?" He began his response to the question of God's reality by introducing the initial concept of divinity (some divine being or thing expressed as a god) through an explanation of the origin of religious thinking and practice beginning with the primordial culture of the ancient Near East. Olan's explanation, of course, is not unique for it is analogous to the wisdom presented by both current and previous generations of religious scholars. Their teachings remind us that in ancient times man reacted to the wonders of the universe, his necessities of life, and his fears in the world, by devising what subsequent cultures referred to as primitive spirits and powers, encompassing society with all kinds of fetishisms, including animistic type influences and totemic creatures of one kind or another. These fetishisms were both awed and feared and responded to the needs, curiosities, and uncertainties of the people.[1] This was the period of pagan mythology and idolatry where the gods were conceived as powers embodied in nature or as separate god-like beings connected with nature and limited by the laws of nature. In these mythological views, the purpose of the gods was to assist man in conquering other men, or to help him survive against the unfavorable and harsh powers of the universe. This ancient period embodied the initial stage in human history that portrayed man's perception of the god or gods he was seeking.

With the gradual development of the religion of Biblical Israel, biblical literature penned by religious thinkers not believing in magic and necromancy became a polemic against idolatry and the worship of fetishes. Evolving theological ideas provided the groundwork for a new understanding of one's concept of divinity. It was during the biblical period when man conceived of God as one who could provide whatever man needed: "rain for the crops, safety on a dangerous journey, a cure for his diseases — these and similar needs were expressed to a deity who had the power to grant them. It was a view quite in keeping with man's understanding of the universe."[2] This was the period when the Bible was regarded as a divinely revealed document, and with no systematic Biblical criticism, every word was deemed to be a recognized truth.

The years following the biblical period reflect the reverence of centuries of devotion. However, man's understanding of the universe began to change with the introduction of the concept of natural law by Isaac Newton (1643-1727) in the late 1600s. Writing a number of religious tracts dealing with the literal interpretation of the Bible, Newton's conception of God was that of a masterful creator and intelligent Being whose existence could not be denied in the face of the grandeur of all creation.[3] Some biographers viewed Newton's assessment as tantamount to a dualistic view approaching deism,[4] the system of thought advocating that God set the universe in motion without interfering with how it is run. However, he differed from strict adherents of Deism in that he viewed God's involvement as the active intervention in the movement of the stars and the motion of the universe to keep the planets in orbit.[5] Yet, Newton also believed in a rationally immanent world in which the ordered and dynamically informed universe could be understood by active reason rather than divine revelation,[6] a concept later embraced by the Reform Movement.

Every generation confronts the religious issues in terms of its own culture while seeking solutions within those existent cultural conditions. This means that society or a particular group within a society share common beliefs, customs, practices, language, and attitudes, while recognizing a particular place or time to which they belong.[7] As these characteristics vary and change, it is imperative that man respond in a manner favorable and intelligible to his new cultural environment. Olan understood the classical view of God as a supernatural, omnipotent, and omniscient being was generally acceptable to the "cultural milieu" of the western world until the twentieth century.[8] But since much of the cultural climate of the twentieth century was unable to submit to this classical view, numerous scholars and religious leaders rejected "the idea that there is an ultimate, perfect, unchanging, supernatural being that is self-sufficient, adequate to himself without need of all else, an uncompromising absolute."[9] "To ask God to set aside, in some whimsical fashion, the regular operation of the laws of nature (as man sought God's direct intervention) made little sense to the modern world."[10] This was the time posited by Olan in which it became no longer possible to ask God to grant something that men of an earlier period found natural. "The theological frame in which the prophetic doctrine is disclosed tends to disconnect the mind of modern secular man. The idea of God omnipotent and judge of history is alien to the culture in which he lives. Meaningful to an earlier generation, it is meaningless in an age pervaded by science and reason."[11]

Reflecting on the view of God from the Bible, there were, and possibly continue to be, many people affirming their faith in an omnipotent and omniscient deity who can both bless and curse His creatures on earth. Yet, Olan, like so many other religious scholars, reminded us that there are many people who have serious doubts about the power of God, as well as God's existence, including those with knowledge of or who experienced the many tragedies of mankind, the foremost of which was the Holocaust.

A Life without God?

Modern people are doing well without God, Olan said, citing the example of those individuals content with having a truly secular view of life "which says there is no God."[12] The significant reality is that since many people live their lives as if God does not exist, at what point does the presence of God seem to matter? If there is no God, Olan said, the universe is without meaning and purpose, then everything is permitted as there is only fear, and wrong is no more real than right.[13] Furthermore, he suggested that if the universe is not the outflow of one unifying spirit and man is a thing among things, then there really is no difference between "duck hunting and man hunting."[14] And without meaning or purpose, the significance of man is meaningless.

> "He has no more regard for a bug than for a person. Man, then, is a thing among things. He is no more significant than the slime that oozes or the rhinoceros that roars. If man is of no greater or lesser worth than anything else, then what difference does it really make whether we kill five thousand chickens or five thousand children? If there is no more meaning to a flea than to a man, what difference does it make if we step on the flea or rub out the man? If man is a thing among things, then why is man shooting a crime and duck shooting a pleasant, legitimate sport?"[15]

As for morality, if there is no God, the guiding principle is opportunism, that what is right or good becomes practical at the moment, inviting possible anarchy while questioning the validity of a just society.[16] Positing the hypothesis of atheism, Olan said that all is an accident derived from a blind machine. "Ideals, love, hope, then are matters of chance. All our dreams are illusions; all are set in a soulless, meaningless, purposeless, accidental collection of atoms. What is there in all of this but discouragement, despair, and demoralization?"[17] Furthermore, if there is no God, society must respond to the relevant and central questions of all religions regarding the meaning of life, suffering, and death. It relates human existence to a reality which gives "purpose to man's journey on earth, to his failures and successes, to his agony and joy."[18] Olan acknowledged that accepting the view of the atheist suggests that love and ideals have no place in society and that "if all is chance then it finally adds up to nothing."[19] The God believer, Olan said, knows that he is not alone; he lives surrounded by a power that directs the universe towards the good, the true, and the beautiful. Despite all the problems which religious faith arouses, there is little doubt that without God we accept defeat before we begin.[20]

The Nature of God

While much has been written and said about living a life without God, Olan alleged that intellectually the premise that God is a reality is far more satisfying than the assumption that God does not exist. A recurring theme in his numerous teachings described the individual as part of something larger than himself, while asserting that the universe is the outflow of one ultimate reality. "The meaning of our existence, its tears and joys, derives from the fact that we belong to some total reality. Our ideals, hopes, morals are rooted in the larger reality; they are not the whims of men or the results of chance."[21] His concept of reality included unexpected life moments, mental awareness, self-determination, and natural resolve, with the universe being seen as the reflection of one universal will. "Within this one reality, there exist elements of chance, mind, creative freedom, and cosmic purpose. There are intimations that God is supreme and ultimate, but never beyond. He is part of reality, not apart from it. He is best described as transcendent–immanent."[22] Olan's transcendent-immanent view of God was dependent upon both human feelings and knowledge. Man's reason, freedom, and creativity derive from the being of all beings, he believed, all of which is implied in the belief that there is a God and projects a view of the world as orderly and rational.[23] Once one says God is real, Olan said many questions can then be asked. Does God hear prayer? Is He a good God while permitting innocent people to suffer and die? These and other questions about the nature of God are important and call for sensible answers.

Accepting a positive affirmation for the existence of God, we can review a variety of descriptions of the nature of God in Jewish thought. In addition to being described as transcendent or immanent, or some combination of both, God might have been personalized or abstract, omnipotent or more or less limited. And there has always been room for differences. This expanding view of the nature of God led to the perpetual stumbling block of all theology — theodicy — the defense of God's goodness and omnipotence in view of evil.[24] The tension between God's power and His goodness has concerned scholars and religious thinkers for a millennium. God's omnipotence and His unfailing love are often challenged by the injustices of life. If God is omnipotent and good, then why is there so much senseless suffering? This is an old problem which has been addressed in a variety of theological prescriptions, all of which retain some semblance of omnipotence, omniscience, and goodness. While Olan admitted the essence of God is evident in nature, in history, and in man, and therefore sufficient for a faith in the existence of a supreme power or being, to describe that power or being as all-powerful and all good finds a stark contradiction in the manifestation of terrible and useless suffering which is often evidence more of a demon than a loving father.[25] This observation is echoed in many of Olan's programs and teaching, one of which follows:

> "To keep on insisting that He is omnipotent and good in the face of senseless tragedies of life is to alienate ourselves from a living God who has meaning for life today. Let us think of God as a father. When we are children, our fathers seem to be all powerful…when the child becomes an adult; he sees his father with his limitations and views him with even greater love."[26]

It certainly is much easier for many people to maintain the view of God fashioned during their childhood — God is the king, sitting on a throne who can work miracles when He chooses. If a catastrophe occurs, the childlike response asserts it was God's will. For Olan, this view was not adequate to the demands of the twentieth century. Too much has happened and continues to happen for the modern mind to take seriously so naïve a view of God. Yet, there are many people who live as if this naive view still exists. Olan responded to the above premise as follows: "It is the pity of our time that it reveals the true reality of God in a more real sense for the first time in human history and men go on and on clinging to a God which their ancient ancestors fashioned."[27]

One might conjecture that the whole concept of omnipotence arose in response to origins which, in hindsight, were unsupported by realities of the times. Olan paints the universe as a changing and growing phenomenon that presented problems generations ago to an unchanging God.[28] With this in mind, he poses the question of whether the principle of evolution applies to the Creator as well as to His creation.[29] While the evolution of life presents great strides in education, science, and technology, it also reveals awful waste, terrible cruelty, futile pain and destruction. Olan, as well as other religious thinkers and philosophers, inquired as to the reasonableness of crediting these advances and regressions to an all-powerful and all loving God. If we had only the facts before us and had never heard of the God of yesterday, Olan wondered if we would have arrived at that perfect Deity of classical theology.[30] "There are too many instances of unnecessary sufferings, of waste, and downright injustice for the mind of man to be satisfied with the traditional insistence upon omnipotence. It may be that a God, finite in power, who is unlimited in love, is more approachable, more understandable, and more real."[31]

Although numerous and diverse theological interpretations of the nature of God have existed over centuries, religious scholars acknowledge two different understandings or interpretations. One opinion is analogous to conventional and more traditional theism in which religious or revealed theology stems from sacred scripture. This view is explained as the belief in the existence of one God as the omnipotent Supreme Being and Judge of the universe. In this connection, God is regarded as the creative source of humanity and the world; transcending yet immanent in the world. The second view is a theology derived from reflecting on experience and reason available to human beings rather than from some special revelation. This assessment describes the philosophy of an emergent God, a God in the process of change who needs assistance from mankind, and the evolving thought process of the human being. This has been explained as follows:

> "To regard God as perfect in power, as he is in vision, at the very beginning, is the most disastrous of superstitions…God and man are a polarity. They are both heroes in the same drama. They need each other, they grow together, but they also suffer together. Hence they need consolation, Benedictions and Consolations. That the Midrash is designed to supply."[32]

Evolution of Limited Theism

The understanding of God by early religious thinkers as being omnipotent and omniscient required a reexamination with the development of monotheistic religions since much in modern society's experiences justified doubt about those specific characteristics of God. Olan believed that change is fundamental to reality and instead of the unconditional view of the divine, we are nearer to the truth if God is viewed as not being absolute, nor perfect or self-sufficient. Society only has to be reminded of the many atrocities and catastrophes experienced by humanity during the course of history. It certainly is not a perfect world and someone, someplace, is waiting for man to assist in the attempt to achieve perfection. Olan described this as follows:

> "In the first place, the evolutionary nature of the universe and of life suggests that the world is imperfect, incomplete. It is true that the Bible records that on the sixth day God finished making the world. But the world is not finished at all, it is terribly incomplete. Furthermore, it reveals in its long evolutionary process many blunders, cruelties, and much waste. A perfect, all-powerful God ought to do better than that."[33]

In Olan's view, God's reality was pictured as having definite or definable limits with a number of possibilities; in effect a limited nature or existence. Henry Cohen described Olan's view of God as "theistic finitism," in which God's reason is expressed in the rationality of nature.[34] In this connection one could have a deep faith in a God who is not all-powerful, and therefore just not able to do everything. God, therefore, is "a limited God, not an absolute one. He is part of the painful process of growth."[35] Man's understanding of God had now evolved into a limited theism characterized by a God who both directed and depended upon human action. "He too is a part of a creative world which is always becoming but never complete. He is involved with man in a great adventure and He is dependent upon man's moral choice and freedom."[36] In this manner, God is a being who cares about mankind, who makes for order and for love, but since He is not in complete control of the universe, He needs our assistance.

Olan also believed that God must be known in personal experiences just as the Hebrew prophets knew and experienced God. "That God is, that He is real, is as valid an assertion as that the world itself is and that it is real."[37] The reality of God's existence is a belief evidenced by the world of nature itself. In this sense, Olan stressed that one's faith in a God is no different than one's reliance on science, both of which ultimately rests upon assumptions that cannot be substantiated.

> "The only valid requirement for a hypothesis, whether in religion or science, is that it be treated with critical discipline and come under logical restraint. If we are faced with a choice between theism and atheism, and a thinking person must confront just that, there is little doubt as to which postulate better fits the facts. To affirm that the universe is matter without form, or purpose, or life, or creativity, or unity, that it is a 'tale told by an idiot,' just will not satisfy the data of reality. That God is, that He is real, is as valid an assertion as that the world itself is and that it is real."[38]

In Olan's view, the early childhood picture of God sitting on a throne was nothing but persistent blindness by clinging to a religious faith which arose when men knew nothing about the true nature of the universe before science. He understood the reality of God coming from convincing evidence, not just from theologians or philosophers, but from the scientist who revealed a universe in which God is as real as any scientific truth.[39] This meant that science acknowledged the universe: as an organism, not a mechanism; of possessing vitality, in other words characterized by life, moving from the inorganic to the organic, from the animal to the human, in effect a process.[40] "But at the heart of everything is life."[41] Olan understood that science revealed the universe as an orderly place with laws, leading one to conclude that there is no such thing as an accident. If one stumbles and falls, it is not an accident; it validates gravity's laws at work. The time to worry, Olan said, begins if one did not fall. "The orderliness of the universe has led scientists to speak of it as being like a thought. What they seem to be saying is that it has both life and mind as demonstrable realities."[42] Finally, Olan said, the scientists disclosed a universe with a purpose, and calling teleology a scientific proposition, he believed that evolution and growth with an ending goal are built into nature. "The seed grows into the flower, the acorn into the tree, the child into the man. Indeed the whole story of evolution from the amoeba to Albert Einstein is a remarkable process from the simple one cell to the conscious, sensitive creature called man."[43] In fact, and as Olan continually stressed, God is not an omnipotent and omniscient God who can do everything; He is a limited God.[44] However, he understood God as still being omnipotent, exerting control over Himself not to act on such authority. The notion of Olan's limited God appears paradoxical but it leads to his fundamental concern during his rabbinate: social justice activism and his understanding that man has the responsibility for implementing actions to make the world a better place.

Olan advanced the proposition that all known reality, including God, is relational, not absolute. With the universe existing as an "eco-system" in which all parts are interrelated, interdependent, and interpenetrating, no one part exists in isolation for it is affected by, and itself affects, all others and the system as a whole.[45] Therefore, from this interrelationship, what God is or will be is contingent upon the actions of mankind. "God's being, then, depends upon what happens in the uncertainty of time. What God will be is contingent, in large measure upon what man does."[46] In responding to Rabbi Erwin L. Herman's letter of January 13, 1966 seeking the criteria giving direction and influence to an evolving God, Olan responded:

"The answer, of course, lies in the use of it on the epistemological (knowledge with reference to the limits and validity) approach to any of the ideas that we have. Our understanding of God at any time is subject to the empirical, the rational, and the intuitional, and the authoritarian approach. At each stage in the evolution of our understanding of God, we have, for that time, the best that we can achieve. This, it seems to me, ought to be satisfactory and a good platform from which to establish a religious life."[47]

Olan did not refer to God as an "entity," but he insisted on the existence of a personal God. "God is personal, not abstract. God, like a human person, is self-identical. Although he changes, unity in continuity persists. He prehends all; He is aware of what is going on in our inmost mind; He can feel for us and sympathize with us. He is the fellow-sufferer who loves and is loved."[48] Although Olan's proposal that "God is personal, like a human person," emits the specter of anthropomorphism, it is evident that he did not represent God and a person to mean the same thing. One can experience God as a person experiences another person without concluding that God is a person. His assertion on the existence of a personal God may stem from his conclusion that human experience is a valid source for acquiring knowledge of God.

Process Thought

With the arrival of modernity the discussion on the extent of God's omnipotence and omniscience continued to flourish in philosophic and religious deliberations. The approach to the concept of God, as well as the problem of evil, began to change the way one understood and viewed the Divine being. This developing methodology, having found prominence from the time Newton's concept of natural law was introduced, was not in conformity with the traditional dogmas or beliefs of previous generations. The successful introduction of the theory of evolution by Darwin in the 1800s triggered fierce debates and raised many questions about life and its origins. Countless people began to reconsider their overall perspective in how the world was to be interpreted, while others continued to disbelieve the whole idea of evolution. This led philosophers and religious thinkers to consider an innovative approach to God and the problem of evil. This new methodology, borne from the evolving knowledge of mankind, was generally known in philosophic circles as process thought, and in religious circles as process theology. As it relates to Judaism, it became known more specifically as Jewish process theology.

The philosophy of process thought initially developed in the late nineteenth century and continued through the twentieth century. This school of thought was originally influenced by the metaphysical cosmology developed by English philosopher Alfred North Whitehead (1861-1947) and, although somewhat independently and with some differences, by American philosopher Charles Hartshorne (1897-2000), the term was generally applied to the Whitehead school.[49] Process thought refers to the "way of understanding reality that emphasizes the changes in the nature of the universe and interprets such change as the natural consequence of real and essential freedom, novelty, purpose, and experience."[50] In effect, process theology, stemming from process thought, is the result of proposing that the fundamental nature of reality is understood to be a series of processes, with life, for example, being described as consisting of the processes of birth, growth, maturity, and decay.[51] This means that the universe is characterized by processes and changes over time from the actions of humanity — the agents of free will.

It should be noted that human thought has been undergoing an evolution for centuries. Over the course of history the human mind and its process of thinking have been growing in self-awareness as society progressed through stages of increased development. So as religious belief and practice went from animism (attribution of conscious life to objects in nature or to inanimate objects) to fetishism (belief in magical fetishes) to polytheism (there are many gods) to henotheism (the worship of one god without denying the existence of other gods) to monotheism (doctrine of one God), new insights relating to the understanding of God were reached. In essence, the growth and intellectual development of society, evidenced by a significant advance in man's ability to reason as well as the development in his faculties of imagination, inquisitiveness, and wonder, resulted in a better understanding of God. In other words, as society progressed, man's comprehension of God differed from predecessors of previous generations. Concerning this progression of man's intelligence, Olan said: "We need to bring our understanding of God up to the level of our better knowledge of the universe and man. We ought to let our religion grow as we mature in science and philosophy."[52]

Process, resulting from the evolution of human thought, can also be understood as a series of experiences or ongoing series of events. The fundamental thesis of process theology is its claim that God grows and is affected by the actions of humanity. "This is what is meant by *process theology: the consequent nature is that aspect of God which is in process with the world, synthesizing and weaving the events of the world, including evil and tragedy, into an ideal harmony. Thus, God, in process theology, represents the pattern of all possibilities and the synthesis of all actualities.*"[53]

Process theology epitomizes a dipolar concept of God. This is described as dipolar theism in which God has two aspects consisting of the Divine existence and the Divine actuality. Divine existence refers to God as the essential existing being while Divine actuality represents the manner of God's existence and consciousness which is contingent upon the world-process. In this concept dipolar theism presents God as having both unchanging and changing characteristics, demonstrating both eternal essence and living existence, as described in the following manner by Alfred North Whitehead.

> "On the one hand, in his *primordial nature* ("God as the ultimate ground of potentiality"), eternally immutable and unconditionally necessary, while on the other hand in his *consequent nature* ("consequent upon world events" and our "constant companion"), ever newly emerging and containing accidents. In other words, God exists necessarily and has necessary attributes, but these are not his sole attributes; he also

has contingent attributes, which are not eternal, although they are indestructible and immortal."[54]

Whitehead criticized the notion that God, as "the *only* ultimate agent or determiner of things and events," possesses "unqualified Omnipotence" (unlimited in creative power) and "that all ultimate agency in the universe is assigned to Him."[55] If one follows this view of unlimited creative power (an unqualified supernaturalism revealing God as the omnipotent creator of all things) then the conclusion leads to God's power as being coercive power, and therefore responsible for both good and evil with human effort deemed insignificant.[56] Contrary to these assumptions, Whitehead conceived God's power as persuasive rather than coercive, and therefore not responsible for evil since human effort, in reality, makes a difference.[57] This concept of persuasive power asserts that God works through persuasion and invitation by persistently inviting us to make the best possible choices. This is consistent with Olan's theology and authentic Jewish theology which professes the belief that the future is contingent upon the actions of members of our society. For example, kabalistic beliefs include the performance of the commandments as having a cosmic effect, namely that of a deity that is shattered or broken and thus in need of humanity to help repair the divine self. This leads to the fundamental theory of process theology: its claim that God grows and is affected by society's actions within the world. What Whitehead was asserting was that we have a role in shaping and participating in the life of God. Jewish tradition preserves the view that man and God are co-workers in the building of the kingdom, and neither can achieve the objectives alone. This was a consistent theme during Olan's rabbinate. "The meaning of human existence lies in man's cooperation with God in bringing near the *malkut shamayim*, the heavenly kingdom on earth."[58]

Process thought was an effort to restore a sense of wholeness to human existence and to understand and reconcile the interrelationship between human experience and nature and God. Critical to the solution of God's omniscience and omnipotence and the problem of evil, Whitehead and Hartshorne wanted to avoid giving the impression that all creativity belonged to God. Their process theology influenced a number of Jewish theologians, including Rabbis Max Kadushin, Milton Steinberg, and Levi A. Olan. In their desire to change the classical view of God as a supernatural, omnipotent, and omniscient being, these rabbis, along with other religious leaders, pursued an extreme Jewish rationalism based on science, nature, and logic.

The Problem of Evil

For centuries many people lived with the perception that God was and continues to be directly involved in their daily actions. This is a misconception, as posited by Olan in the following manner: "The idea that God is directly involved in our daily lives, in our work and play, in our success and failure, is alien to our way of thinking."[59] In primordial times men responded with regard to their culture and civilization. Their gods were capricious creatures, who needed to be appeased and flattered into doing good and not harm. These were mythological beliefs in which the purpose of the gods was to assist man in conquering other men or to help him against the unfriendly power of the universe. Thus, there existed a whole system of animal and even human sacrifices in order to appease the primordial gods. Suffering, then and there, was a sure sign that the gods were discontented. Although current thinking might suggest this to be a simplistic solution, it satisfied man in his ancient society. Later, men began to conceive God as being concerned with moral behavior, punishing the wicked and rewarding the righteous. This undoubtedly satisfied man at one time but it did not face reality. This conception was followed by man's belief that real judgment was postponed to life after death. The wicked may prosper here, but they will be punished in the world to come, while the righteous may suffer on earth and enjoy the reward for their goodness in the eternity of some afterlife. But this thinking was not a good response to the tragedy of the suffering of innocent people and left so much to be resolved. There was no simple and completely satisfying answer to the crucial question involving the righteous and the wicked.

> "Life is too much a mystery, and our minds are too limited, to answer the whole riddle of the universe. At best, we can only get a glimpse of the meaning of our lives and the world in which we live…Our answer to this question depends on what God means to us. If we conceive of God as a being who has the power of life and death, who can reward and punish, then we must submit in a great act of faith. Then we accept faith as just that which our minds question and doubt. For some of us, such a God idea to-day is impossible."[60]

Many people do not have enough blind faith to grant such power to God if He could have prevented some specific tragedy. "God is the power in the universe that gives hope and meaning to our efforts but he cannot save us from the pitfalls of life."[61]

The religious faith of the individual has continuously been under attack from events beyond his control. It is not an infrequent occurrence for innocent and good people to be subjected to cruel suffering while bad people appear to continually prosper and enjoy life. Even for those of faith, there are times when human suffering challenges one's belief in God; but no faith is realistic which seeks to escape the problem by ascribing it to dark, supernatural forces.[62] An innocent child stricken with a fatal disease, a plane crash that takes the lives of many, a tornado that wipes out a major portion of a community without regard for the good or the wicked, are frequent occurrences that challenge the faith of any religious person. This poses the crucial religious question from the Book of Job: "why do the righteous suffer and why do the wicked prosper?" In other words, "why do life and the love of life encounter so many hindrances? Why does God's world contain so much pain and bitterness, so much passion and sin?"[63]

Olan's view of a limited God, and like the other followers of process theology, led him to conclude that human suffering is manmade and not God given. The evolution of knowledge and freedom sanctions the belief of a self-limiting God, an omnipotent God that exerts control over Himself not to act on such omnipotence and ultimately requires mankind to pursue its own efforts and goals for making the world a better place. This view sounds contradictory but it points to the limits of our understanding and the necessity for people to reason, reflect, and act with humility. While ancient man thought in terms of kings who were all powerful, it appears there were some things which God just could not do. Certainly, if God could, like a loving father, He would. In modern society, a father would do anything to help his child, but sometimes he is just not able. Isn't it possible that God, like a father, would save a child from death by disease if He could? But, like the father, He cannot. Olan responded that "if we can grow up in our religious faith by re-examining some old views, we may arrive at an understanding of God which does not shock our minds, and which satisfies our need for an answer to the universe of order, growth, life, and purpose."[64]

One of the principal doctrines of Judaism is the idea of moral freedom, and man's dignity and importance depend largely upon his freedom and power of self-determination and action. For Olan, this meant that man acts from free choice and conscious design, and retains the ability to change his mind at any moment through his own instinct or as new evidence surfaces. Man is therefore responsible for his every act or omission, and this alone renders him a moral being, a child of God; thus, man's moral sense rests upon freedom of the will.[65] Olan's belief in man's moral freedom led to his fervent opposition to the doctrine of original sin — the doctrine that human nature and man were corrupted with Adam's transgression in the Garden, a concept more at home in Christianity — as well as his ardent certainty that man's own character is determined by his own choices. "Adam and Eve rebelled against God…because they desired freedom to sin. The Garden of Eden was a deadly place for man and had he stayed in its comfortable, orderly placidity, there would have been no cultural growth. Man ate from the fruit of the tree of knowledge and then became free to sin, to miss the mark (described as a "glorious fall" or "fall upward")."[66] Olan did not accept the premise that man enters the world with the irreversible taint of transgression from the Garden. On the contrary, he professed that man's "entrance is in innocence endowed with the capacity to subdue his inclinations towards evil, and ultimately to return his soul in purity."[67]

"Each person," he said, "is endowed with a capacity to learn and to know good and evil, and to grow up to choose the good."[68]

"Freedom," Olan said, "limits God's omnipotence and well-nigh ruins His Omniscience. Given a choice, Judaism never wavered: 'All is in the power of heaven, except the fear of heaven.' It is really unimportant to ask whether God limited Himself or is limited naturally. The point is that God is powerless to take from man his freedom to choose between good and evil."[69] This idea of moral freedom is expressed as early as the first pages of the Bible, in the words which God spoke to Cain while he was planning the murder of his brother Abel: "Surely if you do right, there is uplift. But if you do not do right sin couches at the door; its urge is toward you, yet you can be its master."[70] In essence, man is told that he is responsible for the choices he makes. This passage, as well as other similar passages, presents the often repeated idea that man stands at the threshold of choosing either good or evil.[71] The entire structure of the covenanted relationship between God and man, which is basic to Judaism, is inconceivable without the affirmation that the human being is free to choose whether or not he shall obey the commandments. Jewish teachers throughout the ages recognized the problems of free will and therefore one must conclude that Judaism is unwavering in its rejection of any kind of moral fatalism or pre-destination.

While the sin in the Garden of Eden may have brought adverse consequences, with some sages accepting death as the most serious, it did not necessitate a belief that man inherits sin. "He may be burdened by the fruit of the wrongdoing of his forefathers, but Judaism could not assent to the doctrine that a man can do a wrong for which he is not personally responsible. That man is happy, according to the tradition, whose hour of death is like the hour of birth, that is, free of sin."[72] The concept of original sin was not a valid picture of human nature for Olan, and it certainly was of little or no encouragement to an age confronted with real situations.[73] This meant that the continued advances in scientific disciplines and growth in man's intelligence revealed the fact that human behavior may be changed, and that one is not doomed by any inborn quality. In this respect, man has the capability not only to sin, but also to perform good deeds.

Our religious leaders teach that in the Jewish view of the nature of life man is endowed with two "*yetzers*," that is tendencies or inclinations: one towards evil, *yetzer ha-ra*; and the other, *yetzer ha-tov*, towards the good. The foundation of their wisdom originates from Deuteronomy 30:19: "I have put before you life and death, blessing and curse. Choose life." "The opportunity to sin is real, and the desire on man's part to follow it is very strong, in fact stronger than his desire to choose the good."[74] Olan, like other religious thinkers, continued by positing that Jewish tradition gives priority to the *yetzer ha-ra* in the development of man and permits him thirteen years of maturation before the *yetzer ha-tov* appears on the scene.[75] This means the impulse to sin can originate at birth and remains the primary desire until the person matures at age thirteen, at which time the inclination to do good is born. The implications of the monotheistic faith hold that the one God responsible for all of creation is also responsible for the evil as well as the good. Therefore, evil and sin become as much a part of life as goodness and justice. "There is a strong indication that the *yetzer ha-ra*, the inclination toward sin, is a necessary ingredient of life. Sin begins when men abuse the sanctity of life."[76] This suggested that even the evil inclination may not be totally absent from its positive effects to life. The rabbis, Olan said, did not view the self-centered *yetzer ha-ra* as entirely evil, for "even the evil inclination can be employed to serve God and become a means of demonstrating love for Him."[77] This thought process might suggest that the evil nature of man can result in his desire and ability to become creative and, through contrition, alter his way of life.

> "Indeed, the largest portion of the tragedy of human life is the result of human failure. If man could fulfill the potentialities for good and decency, for love and sympathy that are inherent in his nature, the vast and overwhelmingly largest portion of human misery would cease. Greed, ignorance, jealousy, hate, how much suffering do they cause upon earth...Certainly, the largest measure of suffering is in the hand of man."[78]

But as a result of man's failure, one may ask what, if anything, is God doing as the innocent suffer? Olan associated the suffering of mankind with God's trauma and anguish: "God is painfully, and with agony, there to help man grow up and reach out for a better way of life. God cannot do it alone. He must work through man. He is there to help man but man must help God. Neither can do it alone."[79]

Since the largest measure of suffering results from the hands of man, what can he do in order to rectify his failings and inequities? The opportunity for repentance and forgiveness is significant in the Jewish tradition, and in simplistic terms redemption from sin is divine grace that is obtained not on merit but solely when man acknowledges his sinful self. Our rabbis tell us that regardless of the distance one falls, man is always free to knock on the gates that lead to God's mercy. Sincere repentance, followed by forgiveness, is integral to the entire structure of Jewish theology and runs from the Bible to modernity. It stems from the honest recognition that man was created with an evil impulse that makes him prone to sin. Justice, then, demands that a remedy should be provided for his salvation, and that remedy is repentance. Olan alluded to the rabbis' suggestion that repentance is one of the things created before the world was formed; and, because of man's tendency to sin, the world cannot hold together. Penitence, then, is the cement that keeps the world from falling apart.[80]

Repentance includes a wide range of actions, from the act of sacrifice during the priesthood to the prophetic moral prescription of turning from the evil and seeking the good. "The significant point is that at no time was man deprived of the privilege and opportunity to reject his choice of the wrong path, and to retrieve his steps and put himself on the right one."[81] One can look to the Bible and the evils of the people and their subsequent punishments to see that at no point was the door closed to redemption. "The call of God to man which Hosea recorded for all time is the central doctrine of Judaism: Return O' Israel, unto the Lord thy God; for thou hast stumbled in thine iniquity."[82] Jewish tradition conceptualizes God as a merciful father who judges His children, whom he loves, with kindness. This is convincingly pointed out, Olan suggested, in Exodus 34:6 where the Lord passed before Moses and proclaimed: "The Lord, the Lord, a God compassionate and gracious, slow to anger, abounding in kindness and faithfulness..."[83] Olan goes on to say that iniquity must be punished, but it is tempered by mercy and the ever present possibility of reform and forgiveness.[84]

The Jewish tradition holds that repentance — *teshuva* — consists of several stages and allows man to change his ways. For Olan, like the classic Jewish sources, repentance was condensed into a three step formula consisting of remorse, supplication and actions.

> "Man's hope is suggested by the three-fold formula which is the center of the High Holy Day's liturgy. Being human, man tends toward sin and invites punishment, but he can do three things to avert the judgment: penitence, prayer, and kindly deeds. In essence this says that a man can recognize that he has gone wrong, confess it to himself and God, and return to the right way."[85]

Tradition teaches that through prayer, man is able to enlist God's help, as His mercy and grace is available to those who seek Him. Olan projected there is no real change of heart unless a man goes out among other men to do God's work in performing deeds of loving kindness. The significance of repentance, Olan said, is that it obligates both man and God in the experience of life. "God's grace and mercy are available to one who actually does something to change his own behavior...Man and God are covenanted by the law of justice and mercy."[86]

However, two aspects on the matter of sin are uniquely Jewish and warrant further consideration in confronting the issues of the times. In the first place, much emphasis has been on the individual and either his need of redemption or his capacity to overcome his failings. This neglects the possibility of social sin, the collective responsibility of a community for some breach or violation of the moral code. "The social situation makes sinners of us all, no matter how righteous we may be in our personal conduct."[87] As an example, Olan stressed that individual virtue is lost as the fabric of society is diminished by the manner in which the poor and helpless are treated.[88] He questioned whether or not we share group guilt in the evil that results from war, from race prejudice, or from industrial injustice. The difficulty, Olan believed, lays in allocating the blame, for when no one is guilty directly we are all guilty collectively. This is illustrative of the teaching of the prophets who held the entire people responsible for the sins of their day. The rabbis teach that our decisions and actions not only affect ourselves as individuals, but also indirectly affect society as well. "The rabbinic suggestion that Israel is like one body and one soul, where if one of them sins, they are all punished and all are surety for each other, is a necessary check upon the limited concept of individualism which is dominant in theological thinking today."[89]

Precedent for man's collective responsibility was set long ago when, on the Day of Atonement, the High Priest prayed for all the people while invoking repentance for their collective sins. While a program of action for the sins of the individual goes beyond confession, forgiveness, and grace, the recognition of a community's common sinfulness should lead men to a positive course of moral action. For Olan, more than a simple admission of societal neglect was needed in order to remedy man's evil and his search for forgiveness. "It is not enough to acknowledge our share in the sin of war and implore God to forgive. Men are obligated to work and to continue working until the memory of war will be a bitter memory. Man's atonement comes only when the society in which he lives stops hurting people."[90] Judaism has a pertinent and effective remedy for society's failure to deal realistically with the nature of man. Man's pursuit of justice, which is a practical program of establishing order within society, has long been an essential part of Jewish tradition. This remedy, Olan preached, required compliance with God's teachings and adherence to the demands of social justice.

> "Man as a creature who is neither angel nor beast must pursue justice which is a practical program of establishing order among men. It is by obedience to the commandments that man's need for peace is satisfied. Justice is a practical, work-a-day demand which is involved in all social situations whether

business, war, or race. It is the duty of all men and within the capacity of every man. Love, however, is an ideal, and a necessary one, but it is attained by the few only. Charity is a commandment; righteousness/benevolence is a goal towards which man must strive."[91]

In the famous program of Micah, justice precedes the requirement of love and mercy. "He has told you, O man, what is good, and what the Lord requires of you: Only to do justice and to love goodness, and to walk modestly with your God."[92]

While the above paragraphs relate only to the suffering caused by man, some thought must be given to the tragedies caused by nature: earthquakes, floods, and other destructive natural phenomena that are beyond the control of man. Perhaps it boils down to just a matter of luck. "Tragedy is an inseparable ingredient of freedom, which along with chance, is bound together with law and design…Born to freedom, man is born to tragedy; but he is born, also to opportunity."[93] "One can't escape the suggestion that injustice is an essential part of life. Nature seems neutral to good and evil and vents her fury upon the righteous and the wicked without any moral concern."[94] Real life includes challenges, struggles, and disappointments and we contend with each crisis as it appears before us. The innocent suffer for the sins of the guilty, as is so clearly apparent in the cases of war or massive catastrophes. "To the person of unquestioned faith in an omnipotent and just God, the answer is simple. God has a purpose which we human creatures cannot comprehend."[95] For many of us this response fails to deal with reality as we suffer through tragedy. Olan deferred to the lessons from Job that both good and evil come from God. "We tend to forget that all of life is a gift, the whole universe, the world, the beauty, the love, the very food and clothing, yes, the mind itself is not of man's making. Even a moment of life, a moment of joy is a gift."[96]

Another response presented by Olan to the question of natural calamities suggested that the whole drama of life does not exist for one's own selfish being. In essence, the individual is a very small and insignificant part of a tremendous life that is endless in time and limitless in space. Each person, with his own individualized itinerary, is created with his own unique path in life.

> "Too much of our modern thinking is ego-centric. We are too greatly concerned with our little selves and give too much importance to them. The world was not made for me. I have no cause to complain and if I am reasonable, I can only give thanks for the little satisfaction I receive from the blessing of life itself…The fact about life is that tragedy is an essential part of it."[97]

If life itself has God-given meaning, then every aspect of life, including pain and suffering, must be considered a part of the gift of life.[98] In Olan's view, a person who focuses on his own individual growth, both ethical and religious, understands that pain and suffering is part of life, and as such should be able to tolerate it and possibly turn the suffering to some good end.[99] On the other hand, if tragedy is integral to life, why believe in God? "We need God to help us face the tragedy and suffering of life. God suffers along with us, but He is there when all else fails us. It was in such a moment that the man of faith says 'The Lord is my Shepherd, I shall not want.'"[100]

A significant aspect of life is that its meaning arises out of man's triumph over evil. Olan stated this understanding as follows: "The supreme value of any life and of all of life is man's persistent struggle against and conquest of evil."[101] Although man may be led to believe in a panacea that guarantees a life of freedom from all troubles, Olan asserted that it was "downright naïve" and "a form of moral escapism" for man to dream about a day free of all struggle and challenge.[102] This, Olan said, is the real opiate that existed during his rabbinate and Judaism has something to say to modern man about the face of sufferings in the meaning of life. "Good and evil, joy and sorrow, life and death are integral parts of the same creation."[103]

Understanding Judaism as a covenant between man and God explains why modern Jews believe in the continuing worth of morality and justice in spite of the presence of suffering and sin. Yet, one cannot overemphasize the role of either, as undue reliance on one or the other will, in all probability, impact in a negative manner the actions of both God and man. Eugene Borowitz explained as follows:

> The reliance upon God alone in times of oppression and persecution has often acted to reduce the role of *mitzvah*, to relieve the people of its responsibility to use its own powers for justice and peace. And the insistence upon man as the master of history explains the continuing stream of false Messiahs and of the spiritual ordeal which inevitably follows their exposure — for example, the prophets of social change and scientism of the thirties, followed by the despair of the forties. But it is true that despite our best efforts the Messianic era does not arrive."[104]

Conclusion

Monotheism is the foundation stone of Judaism and basic to the Jewish view of nature, of man, and of society. Olan, like many other religious leaders, believed God as creator, not in the mythical account of the one act of creation, but as the source of continuous creativity which men see every day. The universe is not stagnant; it evolves and changes and what is not here today may appear tomorrow. In this manner, life is continually encouraged because new creation is always possible. It is important to believe God is real, Olan said, for if man does not experience Him in worship, His reality is without meaning. God must be known in personal experience…"religion is the art of experiencing the God who is."[105] Sandra B. Lubarsky and David Ray Griffin describe Olan's view in *Jewish Theology and Process Thought* as follows:

> "We are at an "*axial point* in time, precipitated by atomic fission and requiring a 're-evaluation of our basic understanding of man's place in the universe.' Neither classical supernaturalism nor the 'empirical-rational epistemology' of the sciences that explained away supernaturalism is satisfactory. Rather the *neo-classical* picture of the divine as transcendent-immanent, relational, personal, mutable, and persuasive (not coercive) is

both more adequate to what we know about reality and 'readily appropriated by the prophetic faith' of Judaism."[106]

An interesting twist to Olan's views occurred in his December 16, 1951 radio sermon titled "Is Anything Too Hard for God." What we are saying, he preached, is not that God changes, but rather our understanding of Him changes as we learn more about nature and life. It would be unusual, Olan continued, if everything around us was subject to evolution, growth and change, leaving religion alone, fixed and immutable forever. One of the serious causes for modern man's lack of religious faith arises from his denial of a God who satisfied his grandfather. What man now faces is to find a God who will satisfy him. God is limited by man's freedom, for if God could do as He wills, what need would there be for man to choose between right and wrong?

> "God, however, cannot prevent man from choosing his course in freedom, and making a mistake in his choice, thus, God is limited by man's freedom. He is also limited by the laws of nature. If the world is to have form and order, there is no room for a power who, at will, can set aside the laws of nature. God must work within the realm of natural law... Thus, we are faced to-day with a God who is limited and finite."[107]

Olan recapped his conclusion of a limited God in his October 10, 1976 interview with Peyton Davis of the Dallas Times Herald newspaper, confirming that God and man struggle together to overcome one little evil after another. Concerning the simplicity of his answer, Olan said: "The world is what it is. If you are going to confront people as a religious teacher, you can't go around with a big grin on your face and say everything is all right. It isn't."[108] But in Olan's view, an understanding of God's limitations bears refinement and understanding. "Although Judaism has been receptive to a *self-limiting God*, and made it a necessary condition for a moral universe providing freedom to the individual, the idea of God who is *limited in power beyond His control* is not within the body of Jewish tradition."[109]

Olan was a staunch believer that the Jewish view of the nature of man offered a realistically optimistic view of man's possibilities, taking serious note of the tendency toward evil in every man. Acknowledging that the rabbis recognized man's potential for evil, he indicated the odds are that man, when confronted with the choice between good and evil will often choose evil. "Judaism is not naïve, but it is also not compelled by anxiety; it recognizes that man tends to do the wrong, but it does not make an ontology of it."[110] Though man has the freedom to sin, he certainly is not helpless as he stands in need of God's assistance. Sin opens the doors to penitence, prayer, and ethical action; and in this manner we learn that Judaism is concerned with upholding God's will and instructions. In his address to the Super Market Institute Midwinter Executive Conference in Florida, January 1969, Olan suggested that one must ask the basic questions of life: Who am I? What is my relationship to the universe in which I live? Do my aspirations, my loves, my hopes have a reality? "I have a feeling that if we begin to ask the right questions about ourselves we will move towards answering the questions that plague the cities, or plague the nation, or plague the world."[111] Olan's responses to these universal concerns represented the core values of his social justice activism during his rabbinate and are reflected throughout this document.

CHAPTER 9

The Nature and Destiny of Man

Introduction

Previous pages of this manuscript discuss Olan's background, the development of Reform Judaism, liberalism, Olan's views of the relationship of religion to social justice, the search for truth, modern theology, and God and sin. None of these topics specifically addresses the nature and destiny of man, another noteworthy theme offered by Olan over the course of his rabbinate. His views on this topic were eloquently presented in commentaries, lectures, and monographs, the more prominent of which were: "On the Nature of Man" (1948 presentation to the annual convention of the Central Conference of American Rabbis); "Judaism: A Religion of Realistic Hope for Man" (June 1953 commencement address at the Hebrew Union College-Jewish Institute of Religion); "Hope for Man" (1954); "The Future of Man" (1962 lecture at Dallas College of Southern Methodist University); "Creative Hope," (1962 presentation at the Rockefeller Memorial Chapel of the University of Chicago); "The Scientific Revolution and Hope for Man" (1963); "The Nature of Man" (1964); "The Jewish View of Man" (undated, but after 1972); "Man, His Nature and Destiny" (undated); "Prophecies of Doom — A Critical Examination" (undated); and "Literature and the Condition of Modern Man" (undated).

As a starting point it should be noted that the foundation of religious thinking begins with the conception of man. Although God represents the pinnacle of the religious pyramid, man stands firmly at its foundation, and without a thorough concept of man, a meaningful theology is problematic. Instead of responding to the question of "what is God," Olan focused on man's relationship to God, illustrated by the exclamation of the Psalmist:

> "What is man that You have been mindful of him, mortal man that You have taken note of him, that You have made him little less than divine, and adorned him with glory and majesty. You have made him master over Your handiwork, laying the world at his feet."[1]

Although one may question the significance of the individual in the overall scheme of things, his place and function in the community of the divine was predetermined. In this regard, Jewish religious scholars believe that man was chosen to be God's ambassador in the world while being charged with the responsibility of both protecting and improving the results of His labor. "In other religious cultures God fulfills His purpose without man, but in Judaism God and man are partners, co-workers in the building of the Kingdom."[2]

Incompatible with the above thinking and citing the years of mass cruelty and destruction of two World Wars, of Nazi gas chambers, the development and delivery of nuclear weapons, of rising Russian communism as a world power, the volatility of Korea in the 1950s and Vietnam in the 1960s and early 1970s, and race and class rebellion, Olan echoed the problems of mankind as not only one of believing in God, but also a despair about the nature and character of the human condition. In essence, in what sense can we have faith in man? While catastrophic social and government actions, like Russian pogroms or Nazism, were subject to perceptive analyses by economists, sociologists, anthropologists, and psychologists, Olan believed the concepts of man and nature, which form the foundation for the formal patterns of history, were rarely, if ever, the concern of modern social scientists.[3] This was a limited approach, he said, calling it a "logical absurdity" revealed in the writings of Bertrand Russell, "the otherwise profound student of social movements."[4] The failure to relate ideas and social phenomenon to the underlying concepts of man led to an irrational dualism of social progress in a universe that was essentially unfriendly to human life without purpose and perpetuated a speculative view of history in which structure was divorced from thought.[5] Olan found this view to be hypothetical, limited and invalid, and therefore responsible for the presence of social confusion.[6] Fundamentally, man's confidence had been impaired and the age of anxiety had been authenticated.

> "The vision of what was once called the 'liberal imagination has been replaced today by the imagination of disaster. The modern liberal seems to have lost the unique characteristic of liberalism — the ability to fill the imagination of his time with programs which are daring and attainable. Frightened by the disasters of recent history he has relinquished the stage to prophets of despair and to totalitarians who exploit the utopian vision in order to maintain a society of slaves. The evils of our time are real enough and science has armed them with a dreadful power."[7]

For one to say that this was an apocalyptic view of the nature and destiny of humanity was no exaggeration and Olan continually lectured about the pessimism concerning man's moral possibilities bordering on hatred or contempt for mankind. Although every generation conceptualizes itself as living with apparent unsolvable and difficult problems, a radically different cultural climate developed in America during the twentieth century. Society was engrossed in a dilemma different from anything experienced before in all history. Olan attributed this dilemma to two major revolutions which, coincidently, continue in varying degrees to today's post-modern era. One revolution was the rapid development of science and technology that provided society with, among other things, the means for achieving the final nuclear holocaust; and, the second revolution was the steady shift from theism to secularism.[8] The questions posed by these events centered on whether or not the existing human condition was serious enough to be called a crisis, and was it a time of judgment for life or death of an age in history. "The continuance of our present downward course at the accelerated rate that marks the last half century announces not only the end of Western civilization, but in all probability, the end of all civilization for another millennium."[9] The rapid progress of science and technology along with society's shift from theism to secularism were foreseen, gradually emerging over time, and appearing more friend than enemy through their developing stages.

Science and Technology

Prior to the twentieth century man's needs rested solely on the conviction that an absolute relationship existed between cause and effect in all of nature.[10] This view transmitted the belief that "there is nothing new under the sun"[11] and everything had already been created. It was a determinist approach based on an understanding of nature whereby the ends were pre-determined by nature, by God, or by fixed natural laws of the universe.[12] This was the common view of the nature of man and the universe by theologians, philosophers, and scientists of the pre-modern era.

The increasing development of man's intellectual capabilities over many generations gave him the ability to control his own destiny to a greater extent than was previously possible. The contributions of science and technology have benefitted society and human nature in a continuous process of change. Man now had the ability to define objectives and set goals for new achievements. "After all, man himself is the result of a mutation in the process of evolution. His introduction was a change."[13]

Generally speaking, science is experimental and operates under conditions controlled by the scientist. One might view the scientific laboratory as a small reproduction of nature with a corresponding freedom applying to both the laboratory and nature. While, in previous generations, "the ends were predetermined by nature, by God, or by the fixed laws of the universe," in the modern view it is man who can select the end or the goal (from a number of alternatives) toward which he may direct his abilities."[14] Science constantly moves society from the unknown to the known and has exposed nature and life and many of their traditions more than ever before.

> "The newly reported theories in the sciences of physics and biology have destroyed the foundations of a fixed concept of nature and life, moving swiftly into the more uncertain areas of relativity. The rapid progress in dynamic psychology and cultural anthropology has violently disturbed our thinking about the nature of man. This much seems certain: though we cannot comprehend with precise clarity the nature and extent of the upheaval in Western culture, we are faced with fundamentally radical changes."[15]

"Proliferation of nuclear weapons, exhaustion of resources, and pollution of air, water, and earth turns the future into a nightmare. It now takes more courage to live than before."[16] And the rapid progress in industrial technology threatened to dismiss the human being as a necessary element in the production of goods and services.[17]

For Olan, it was the best of times and the worst of times.

> "Science has presented man with the opportunity to fulfill his oldest dream — to achieve the satisfaction of his basic needs and to live in dignity in a brotherhood with other men. At the same time, however, science has rendered him superfluous. It has freed him from his bondage to superstition, ignorance, and blindness which opened for him opportunities to investigate the mystery of nature and to give him increasing control over it. It has shown him a way to a better knowledge of himself and some possible ways to live in a healthy relation with the world of nature and men. Unfortunately man pushed beyond the legitimate boundaries of science and robbed himself of a faith which gives meaning to his existence, and purpose to his adventurous journey through life."[18]

The tragic irony lay in the fact that science and technology, the very instruments which promised man's liberations from most of his distress, held the most serious threat to his continued existence on earth. "The prophecy of doom does not come from the prophet who speaks in the name of God, but from scientific laboratories and the pronouncements of social scientists."[19] Science has made vast strides in creating power enough to destroy the world. The moral growth of man necessary to control that awesome power has lagged way behind. So we live perched on the brink with great power and little or no moral control."[20] Olan recalled the Norse myth describing the twilight of the Gods, the *Gotterdammerung,* which foretells the setting of the sun upon humanity and the beginning of an eternity in which the world, empty of deity and humanity, will endure in a formless void. Attention was directed to the development of nuclear power and the social, political, and economic upheavals existing in the world in posing the question whether the end of the human era and the coming of oblivion were just a stone's throw away. "The rapid exhaustion of the earth's resources; increasing pollution of the air, water, and the earth itself; and the imminent threat of worldwide nuclear war suggest the fulfillment of the doomsday prophecy of the Norse myth in the not too distant future."[21]

The scope in the campaigning of modern prophets of pessimism was a harsh and disapproving reproach to the liberal who placed his faith in progress, reason, and freedom. The naïve hopefuls who had confidence in the premise of science to heal our diseases both physical and human had to face a world in which all their dreams were turned into nightmares. Science, it seemed, had become a golem created by man which, in the eyes of many, could not be controlled. This can best be understood by revisiting a most horrid event of the twentieth century. Instead of growing up and becoming a creature in control of his inner urges, man exhibited a devilish combination of technological brilliance and sub-human bestiality which ended demonically in Hitler's gas chambers. Dazzled by a few gadgets and intrigued by mental cleverness, he had forgotten the terrible truth of his own nature and that of the universe.[22] This begs the question of man's maturity and growth, and his ability in handling the power conveyed by rapidly advancing science and technology.

The question of one's place in the scheme of things had been thrown wide open by the revolution in science and technology. The prophets of doom pointed to a human condition dangerous enough to warrant the prediction of the final extinction of human life on earth. The increasing population growth and decreasing natural resources would, in Olan's pessimistic view, lead to a "Malthusian struggle" for survival, with the smallest and largest nations possessing nuclear bomb capability. His calendar for a nuclear holocaust and redistribution of essential resources read like this: "in 1970 it is the politics of despair, in 1980 the politics of desperation, in 1990 of catastrophe, in 2000 of annihilation — give or take a little."[23] With the rate of exhaustion of natural resources rapidly reaching the limit of safety, Olan stressed the concern for the limitation of natural resources in supporting society's industrial growth and increased population. The environment also was under attack from the growing use of energy. Thermal pollution, then as it does today, represents a lethal threat to human existence. "The time is not distant when we will be forced to limit our industrial growth in order to survive."[24] Science it seems represented the False Messiah, holding great promise for the continued enhancement of society while, at the same time, providing the means for the annihilation of mankind. "Man has eaten of the fruit of the tree of knowledge and finds that he cannot digest it."[25]

The difficulties and injustices of the times were certainly nothing new in character. History revealed that components of previous societies had acted unintelligently, thoughtlessly, and immaturely numerous times. In effect, Olan presented man as having a dual nature, a higher and a lower, and it is not surprising that in the process of history one age stressed one side of that nature, and the succeeding age the other side. The tendency, then, was to think well of human nature while civilization was prospering, and to think badly when things went wrong.[26] The only new aspect was society's ability through science and technology to give those earlier and lower motivations an efficiency they never had before. Although the foolishness of men who have missiles and bombs in their hands is frightening, by the same measure our knowledge and technology should be applied equally to the problem of controlling potential threats.[27] There is something masochistic, Olan posited, in the rush and excitement with which the pessimists have adopted the fusion of human depravation and scientific achievement. Society needs to be more sensible in organizing themselves to make the new knowledge of nature and of man to work for the improvement of the existing human condition.

Olan highlighted science's revolutionary discoveries from nuclear energy to genetic material as challenges to our moral values and religious ideas. "Science is the most poignant expression of modern secularism."[28] For example, various contraceptive devices have required men and women to question the validity of intimate values which have been socially approved for millennia.

> "Indeed, the possibilities of modern medicine and the life sciences in general confront us with a need to re-evaluate our ideas of the meaning of life and of death. The increased practice of transplanting parts of the body from one person to another raises many questions, not the least of which is the nature and realization of man himself. Does man have a constant, unchangeable quality which is to be respected as the sign of dignity? At what point does life end and death begin?"[29]

Another issue, Olan believed, addressed the relationship of what he termed social functionalism that would determine the kind of individuals ultimately constituting society. Scientific technology, through biological sciences, has empowered man to determine within limits what he shall be, who shall live or who shall die. Advances in biomedical science involving the end of mortality and the mechanical manipulation of human feelings and behavior present ethical issues never before confronted by society. Is it right or wrong; is it good or evil? The changes in life sciences have altered the genetic quality of life and require different standards in determining what the nature of man shall really be. "The seemingly naïve inquiry of the Psalmist "What is man?" has now become a complex and a very crucial matter."[30] No ethical code or principle of the past was adequate to deal with these aforementioned issues, and it was clear during Olan's rabbinate that much was needed other than what existed to meet the radical changes resulting from advancing scientific and technological achievements. While work still needs to be done, many of the legal, ethical, and religious issues have been addressed by religious and government leaders during the years succeeding Olan's retirement from the pulpit.

"The fact is that science, the epitome of secularism, has achieved what God never could. It has cured diseases once declared incurable; and it has made it possible to raise enough food to still the hunger of every human being on earth. Secularism is the success story of today. Man is doing very well without God."[31] Essentially, Olan continued, "what prayer could never achieve, science has achieved."[32] In man's secular pursuits he shaped his view of the world in scientific terms which led him to either phenomenal success or potential disaster. "Unfortunately, and unexpectedly, they (science and technology) have also led him to a secularism which has eradicated everything beyond the secular, beyond what science and mathematical logic can validate."[33]

Secularism

Secularization was the dominant social pattern of the contemporary society in twentieth century America. And as it related to Olan, Sidney L. Regner put it in perspective: "Again and again in his writings he called attention to the shift from theism to secularism as one of the major revolutions accounting for modern man's dilemma."[34] Olan proposed that secularism suggested a view of the universe as an unplanned chain of particles devoid of either purpose or goal. In the view of the secularists, man was described as a thing among things, a by-product of a blind machine.[35] He also described it as "an irreversible historical process in which society and culture are delivered from tutelage to religious control and closed world views."[36] The release of the natural order from control by the supernatural, which dominated the past, encouraged the freedom and refinement of the human spirit, placing restraints upon those forces that degraded the stature of man. This was a process of "desacralization" that opened the universe for man to investigate, understand, and, to an increasing measure, to control.[37]

The erosion of the theistic view during this period of history, beginning with the Enlightenment and Emancipation, was characterized by

Olan as a fragmentation of human culture — a modern society morally adrift and spiritually sick. Accordingly, the church and synagogue were not in the position to offer spiritual revival, for at the time it experienced a vague and undefined mood without substance and direction. There appeared to be a growing recognition that the foundations were being destroyed, that the causes of man's modern malady went deeper than politics, economics, sociology, or psychology. The human situation was sick at the roots as man had lost his sense of relatedness to destiny and his understanding of the basic meaning of his life.[38] The corruption of human existence and failure of justice presented frustration in the face of potential unlimited abundance[39] as society witnessed "the corrosion of urban centers, the awful presence of hunger amidst affluence, the failure to take seriously the freedom of the black community, and the continued fiasco in Vietnam where death and destruction are the cruel order of the day, these are, all of them, cut of the same cloth."[40] The agony of the times required a restoration of our prophetic tradition as Olan cited the similar situation when God admonished the ingratitude of Israel by declaring to Amos: "For three transgressions of Israel (I will forgive), for four, I will not revoke it; because they have sold for silver those whose cause was just, and the needy for a pair of sandals."[41]

Secularism has been described as the organization of life as if there is no God. "For the first time, men have left their God not for other gods but for no God at all."[42] A critical concern posed by the transition from theism to secularism was no longer whether we can believe in God, but whether and in what sense can we believe in the human being. Olan believed that the efforts to resolve the overwhelming crisis had fashioned a hopeless view of man that pervaded existing cultural expressions of the period. Man appeared to have lost faith and there was no real sense of self at the core of ones' life. While science and philosophy explained a universe without God, society experienced a shrinking of Biblical authority; and the church and synagogue showed themselves to be human, at times to be too human, with the rites and ceremonies becoming less meaningful. There was a pervasive mood of despair that characterized the period.

The rapid displacement of a theistic view of the universe by secularism induced the gloomy prospect that the world had no room for man's ideals or his noble plans.[43] Ultimately, disenchantment from the shifting landscape resulting from science and increasing secularism was expressed by the authors in their novels, by the writers and producers on the stage, and the creators of popular arts. "If you read the great scientists, the great artists, you find a mood of doom hanging over everything they write."[44] Many people said that modern man was not alive, and Olan, like Arnold Jacob Wolf, directed his audience to the artists whose works revealed the true human situation of despair — the major mood of modern culture. "Whatever the experts may say about modern art and music, this much seems patent — it is permeated with everything but a spirit of triumph and confidence."[45] As an example, Olan pointed to Pablo Picasso's "Guernica" depicting a bombing in Spain by twenty-eight German bombers on April 26, 1937 during the Spanish Civil War. The painting summed up "the agony and loneliness of modern man who is engaged in a terrible struggle between hope and despair, where the hunger for order is constantly frustrated yet is never denied, the experience of the void."[46] As for the sculptor, he molded forms misshapen and deformed to reflect the world visualized through his own eyes. In both art and modern music, one heard the cry of despair, maledictions upon life, the conflict of nature and man, the cynicism of the soul; what Paul Tillich called the "experience of the void."[47] Much of the modern literature, obsessed with violence rooted in the ground of evil lying beneath the surface of contemporary existence, typified the lonely person in the world of terror and dissolution.[48] The artist responded to man's life by way of his own distinctive instrument fashioned by imagination, sensitivity, and talent. "From Kafka to Mickey Spillane, man is pictured either as an insensitive brute or a helpless victim of demonic powers."[49] "The modern artist possesses the singular sensibility of the creative genius to feel in his bones, as it were, that something terribly dark and sick has engulfed the life of man…The artist and the scientist are today's prophets alerting us to the doom ahead. While they draw upon two very different sources of experience, they are one in their unveiling of the explosively dangerous human condition."[50] These artistic references can be summarized in one brief comment preached by Olan in 1961: "Our culture is pessimistic, the stage, the fiction, the poetry, the music all combine to reveal a human being who is not only hollow, but corrupt and evil."[51]

The implication of a change from a culture of theism to one of secularism has been suggested as the most radical revolution of modern times and the major confrontation which Judaism had to meet. Many people who belonged to a religious community lived secular lives and their religion had become a symbol of conformity. "Its adherents do not arrange their lives around the belief that there is a living God."[52] This could be catastrophic for the Jews. "If there is no God, the election and covenant of Israel is a fantasy and the Kingdom of God in the end of days a delusion."[53] The encroaching secularism also raised questions concerning the continuity of the declaration of the Pittsburgh and Columbus Platforms supporting the theistic view of the nature of One God. "Today the affirmation of our faith in the reality of a living God must be announced against the background of a secular wave without and within Judaism. It must spell out the implications of the God faith upon the nature of man, society, the covenanted people, and the meaning of death."[54] Reminding us of the Jews' survival from numerous attempts at destruction and annihilation, Olan thought secularism to be an enemy yet to be tested.

The increasing crisis of the period produced an almost complete distrust in human reason as a useful weapon in man's struggle to overcome his difficulties. The pride which for some time had been society's response to the achievement of intellect and of science was under suspicion in many quarters. "Man as a rational being is under heavy attack, and the irrational has become the fashion in philosophy as in religion. If this tendency is permitted to continue, man forfeits the only weapon with which he can effectively meet the issues before him. If he cannot use reason to measure his place in the scheme of the universe, and to meet the dangers that beset him, he has little or nothing left but despair and defeat."[55] As man's disposition was mired in hopeless despair the times called for a more reasonable and less emotional approach for the concern of humanity's destiny.

Hope for Man

A more realistic view of human nature can be gleaned from common sense and an added objective look at some facts. Although the human is often encouraged by pride and acts out of hypocrisy and lust for power, he is unlike other animals. It is important to consider him, not only for what he was, but also for what he is and what he can become. Because we know more today about the primitive urges embedded in his unconscious, we tend to blind ourselves to his specific human qualities. His uniqueness lies not in the person that he is but in his capacity as a creator of culture and endowed with the ability of conceptual thought that can only be achieved by the human being. Consequently, he has previsioned goals which he seeks to satisfy, and his knowledge and energy are directed toward successful completion. Man is not a passive creature of his culture, but a striving being busy devising means to achieve new ends and to preserve his creativity from generation to generation.[56] His sense of time enables him to look back into the past and to plan for the future.

The Jewish concept of the nature of man is the foundation upon which the progressive and optimistic movements of western civilization were established. The native Jewish tradition endows man with the capacity to determine to a large extent the nature of his destiny. Judaism places him in a unique status in relationship to the other creatures and to God. Beginning with the concept that man is created in the image of God, Jewish tradition endows him with perfectibility. From the doctrine of *imitatio Dei* (the creation of man in the image of God), the entire structure of Jewish ethics rests. It makes man pre-eminent in the animal kingdom by endowing him with self-consciousness and a potentiality for infinite development.

The loss of faith in human destiny was reflected in the cry of despair that dominated the period's cultural expression. From the cataclysmic events of the first fifty years of the twentieth century many people exhibited a "failure of nerve." This phrase was a reflection of thinking that was pervaded by futility and disregard arising from a lack of faith in the value and meaning of life.[57] The times called for a new faith and a more reasonable and less emotional approach to the matter of man's destiny.[58] Man needs to see the sun that shines and lightens the possibilities of a new day.[59] In order to accomplish this task, Olan presented the three following criteria or benchmarks in the process of achieving hope for mankind.[60]

In the first place, Olan recognized that part of the solution resulted from the work of the scientific laboratory. With the increasing evidence that the universe was a cosmos and not chaos, science revealed a universe or order subject to mathematical comprehension. Man, whose life was not at the mercy of whimsical spirits or capricious powers, was a thinking being and an essential component of the universe. His hope and destiny were part of a universe which was subject to some order or control. Science revealed the possibility of the individual fitting his life into a cosmos, a universe of order, of growth, and of promise. In fact, man was able to depend upon nature and he need not fear the "vagary or whimsy" of some mysterious power.

In the second place, the universe was not only dependable, it was creative. Man was a value seeking creature, not only comprehending nature but seeking to control it toward some desirable end. With his nature to seek the truth, and his creativity in a creative universe, he projected ends and set out to achieve them. In a real sense it was this creative element which was the foundation and essential characteristic of scientific exploration. The essence of it all was the expectation of something new. A creative universe is a hopeful one for what is not here today may be achieved tomorrow. Man's progress is from the known to the unknown,[61] but it is with promise and not with doom. Indeed it is upon this great adventure that man stakes his life. It is this venturing forth into the unknown with expectation that characterized art, philosophy, and ethics.

Finally, hope for man rests not only on the fact of the orderly, vital, creative universe he inhabits, but also upon the unique quality of freedom that he cherishes. Although man is considered part of nature and subject to its laws, he is unique in his freedom to choose, to make decisions, and to assume the risk of the consequences. Yet, Olan questioned the individual's pursuit of freedom. Like Adam, man sought the security of paradise where there was no need to choose and where he felt secure. In a real sense he rejected his essential human quality and yearned for the safety of his animal nature.

Conclusion

Olan stressed the importance of man's understanding of the meaning of human existence. If man is convinced that he is an integral part of the *whole* and the *One* (referring to God) whose purpose is creation through liberation, he will then fashion a code of ethics adequate for the life crisis which confronts humanity today.[62] Olan believed that ethical monotheism, the essence of the Prophetic faith, could save mankind from impending holocaust which threatened the end of all life on earth. This required a covenantal community that continued to be fiercely passionate in its witness to God, the Creator and the Liberator. This symbolized the Jews historic role of the mission of Israel: "It is not incumbent upon you to complete the job, but you are not free from beginning it."[63]

Yet, in "Prophecies of Doom — A Critical Examination," Olan probed the morality and ability of modern society. "The moral issue today is totally different than anything mankind has experienced in the past — responsibility for the survival of generations yet unborn…We are doing very poorly in meeting our responsibility to our living neighbors, is it realistic then to expect modern man to make real sacrifices to secure the existence of generations centuries in the future?"[64] "The moral question we face today is the right of unborn human beings to life on earth."[65] In effect, the modern view of the nature of man raised serious doubts about his ability to handle the power that science and technology placed in his hands. Olan attributed the motivation for ethics in the roots of fear and expediency. "The hesitancy to use the atomic bomb is not due to a conviction about the sanctity of human life. It is not dropped because there is fear that it will be dropped on us. The ethics of expediency is expressed in the popular maxims of the day — enlightened self-interest, and honesty pays."[66] And in one of his final interviews just prior to his death, Olan saw an imminent catastrophe on the shift from theism to secularism and the rapid growth of science and technology. "Theism is practically out of existence. However, science has produced a weapon that ends all life on earth, and the probability is I don't see how we can avoid blowing it up."[67]

In spite of the doom and gloom, Jewish scholars describe man as a microcosm, in whom is reflected the whole creation of God. In this regard, "Judaism, following its traditional attitude toward creation, looked upon man's physical nature as divinely formed and worthy of respect…What God created was for man's enjoyment so long as he did not abuse the privilege."[68] Scientific and technological disciplines, in conjunction with the freedom emanating within secularism of American society, endowed man with the capacity to change his characteristics and provided him with the powers to learn from experience. "There is nothing fixed or unchangeable about man. In a real sense, they disclose him as a free agent in nature in that he is the maker of the instrumentalities which form the cultural milieu which in turn determines his character and much of his destiny."[69]

The findings of modern science tend to support the basic affirmation of the Hebraic-Liberal concept of the nature of man. "In the face of a growing mood of disenchantment, the Jewish belief in man's worthiness and hopeful destiny needs emphasis and propagation. Liberalism, like Judaism, when it is rooted in its basic affirmations is a faith which articulates a realistic hope for man."[70] Realistic hope tells us that man must face the reality of danger and be ready to make decisions and take risks that go with them. While the life of the Jew is nourished on faith, the moment he accepts fatalism his history ends. The faith is woven into the whole history which he has written in letters of pain and suffering.[71] There was only one way out for man and that way was a total commitment to God, the existential moment when "man stakes his life on his thinking. Another term for this process was the popular 'leap of faith.'"[72] This leap of faith stems from an understanding of Jewish theology and the related interpretation of faith, practice and experience. In the final analysis, Olan desired to put the human condition of the times in a more realistic perspective, suggesting that one must learn to distinguish between change and the "crack of doom."[73]

> "The darkness is real enough, two world wars and a hydrogen bomb are devastating facts. But it is willful blindness to neglect the progress which man has achieved. The basic conditions of life have improved immeasurably; we live longer, have more leisure, do less backbreaking labor, have more literacy, and show more concern for the underprivileged. All of this may not be paradise, but stubbornly to ignore it in favor of a philosophy of Nihilism is irrational to say the least."[74]

CHAPTER 10

Judaism and Immortality

Introduction

The subject of immortality has been a topic among scholars in nearly all religions for many centuries. While Judaism has always maintained a belief in the afterlife, the forms assumed and the methods in which it has been expressed varied greatly and differed from one period of history to another. Although Jewish religious leaders over the years attempted to understand and present their ideas of immortality, it was not the most frequent theme of Jewish thought and scholarship during the twentieth century.

Olan read about immortality throughout his years in the rabbinate, yet the subject was an infrequent theme for his pulpit and in the liturgy of the synagogue. It never occurred to him to write about it as it did not appear to be a theme that called for major treatment.[1] His interest in the subject was amplified by an invitation of the Commission on Jewish Education, under the joint auspices of the Union of American Hebrew Congregations (UAHC), the predecessor of the Union for Reform Judaism (URJ), and the Central Conference of American Rabbis (CCAR). He was invited to prepare a manuscript on the concept of immortality in Judaism and Jewish thought. The result of this invitation was his text entitled *Judaism and Immortality*, published by the UAHC in 1971.

Rabbi Robert Gordis, former president of the Conservative Movement's Rabbinical Assembly and the Synagogue Council of America, described Olan's text as being "lucidly written and well documented book" and "the rise of the traditional belief in the resurrection of the dead and the development of the faith in the immortality of the soul in its various forms are clearly and interestingly delineated."[2]

Olan's study demonstrates that during the different ages of Jewish civilization the evolutionary aspects of life challenged the concepts of immortality and the afterlife. It also reveals the depth and breadth of Olan's probe and supports the fact that there have been and continues to be great diversity in Jewish thought about immortality and the afterlife. Beginning with the prophetic vision of the Bible, Olan continued his exploration through the literature of the Apocrypha (200 BCE-100 CE), to the teachings of the rabbis of the Rabbinic Period (300 BCE-500 CE), to the wisdom of the Medieval Jewish philosophers from the sixth century CE to the sixteenth century CE, to the mystics of the fourteenth and fifteenth centuries, to the modern period and the age of reason beginning with the eighteenth century, and finishing with the postmodern period encompassing Olan's generation. Concerning the breadth of the conceptual matter of his text, Olan wrote:

> "Judaism, which has been contemporaneous with all of recorded history, has reflected the total philosophical and cultural history of civilized man in its views of immortality. Jewish thought on the subject has spanned every position from complete rejection to fervent and sometimes extravagant acceptance."[3]

While Olan's study is rather exhaustive, it should be noted that it unveils his sole comprehension and interpretation of the written tradition regarding the afterlife and does not represent a consensus of scholarly thought throughout the periods of Jewish tradition. As his study demonstrates, the idea of life after death was never really absent from the tradition, and its nature and prominence varied through the centuries as political and social surroundings dictated. Whereas Olan's text delivers authoritative Jewish scholarship as requested by the Commission, it fails to conclude a systematic and coherent view of the afterlife.

When discussing immortality, it follows that resurrection must also be included in the conversation. According to the doctrine of immortality, there is no death at all except for the body; the soul never dies. In the doctrine of resurrection, death ends both body and soul, and the whole person, body and soul, is "resurrected" and brought back from the dead to live again in some future period. Over 2,000 years ago the two ideas were combined to generate a traditional Jewish view that the soul lives on when the body dies and is reunited with the body at the time of resurrection. These two separate ideas have inspired considerable thought and commentary throughout Jewish history. Rather than an extensive review of the study, the following pages represent brief capsules of Olan's analyses from the literature of the Bible through the postmodern period.

Literature Relating to the Afterlife

While neither denying nor accepting the belief in the continuation of life after death, the Bible contains almost no references about it.[4] Yet the Biblical writers certainly had some awareness about the concepts of both immortality and resurrection. One suggestion, which offers probable support for the omission of explicit biblical references, posits that the relative silence of immortality in the Bible stems from its protest against the pagan conception of life in the hereafter as being bound up with pagan religion and pagan gods.[5]

> "The Egyptian cults of the dead were overly obsessed with death. The Babylonian culture...attempted to deny death by seeking to avert it through discovering the secret of eternal life. The religion of Biblical Israel rejected both extremes and sought to lay the foundation for subsequent Jewish views of death and dying. From the perspective of the biblical mentality, there was the perceived danger that either the death-avoidance of the Babylonians or the death-obsession of the Egyptians might preempt a preoccupation with life and living."[6]

Another reason, Olan suggested, results from historical material reflecting both early pre-prophetic tradition (no distinctive concept of life after death) and late prophetic concept when the function of the soul, sent by God, became characterized as the "source of spiritual life" rather than the "bearer of life."[7] The prophetic influence on Olan is captured from his explanation that the above notion places man in a special relationship with God, distinguishing him from the rest of the animal kingdom.[8] Although this was not a clear separation of body and soul, it created "some sort of independent existence for the soul."[9]

From Olan's survey of the biblical material it becomes evident that the theological doctrines of the Pharisees — beliefs in the resurrection of the dead, the Day of Judgment, reward and retribution in life after death, the coming of the Messiah, and the existence of angels — were giving expression to the hopes of the underprivileged and oppressed common people. It was during the period of the Maccabean Wars when the Pharisees introduced the above concepts leading to the bodies of the dead rising from their graves upon the arrival of the Messiah.

Following the fall of the Northern Kingdom in 722 BCE and the Babylonian exile in 586 BCE, with the destiny of the nation in doubt, the Prophetic doctrine was reinterpreted by introducing the idea of personal responsibility whereby everyone was responsible for his own deeds and no one was to be punished for the sins of others. Under these new conditions the Israelites began to question their relationship to their God and the problem of individual fate, apart from that of the nation, began to emerge. Although slow in development, the groundwork was now laid for a concrete formulation of immortality and resurrection.

With the personalization of the covenant from that of a nation to that of the individual, a tension developed between the vision of national destiny and the demands of individual reward and punishment. "For the first time," Olan pointed out, "the idea appears that the righteous individual as well as the righteous nation will share in the Messianic kingdom and rise from their deaths for their reward and God's glory."[10] Although the Bible does not offer a solid, well-integrated concept of either immortality or resurrection, the material is present Olan said, and ultimately formed the basis for the formulation of both ideas in the literature of the Apocrypha and the Talmud.[11]

The collection of Apocrypha literature, which the tradition calls "outside" or "hidden books" (*sefarim chetzonim*), represents writings that were not canonized and "are not in the same caliber either in content or style as the books of the Bible."[12] Suggesting a time frame of 320 years from the canonization of the Scriptures to their finalization about 180 BCE,[13] nearly all of the apocryphal books include ethical elements that indicate they were written under the influence of the Scriptures.[14]

While apocalyptic literature concerns itself primarily with the problems of individual destiny, the problem of theodicy forms the major interest with the future of the nation playing only a minor role. Olan captured the essence of portions of the Book of Enoch (166-161 BCE) revealing the apparent conflict between the righteous victims and their belief in God's goodness and omnipotence,[15] and II Maccabees (100 BCE-40 BCE) concerned primarily with the destiny of those who sacrificed their lives for the glory of God. II Maccabees portrays a resurrection to eternal life, foreseeing "the gathering of the dispersed into a 'holy place,' the nature of which has not been described, but which is expected 'for God has established Israel forever.'"[16]

Living in the environment of Hellenistic culture during the first two centuries of the Common Era, Greek thought influenced the Jewish view of immortality and the soul. This is evident in the Book of Wisdom, in which Olan posited the author's view that the "soul is preexistent and only temporarily incarcerated in the body and, therefore, that a resurrection of the body would be undesirable because of its evil nature."[17] Olan's commentary moves to II Enoch and the work entitled *The Book of the Secrets of Enoch*. This text, predicting the existence of the world for six thousand years, followed by a thousand years of the Messianic kingdom, identifies that the righteous alone will escape final judgment and enter their eternal home of Paradise.[18]

Brief consideration is afforded to IV Book of Maccabees (70 CE) and II Baruch (50-100 CE). IV Maccabees, characterizes this life as one of joy in communion with God while the wicked are doomed to be tormented in fire forever.[19] II Baruch provides an account of the Messianic kingdom where the righteous will be preserved in chambers to enjoy peace while angels guard them and the wicked go to Sheol to recline in torment and anguish while waiting for the final judgment.[20]

Olan closes the section of apocryphal writings of the first century CE with the Book of IV Ezra and the writings of Josephus. The text of IV Ezra suggests that following the destruction of Rome, there will be a four hundred year life for the kingdom, after which the Messiah and all men will die and the earth will return to primeval silence for seven days, to be followed by the judgment of all men.[21] The wicked are subjected to the furnaces of Gehenna and the righteous go to a Paradise of delight. Josephus' view of life after death is described as projecting "an intermediate stage of happiness for the righteous, who will then rise and enter other bodies, and a Sheol reserved for the wicked, which is the hell they enter immediately upon death."[22] Josephus believed the soul had an everlasting energy and that individuals lived with the concept of reward and punishment. If they lived virtuously or viciously in this life, the vicious would be in custody in an eternal prison and the virtuous will have power to revive and live again. [23]

Olan's survey of the apocryphal literature disclosed a significant departure from any biblical references of life after death. The desperateness of the people provoked concern for a remedial judgement in life after death and the idea of the Messiah gained some prominence. In the Hebraic tradition, and during the rabbinic period, resurrection and immortality were firmly allied to the idea of individual reward and punishment, and by the first century CE the idea of an afterlife had become a fundamental doctrine of Jewish faith that remained essentially unchanged for one thousand years.[24] "There is a just God who rewards the righteous and punishes the wicked; and in a variety of forms, the moral demands of life are satisfied in the accounts of the life which follows death."[25]

"The prophetic vision, which was a Kingdom of God on earth, as opposed to one in heaven, became the heritage of the rabbis and remained uppermost in their teaching."[26] The prophetic emphasis was the importance of life on earth rather than the afterlife. Demonstrating the significance of ethical conduct by the living, Olan cited Rabbi Jacob (circa 150 CE) in the Talmud.

> "This world is like unto a vestibule before the world to come; prepare thyself in the vestibule, so that thou mayest enter the banqueting hall. More beautiful is one hour in repentance and good deeds in this world, than all the life of the world to come; and more beautiful is one hour of the even-tempered spirit of the world to come, than all the life of this world."[27]

Resisting the emphasis of a future life at the expense of life in this world, Olan pointed to Ecclesiastes 9:4, which reads: "For he who is reckoned among the living has something to look forward to — even a live dog is better than a dead lion."[28]

In spite of the commentary focusing on the life of the living, authoritative commentary exists in the Mishnah and Talmud supporting, or at least providing credence to the belief of resurrection and the world to come. A simple formulation of this viewpoint is provided by Rabbi Eleazar Ha-Kappar (late 2nd and early 3rd century).

> "He used to say: the born are destined to die, the dead to be brought to life, and the living to be judged, to know and to make known, so that it become known, that He is God, He the Fashioner."[29]

Olan also provided the "dogmatic formulation" of Mishnah Sanhedrin 10:1: "Whosoever says there is no resurrection of the dead mentioned in this Torah…will have no part in the world to come." The inference here, Olan wrote, "is that a person who believes in the resurrection of the dead but does not acknowledge that it is revealed in the Torah is a nonbeliever."[30] An interpretation from Tosefta Sanhedrin 13 means the "righteous of all nations of the world will have a share in the world to come…"[31] According to the rabbis the doors to Paradise will always be open: "All Jews go to heaven because God always accepts the repentant sinner, and surely every man repents at the moment of death. Even at the gates of hell one may confess and return to God."[32]

Olan understood the rabbinic period was pervaded by a strong belief in resurrection, and whatever ideas existed of the immortality of the soul during that period was rarely separated from the body's existence.[33] This followed the rabbinic idea of man's unity, a combination of a divine soul and an earthly body in one being. This represents a moral dualism resting on a distinction between heavenly and earthly, between the divine and the human, characterized primarily from a difference between moral and religious values.[34]

> "In the rabbinic view good and evil are implanted in man, whose purpose it is to subjugate the evil. This is a function of neither the soul nor the body separately, but of the total organism. The soul and the body are not two unrelated facts; rather, the visible and invisible parts of one being."[35]

The medieval period (650 CE-1650 CE) was the time the Talmud was recognized as the center of Jewish religious authority.[36] It is in this period when it became necessary for linguistic analysis and philosophical speculation as religion was confronted with the need to find answers to rational arguments of "why." Why we do what we do and why do we believe what we believe? It became the task of distinguished philosophers and religious thinkers to demonstrate that Judaism met the standards of rational thought, as their rational-oriented philosophy of Judaism examined its truths and teachings in light of reason. While a major emphasis of the rabbinic period was the resurrection of the body and the belief in a life after death, philosophical thinking now turned to the metaphysical concerns of the nature and destiny of the soul. "What is the soul? What is its nature and destiny?"[37]

Olan introduced one of the earliest of the period in confronting the matter of life after death. Saadia Gaon (882-942), the father of Jewish philosophy who presented a rationalism-oriented philosophy of Judaism that examined truths and teachings in the light of revealed reason.[38] He affirmed the Pharisaic tradition that the idea of another world is reflected in the Torah. Beginning with Leviticus 18:5 ("You shall keep My laws and My rules, by the pursuit of which man shall live"), Olan included Saadia's use of the word "live" as not meaning this world since the wicked live here in this world; it can only mean the world beyond.[39] Saadis'a method of interpretation demonstrated his use of reason validating the existence of another world.

> "The pain which the soul endures on earth, because it abstains from its desires, must be compensated by a reward. It often suffers hatred, persecution, and death because it pursues justice. There must be a reward for this moral activity...Hence there must be another world where inequities are adjusted."[40]

Additional philosophers and thinkers of the medieval period are presented by Olan, all of whom had differing thoughts on the issues of resurrection and life after death. These thinkers include: Solomon ibn Gabirol (1021-1058) projecting the ultimate aim of man's existence to be uniting his soul with the upper world; Maimonides (1135-1204) describing the soul as not immortal in origin, but rather "born with the capacity to acquire immortality when one becomes fully human, that is when one acquires the nature of the perfect human being there is no external power to deny his soul eternal life,"[41] and Joseph Albo (1380-1444) enumerating the three basic principles of Divine religion being God, revelation, and reward and punishment after death ("the soul is uplifted unto God to the point of acquiring the quality of eternal life"[42]).

"The demands of justice still cried for some reward and punishment after death. In this the philosophers added nothing to the rabbinic tradition...The new element was their introduction of the metaphysical problem of the nature and destiny of the soul."[43] Some philosophers viewed the soul as a separate and distinct entity while others conceived of it merely as the form of the essence. The point Olan stressed is that for the first time in Jewish history a body of speculative thought arose that distinguished between body and soul. He concluded this period by suggesting that the distinction between body and soul played a significant role in the development of the Jewish idea of immortality in the modern period.

Although the major expression of Jewish mysticism, ecstatic or prophetic Kabbalah, developed in the thirteenth century,[44] the fourteenth and fifteenth centuries marked a highpoint in Jewish mysticism, briefly described as the religious movement that emphasizes the direct awareness and intimate experience of divine presence.[45] In other words, the real meaning of mysticism is a "direct and intimate contact between two poles: man and God,"[46] a relationship that can be realized only through the soul.[47] Much of the literature of the period dealt with the nature and destiny of the soul more extensively than any other writings in Jewish history.[48] The preexistence of the soul is an integral part of Jewish mysticism; it comes from God and can be returned to and reunited with God when it fulfills its mission of piety and contemplation. "Without Judaism, Jewish mysticism is a soul without a body, a vagabond spirit. Without mysticism, Judaism is a body without a soul."[49] Stressing the significance of the soul, Olan presented Berachoth 10a as one of the most commonly quoted passages:

> "Just as the Holy One, blessed be He, fills the whole world, so the soul fills the body. Just as the Holy One, blessed be He, sees, but is not seen, so the soul sees but is not itself seen. Just as the Holy One, blessed be He, feeds the whole world, so the soul feeds the whole body (intellectually and spiritually)."[50]

Although Olan believed the Jewish mystics of the period added very little to the idea of immortality of the soul, he admitted the Kabbalists advocated a doctrine of the transmigration of souls and reincarnation.[51] "The (*neshama*), soul, is always climbing back towards its source, a goal realized only after death. But a whole lifetime is often not adequate to achieve this, requiring more than one bodily incarnation."[52] The Zohar presents this as a positive doctrine in which all human souls have a common origin and every soul must pass through a series of reincarnations.[53]

Olan continued by perusing through the Safed school of Jewish mysticism and its formulation of a more positive doctrine of transmigration.

From his study of Isaac Luria and Hayyim Vital, Olan presented what he viewed as a more complete understanding of transmigration. The suffering of mankind is caused by the combination of good and evil, and salvation depends upon withdrawing the divine elements from the unclean.[54]

Hasidism, founded by The Baal Shem Tov, arose in the eighteenth century as a vital and mass expression of the Jewish mystical experience. As a deprived and persecuted religious movement, the Hasidim were anxious about the rewards to be offered to the righteous in the afterlife. They confronted the problem of theodicy and attempted to explain the suffering of the righteous. It was a positive and reforming movement among Eastern European Jews for fifty years before it began to decline in importance (although it began to surge again during the latter half of the twentieth century). Olan indicated, however, that it left a lasting impression upon Jewish life because of its simple style and use of epigrams, metaphors, and parables. Hasidim popularized Jewish mysticism, avoiding the complex symbolist and abstruse style of the great kabbalists.[55] Unlike the rabbis concern during the period of the Talmud, the Hasidim did not revive an interest in the resurrection of the dead. For the Hasid, like the view of the kabbalists, the immortality that one receives is for the soul.[56]

While Olan indicated that Hasidism made no original contribution to the concept of immortality, he did stress that the Hasidism placed great emphasis upon the pleasure that a Jew can achieve in this world if he finds the correct relationship to the Divine and enthusiastically cleaves unto the Holy One in his heart.

> "In its most creative period it revealed the bliss which men may attain here on earth if they seek communion with God through earnestness and sincerity. The real joys of this world are not material but spiritual. A proper training in this kind of living on earth prepares a man for the highest bliss in the world to come."[57]

With the introduction of the Haskalah in the eighteenth century, followed by the *Wissenschaft des Judenthums* ("Science of Judaism") in the nineteenth century, the literature of the past underwent a reevaluation and reinterpretation which included a "break with traditional theological modes of historical thought; and the use of history to serve modern social and political ideologies."[58] This was a period of transition in which the concept of immortality was subjected to all the tests of reason and experience.

At the outset of the modern period, Moses Mendelssohn (1729-1786) is presented by Olan as a radical break with tradition by separating the articles of belief in Judaism from the practice of its commandments. "Religious ideas…are arrived at by reason which is universal. Therefore there are no unique Jewish dogmas."[59] From his rationalist approach, Mendelssohn's revived the view of the spiritual substance of the soul, and unlike Maimonides, held that the human soul is by nature indestructible.[60] At death, the soul separates from the body and "is free to contemplate perfect beauty, truth, and goodness."[61] Fundamentally, the soul hungers for perfection which cannot be satisfied in this world, and God, who created the soul for man, must provide a place where its desires can be achieved. Like Maimonides, Mendelsohn emphasized the supremacy of virtuous actions because they are seen as desirable in themselves, and not for the purpose of receiving an award.[62] Furthermore, Olan wrote, Mendelssohn ignored the entire Jewish tradition of the resurrection of the dead. "He is wholly committed to the idea of immortality of the soul which is a distinct entity and is destined to achieve Supreme bliss after the death of the body (a concept in the theology of the Reform Movement)."[63]

The nineteenth century saw the idea of immortality of the soul expanded upon by two liberal thinkers who were influential in the Reform Movement: Abraham Geiger (1810-1874) and Hermann Cohen (1840-1918). For Geiger the spirit was everlasting and he underscored the importance of earthly life over a life in the future, a belief of most modern Reform Jews.[64] Cohen believed Judaism to be a Messianic religion in which one who accomplishes the ethical nature of human existence also achieves immortality. Olan believed that both Geiger and Cohen represented a departure from the mystic idea of the soul as a distinct entity and the projection of a world better than this world for the individual after death.⁶⁵ They conceived the view of the soul as a spiritual expression of one's actions and both ignored the dogma of resurrection.

The subject of immortality in the modern period concludes with a brief view of the thoughts of Leo Baeck (1873-1956), rabbi, teacher, distinguished scholar, leader and hero of the concentration camps. He recognized a unity of mortality and immortality while the spiritual element is bound up with the ethical. "The reward of piety…is now transferred to a world beyond. The 'length of the days' which it promises now appears as 'eternal life,' and the message of happiness which it brings is interpreted to mean 'eternal bliss'…the spirit comes from God and returns to him again."⁶⁶

Olan concluded the subject of immortality during the period of his rabbinate with brief introduction of three modern scholars. Mordecai Kaplan, founder of the Reconstructionist Movement, abandoned the entire concept of resurrection of the dead. His movement eliminated the Hebrew phrase from the *Eighteen Benedictions* and dismissed the entire matter of both resurrection and immortality of the soul. Louis Finkelstein, president of the Jewish Theological Seminary, attributed the concept of immortality, with its accompanying concept of resurrection, to the inability of earlier generations, and particularly the Jew, to conceive of separation of body and soul. Kaufmann Kohler succinctly stated that the belief in resurrection of the body is in direct contradiction to the entire attitude toward both science and religion that it may be considered obsolete for the modern Jew.

American Reform Judaism expressed similar convictions early in its history. Olan alluded to the congregation of Charleston, South Carolina, founded in 1824 and the first congregation on American soil. Rather than include the Maimonidean statement of belief in the coming of the Messiah and bodily resurrection, they believed "with perfect faith that the soul of man is breathed into him by God, and is therefore immortal."⁶⁷ This view was reaffirmed in later platforms of the American Reform Movement, and is most explicit in their 1885 statement that stated that the "soul is immortal" while rejecting as beliefs both bodily resurrection and Gehenna and Eden (Hell and Paradise) as abodes for everlasting punishments and rewards.[68] In 1937 the Central Conference of American Rabbis adopted their latest (up to the time of Olan's immediate commentary) statement of principles, simply declaring that Judaism affirms that man is created in the Divine image and his spirit is immortal.

Olan was grateful to his contemporaries for the opportunity to present his text. "The invitation of the Committee on Jewish Education to prepare a work on this much-neglected subject presented a challenge. I am grateful to the commission for placing renewed emphasis on the importance of the concept of immortality in Judaism and Jewish thought and for awakening my interest."[69]

Conclusion

A review of Olan's study confirms that from its earliest days Judaism had and continues to have an indisputable interest in the subjects of immortality and resurrection, doctrines resulting from the belief in absolute justice and divine mercy. Although no definitive concept of life after death developed during the biblical period, people were influenced by the prophets to obey God's will in order to lengthen the days of their lives. Beginning with the physical concept of the resurrection of a united body and soul, Judaism moved toward a belief in immortally of the soul with varying concepts of bodily resurrection. "The rabbinic period was the first to disclose a clear formulation of the idea of resurrection of the dead, and this concept, whether bodily resurrection or immortality of the soul, has therefore never been absent from Jewish religious thought."[70]

Although it is difficult to assess the amount of influence the historical commentaries had on Olan's own views of the afterlife, his vision certainly warrants that death is not the end. By recognizing the individual as different from other animals, Olan suggested that one who can conceive truth, goodness, and beauty, must himself be as eternal as those values. "Without immortality, man as a creature is an irrationality in the scheme of the universe. The faith that there is life after death, then, is reasonable from the evidence of life itself."⁷¹ Although immortality is not evident by authentic or original experiences, Olan perceived that we may hold it to be a true and valid concept from inferential evidence and indirect data that is available to us. He further concluded that for the Creator to endow man with so much and so many possibilities, that to destroy it all before fulfillment is an irrational act.⁷² "The universe is too orderly for that. The concept that there is life after death is not a wishful idea, a fancy which men adhere too out of fear or ignorance. It is a reasonable postulate, necessary to explain phenomena which are real in man's experience."⁷³

Olan pursues the discussion through an analysis of rationalization and reason. Faith is a rational process, he stated, that can explain the phenomena of the universe, life within it, and the concept of God. Although revealing that God cannot be experienced or demonstrated in a scientific laboratory, Olan said the presumption of God is shown through an orderly universe that exhibits direction and a sense of purpose. "Immortality," he continued, "is also a postulate, a hypothesis which best fits man's experience and nature. It is a belief which men of intellectual integrity have affirmed."⁷⁴ Support of this view is directed to scientist-physician Sir William Osler, scientist-philosopher William Bergson, and from Socrates to William James, as some of the most trusted intellects that have been persuaded by their experiences to believe in immortality.⁷⁵ That they have manifested their faith in the reality of life after death, and the belief in immortality "is, to say the least, proof that this doctrine is not only for the ignorant or superstitious. Modern man, informed by the new sciences and philosophies, may affirm his faith in the reality of life after death without compromising his intellectual integrity."⁷⁶

Reason was also instrumental in reinforcing Olan's view of life and the afterlife. He alluded to some of the things that are reasonable, including the belief in love because it is a reasonable conclusion to what we feel. Though no empirical evidence exists, we believe in God, and there is no scientific evidence to prove that God is or what He is. It seems more reasonable, he said, to believe that the universe is more spiritual than material. There is meaning in the universe, and reason demands that meaning is an intimation of the presence of some spiritual power which we call God.

> "Common sense and reason are best served by a belief that man has a spiritual nature along with his physical being. The body dies, we say, but the spirit lives on with God who gave it. It seems reasonable to believe that if life has produced such spiritual potential, that it will not destroy it all at the grave and begin anew with the next man. It appears more reasonable to believe that there is an eternal nature to man which reaches out beyond death."[77]

"If the religious view of life is reasonable, then immortality is reasonable. If the universe has meaning and purpose, if man is a being with more than cells and body, a being with spirit, then it is reasonable, nay, well-nigh necessary for us to believe that death is not an end."[78]

In addressing the nature of immortality and its relationship to whether or not injustices committed on earth are rectified after death, Olan believed it undesirable to promote the afterlife as an answer to any imbalance of the scales of justice. "There is no warrant in logic or experience to assert that after the grave the just will be rewarded and the wicked will be punished. The baffling problems of theodicy cannot be resolved by postponing them to a non-terrestrial existence."[79] As a practical matter, Olan wrote, the world-to-come is not a viable answer to the imbalance of the scales of justice in this world. He emphasized the significance of morality, absent the objective of reward, as the hypothesis that rational, modern men may accept with intellectual honesty. Death is a mystery, and to be rewarded for doing good things is to rob goodness of any moral quality.[80] Moral values and the good life are independent of immortality. "If the grave ends all, the good is still the good, and evil is still evil. In fact, life's terminus imposes an urgency upon us to intensify and quicken our moral activity."[81] In recalling the prophetic teachings of the importance of justice and righteousness in this world, Olan stressed man must not be enticed away from the battle for God's kingdom on earth by the fanciful promises of a world-to-come.

Human existence, Olan preached, was more than matter that returns to dust. In a universe characterized by laws, minds, and purpose, man must fulfill the unfulfilled. It is both futile and misleading to describe in detail as real what we cannot possibly know by experience; and therefore, we should not attempt to picture the "furnishings" of the life after death.[82] "There is, however, enough in human experience to warrant man's faith that death is not an end. To believe this is to give depth to man's hope in life."[83] "Faith in God is given a deeper dimension by the affirmation that the part of man we call the soul is deathless."[84] The recitation of the *Kaddish* (the "Sanctification") prayer in time of death or in remembrance is provided by Olan as proof text for the expression of the basic faith of Judaism in a future life. It is in this prayer that affirms God, the Creator of all, who is eternal and our Redeemer through eternity. "In a religion like Judaism, which is free of creedal dogma, the belief that death is not the end comes as near to a common principle of faith as that of belief in one God."[85] "The God faith, not only requires the declaration that death is not an end, it adds a dimension to faith itself by the affirmation that what man is, God in miniature, is deathless."[86]

Nevertheless, the presentation of historical ideas and commentaries reflected in Olan's text presents a concern for contemporary society. Characterized by revolutionary scientific developments of the twentieth and twenty-first centuries, what relevance can there be for life after death in a society embraced by secularism and a world deemed an insignificant part of the planetary system. Olan believed the postmodern generation demanded empirical evidence in support of its beliefs of an afterlife. Yet, as he commented, and certainly most people would concur, there is nothing that proves that one can survive death and, on the contrary, there is nothing that proves that one cannot. As far as we presently know, no one has ever come back to give substantive testimony, and neither do we know how to determine the legitimacy of anyone claiming otherwise.

While most Jews share a religious philosophy focusing on what one can and should do to make the world a better place and a social philosophy that affirms life, in all probability they hold little stock in the after-

Rabbi Levi A. Olan

---

life. But even without believing, the afterlife draws concern of anyone in a near death situation. Perhaps it is reasonable to say that what awaits us after we die is immaterial. As Jews, we are partners with God in creation and have the obligation to do our part in repairing the world by living a meaningful, ethical, and fruitful life.

CHAPTER 11

Epilogue

After Olan's first year at Temple Emanu-El in Dallas, he questioned how he endured the painful, up-hill journey. He recalled the burden of an imposed leadership, the arduous task of molding himself to a new environment (or molding the environment to him) and the transition from a life of irresponsible scholasticism to one of responsible production.[1] This early sermon emphasized the busy routine of his rabbinate, which included teaching numerous classes, meetings with directors and trustees, civic and social work, sermons, and a myriad of life cycle events encompassing much of a twenty-four hour day. Although his religious, social, and philosophic views were liberal and presented a major challenge in coming to Dallas, this was instrumental to his decision to come, and he envisioned his task as implementing his liberal views in the conservative environs of his congregation and the city of Dallas. Surprisingly, he found a positive response to his liberal views on social justice and in his responsibilities in the synagogue and its Jewish community.

Olan was a leader with a purpose in which he believed and to which he was committed throughout his life, and for which he was willing to sacrifice. He was a man of great integrity without suspicion of self-seeking motives and a man of courage willing to stand for what he believed even if in the minority. His leadership, evidenced by his own conviction and the sincerity of his purpose, was manifested by his awe-inspiring sermons as he preached not with a promise of wealth or success, but merely with the opportunity of achieving a higher and nobler life.

As a distinguished orator, Olan's sermons touched the heart and minds of his congregants and all of his listeners. The sermon was significant in his rabbinic functions, equal to and at times exceeding the importance of teaching, pastoral work, public relations, community involvement, social causes, and administrative functions, all of which had a proper place on his very limited calendar. Olan firmly believed in the importance and effectiveness of his sermons, that people needed what he passionately offered, and that it made a difference in their lives. His sermonic objective was "to win a response to the demands of the highest. Its appeal is to the will more than to the mind, stimulating the impulse, giving confidence to hope, sensitizing moral feelings, and sending a man out saying, done. The word must lead to the deed."[2] The effectiveness of a sermon, he alleged, necessitated a lifting of spirits, elimination of malevolence, and a realization of ideals among his listeners. "If we are to preach," Olan wrote, "we must rise above our doubts, and feel as though the Kingdom of God depends upon the sermon of the week. Its delivery must be with passion and fire, charged with the feeling that upon it hangs the fate of the 'end of days.'"[3] In Olan's mind, the successful sermon was infused with spiritual motivation that affirmed not only the presence of God, but also the power of God in every instance as a guide and aid to man in his appointment with destiny.[4]

Olan was an effective teacher and theologian because he always talked about things that really mattered in the lives of people: about their relationship to a society where they were concerned that people obtained justice and were cared for. He reached a point where he saw that the function of religion altogether was the prophetic faith, for the prophets were never concerned with an individual's behavior, except as it built the good society. He devoted his life to scholarship speaking in the name of the prophets, and he interpreted religion not as going to church or synagogue, but as putting your heart into it. "Preaching and teaching constituted for him the essential function of the rabbi and it was as preacher and teacher that he left his mark on his congregation and community."[5]

During the course of Olan's years in the Worcester and Dallas rabbinates, sermons, writings, and engagement echoed his religious and ideological precepts, as well as those of the Reform Movement, stressing the doctrines of religious liberalism, the prophetic call for justice and human rights, and man's partnership with God in mending the world. This not only included a broad spectrum of Jewish theology and philosophy, but also concern for the excesses of commerce and industry and the humanitarian need to reduce man-made misery and suffering from poverty, social inequality, racism, and prejudice. Following the Reform Movement's concern for a just society, Olan preached that greater priority should be given to the challenge of social justice. "While we are desperately in need of disciplined worship and observance, our major interest is a world redeemed from war, bigotry, slavery, and injustice."[6] "As a liberal religious movement, we came into history dedicated to liberate all men from all slavery: intellectual, spiritual, moral, and physical. This is still our primary emphasis in Judaism, and our special contribution toward the fulfillment of the Messianic Day."[7]

Olan was an advocate of peace, and totally against war among nations and people as he continually spoke out for the betterment of the human condition and the world in general. When Vietnam became a prominent issue during the mid-1960s, he pointed to the plight of the Vietnamese people supporting a regime and choosing a way of life not approved by our government. Olan objected to our country's disapproval of the Communist leaders of Vietnam rather than viewing the war as a war of liberation by the Viet Cong and people of Vietnam. Following the CCAR's call for a cease fire and a negotiated settlement of the conflict, Olan insisted that foreign and domestic issues could be solved successfully not in terms of practical politics but only in the light of the moral law rooted in the universe by its Creator. His anti-war rhetoric and concern for the hungry people in Europe earned him high praise on a national and international level. Summoned by national political and religious leaders, Olan was instrumental in supporting groups organized to assist in efforts alleviating hunger and working for peace.

Olan was truly an "Untired Liberal" and he continually advocated on behalf of liberalism and the liberal expression of faith. "Our liberalism opens the doorways to many communions and brotherhoods which wittingly or unwittingly are witnesses and co-workers in the building of God's Kingdom."[8] With one of the contributions of the Reform Movement being clarification of the idea of continuous revelation, Olan advanced the belief that the essence of all liberalism is a dedication to the search for truth and a refusal to congeal into fixed dogma. This warranted the Reform commitment for an honest examination of all truths, regardless the form from which it came. "Nothing is unfit so long as it helps make clear the will of God and intensifies the Jew's desire to advance the fulfillment of the covenanted faith."[9] Olan called the Reform a "peculiar treasure" that is committed to a unique faith, and is therefore bound to examine all doctrines not only for their intrinsic value, but for their relevancy to our historic purpose.

> "Reason is a divine gift with the Jew, and is a chief instrument in determining God's way. As liberals, we have the obligation to examine all truths, to relate them to our purpose in history, and to push forward the frontiers of the knowledge of God... One of our greatest contributions to Judaism is our dedication to the possibility of new revelations."[10]

He visualized an opportunity for Reform to provide a path for those who can accept only a voluntary attitude toward discipline; for those who, committed to the reality of the covenant with God, need the freedom to select their program of worship.[11]

Olan's liberal compulsion was influential among Reform Jews throughout the postwar generation of World War II, and his conception of man partnering with an impersonal God and his confidence for the future were widely represented by both religious leaders and the laity. If the challenge of life is how to sanctify life, then Olan lived his life with a life of purpose evidenced by his continued proselytization for what he believed and practiced — sanctifying life as the primary directive of Hebrew Scriptures. He was called an outspoken advocate of equality and humanity who struggled to correct the ills that he felt society had inflicted upon the less fortunate. For Olan, it is the standard of values that judges the worth of our lives and measures our true success or failure. He believed society must have an adequate philosophy of life, recognizing its failures while seeking to find their causes. "Although we cannot control all the circumstances of our lives, we can control the effect those circumstances have on us. And as we are more satisfied, we can be more fitted to create a more peaceful and orderly world."[12]

Olan's addresses emphasized that Reform Judaism had a historic role to play. Although the liberalism of Reform permits intellectual acceptance regarding differences and a clear perspective about fundamentals, he believed the focus of all Jews should be their "Judaism," regardless of the path chosen. Recognizing the denominational differences among various Jewish religious movements, he stressed that the direction which Reform Judaism set for itself is the same as Orthodoxy and Conservatism. "One purpose is common to all of them; i.e., giving witness to our covenant with God and bringing near the Messianic Day. There is legitimate difference in the roads we choose, but there is no possible disagreement upon where we all want to arrive."[13] The peril, he said, is our preoccupation with the road maps and our increasing loyalty to the route we have selected. The important word is *Judaism*, Reform, Orthodox, or Conservative should be only secondary descriptions; the time is propitious for a ringing declaration that the goal is the fulfillment of our destiny as a 'kingdom of priests and a holy people.'[14]

With the unique concept of individual freedom in America, Olan believed American Jewry to be the most powerful Jewish community in the world.[15] However, he alleged that the ever-present consciousness of group discrimination strained the faith of American democracy and, consequently, total freedom had not yet been accomplished. Many human rights goals had to be addressed for the future in spite of the provisions included in the Declaration of Independence and the Bill of Rights. Second class citizens continued to exist in America because of color, national origin, and often creed. Because of the goal of freedom and equality the "destiny of America has yet to be fashioned."[16] Referring to Asser Levy who insisted upon his right to serve in the National Guard after the arrival of the Jews in America, Olan pointed to the role of the Jew and his struggle for freedom over the course of history, saying: "the Jew has been in the center of the struggle to make real the destiny of the nation."[17] Still there were and continue to be areas in American life where color, creed, national origin and class distinctions are barriers to the realization of the sanctity of the human character. Although substantial progress has been made in America since Olan's rabbinate, Jews everywhere, like society in general, have an obligation to remain faithful and exhibit courage in a continued, unrelenting drive to advance human rights initiatives. The essence of religion for Olan was faith — faith in the meaning of life and the ability of man to fashion life so peace, justice, and truth would ultimately prevail.

In the final analysis, Olan spoke out on the concerns of the day, aiming at the relationship of religion to the good society — racism, poverty, social injustice, confrontation among nations, and the quality of education, among others — and let the chips fall where they might. Although he was not always accepted with the approval of city leaders, and even some members within his own congregation, during his 35 years in Dallas Olan won the undying respect of city leaders, as well as prominent state and national political leaders. When arriving in Dallas, he found a city "on the make"[18] as he put it — a city that realized it needed to grow culturally as well as economically. He found a city that was "narrow and bigoted," a very fundamentalist religious atmosphere, a very discriminatory social environment, and a "general mood characterized by immaturity of people who imagine they have more strength than they have.[19] Yet he responded with enthusiasm referring to his new position as "a rewarding experience of tackling a new job and trying to fashion a program on a little larger scale."[20] He was instrumental in opening the eyes of civic leaders to racial injustice, inadequate housing for the poor, and substandard education, as he continually sought remedy for the ills of the community's moral dilemmas. After being called "the conscience of the city" by Fortune magazine, Olan commented: "While I wouldn't have used so grandiloquent a title, I think what I've always done in this city is to confront them with the moral demands of whatever the situation was."[21] Narrowing the division that existed between rich and poor was a priority for him as he continually strove to improve social conditions.

Olan was an inspiration to his congregants and community as he continually gave direction and hope to those seeking a better life. His importance to the Worcester and Dallas communities can best be demonstrated by a letter written by Rabbi Joseph Klein, Senior Rabbi of Temple Emanuel of Worcester, Massachusetts, to Rabbi Gerald Klein, successor to Rabbi Olan, of Temple Emanu-El:

> "It is always risky to indulge in superlatives, but I am personally convinced that Rabbi Olan was the most successful rabbi the Reform movement in New England ever had. He took a very small congregation, which had no physical facilities of any kind, and built it into one of the great congregations of the land solely on the strength of his personality and leadership... In substance, Temple Emanuel in Worcester and Temple Emanu-El in Dallas have been uniquely blessed in having as their spiritual leader one of the truly great rabbis of our time — one whose gifts of personality made him unique not only as leader of the congregation but also as national leader in the rabbinate and the Reform movement in Judaism."[22]

It certainly is not an overstatement for one to say that Levi Olan accomplished his goals during the course of his rabbinate or that his life positively impacted the broad communities in which he preached. He was an inspirational leader, not only in the religious and secular communities of Dallas and Worcester, but also in the State of Texas and the American Reform Movement. Perhaps a fitting summation of Rabbi Olan's legacy can be found in the Jerusalem Talmud. "By three things the world is preserved, by justice, by truth, and by peace, and these three are one: if justice has been accomplished, so has truth, and so has peace."[23]

End Notes

Preface

1. Levi A. Olan, "Philanthropy and the Modern World," p. 3, June 7, 1965 (This composition was presented by Olan at a dinner with faculty consultants to the Hog Foundation for Mental Health, the University of Texas, Austin, Texas, January 28, 1965. Established in 1940, the foundation continues to be an influential grant maker, providing funds for mental wellness for the people of Texas.)

2. Ibid., 13.

3. Levi Olan, "Beyond Cheap Thanksgiving," 1976.

4. Jeffrey Weiss, "Religious Leaders Honor Outspoken Rabbi's Legacy," *Dallas Morning News*, September 2, 2006, 3.

5. David Ritz, "Inside the Jewish Establishment," *D Magazine,* November 1975, 111 and "The Way It Was," *D Magazine*, November 2008, 176. (David Ritz is an American biographer, novelist, lyricist, and journalist who, among other endeavors, has collaborated on the memoirs of numerous entertainers.)

6. Jason S. Auerbach, *Rabbis and Lawyers,* 49. (The most conspicuous spokesmen, Auerbach writes, include Louis Brandeis to Martin Luther King, Jr.)

7. Ibid.

References Cited in Preface

8. Levi A. Olan, "The President's Message to the 8th Annual Convention of the Central Conference of American Rabbis," Houston, Texas, June 16, 1969.

9. Levi A. Olan, *Prophetic Faith and the Secular Age,* xi. (Olan is quoting from E. F. Magnin, "The Voice of Prophecy in This Satellite Age," in *Interpreting the Prophetic Tradition*, 104-105.)

10. Olan in *Prophetic Faith and the Secular Age,* xiii.

11. Levi A. Olan, "The Majority Can Be Wrong," WFAA Radio, January 29, 1967.

12. Levi A. Olan, "Confronting Life at its Depths," undated.

13. Levi A. Olan, "What, After All, is Religion," WFAA Radio, April, 27, 1952.

14. *Levi Olan: Oral History Interviews Conducted by Gerald D. Saxon on February 4 and April 6, 1983*, 16-17.

15. Lev. 24:22.

16. Levi Olan, "Religion and the Social Problem," WFAA Radio, April 10, 1949 and "Theological Foundations for Guiding Principles for Reform Judaism," 1972.

17. Richard Austin Smith, "How Business Failed Dallas," *Fortune Magazine*, July 1964, 163.

18. David Ritz, "Inside the Jewish Establishment," *D Magazine*, November 1975, p. 111 and "The Way it Was," *D Magazine*, November 2008, 176.

19. William Zale letter of March 18, 1960 to Levi Olan.

20. Richard Austin Smith, "How Business," 163.

21. Gerald J. Klein, "Introduction," in *A Rational Faith: Essays in Honor of Levi A. Olan*, edited by Jack Bemporad. x. (Rabbi Klein was the Assistant Rabbi during Olan's rabbinate at Temple Emanu-El, later becoming Co-Senior rabbi after Olan's retirement.)

22. Smith, "How Business," 163.

23. Peyton Davis, "Rabbi Levi Olan: A Conscience of the City," *Dallas Times Herald Newspaper*, October 10, 1976, Sunday Q & A Section.

24. Smith, "How Business," 163.

25. Limited studies or comments have been written and are included in such

documents as: "A Snapshot in Time," by John A. Linder, (American Jewish History — 403, HUC), January 2001; "Levi Olan: Champion of Liberalism," by Evan Moffic (Independent Reading Course, HUC), Spring 2005; and, "Communism and Judaism," by Anne Strauss (Term Paper, HUC), 2009. And of course prominent religious scholars, including Sidney L. Regner, Michael A. Meyer, Abraham Joshua Heschel, William G. Braude, Arnold Jacob Wolf, Roland B. Gittelsohn, and Robert G. Goldy have made brief mention and reference to Olan in various writings and texts. Documentation of Olan's background and secular views can be found in the texts of Hollace Ava Weiner (*Jewish Stars in Texas, Rabbis and Their Work*, Texas A&M Press, College Station, Texas, 1999), and Gerry Cristol, Archivist of Temple-Emanu-El (*A Light in the Prairie, Temple Emanu-El of Dallas 1872-1997*, Texas Christian University, Fort Worth, Texas, 1998.)

Chapter 1

1. Port of New York passenger records of The Statute of Liberty — Ellis Island Foundation (www.ellisisland.org/research/passRecord.asp?:MID=007938074...) provided by Lionel Joseph, son-in-law of Levi Olan.

2. S. M. Dubnow, *History of the Jews in Russia and Poland*, 106.

3. Probate Court Records of the Commonwealth of Massachusetts identify the name of Levy Olan changed in 1940 to Levi Arthur Olan.

4. Levi A. Olan Autobiography, written in the 50th anniversary year of marriage (1931-1981), 1.

5. The badenstreet.org website describes its founding by two women in 1901 as the "Social Settlement of Rochester" to provide cultural, practical and social education to young women of foreign birth. It has continuously and dynamically grown to provide a full range of services and facilities to improve the social, educational and cultural conditions in its community, to relieve human suffering and to foster the growth and development of its participants and community. The goal is to pursue the elimination of the causes of poverty and to reduce the level of negative social problems associated with being disadvantaged.

6. Gerry Cristol, *A Light in the Prairie, Temple Emanu-El of Dallas 1872-1997*, 154-155 and *Levi Olan: Oral History Interviews Conducted by Gerald D. Saxon on February 4 and April 6, 1983*, 7-8.

References Cited in Chapter 1

7. Levi A. Olan Autobiography, written in the 50th anniversary year of marriage (1931-1981), 2.
8. Levi A. Olan, untitled and undated commentary regarding the significance of language.
9. Olan Autobiography.
10. Gerry Cristol, "Levi A. Olan, Conscience of the City," in *Legacies, A Historical Journal for Dallas and North Central Texas, Dallas Historical Society*, vol. 17, Number 2, Fall 2005, 47.
11. Cristol, *A Light in the Prairie*, 154-155.
12. Ibid.
13. Olan Autobiography.
14. Saxon, "Levi Olan: Oral History Interviews," 9.
15. bid., 8. (Sidney Regner was a prominent Reform rabbi ordained by the Hebrew Union College in 1927. In 1985 he wrote a memorial tribute to Rabbi Olan appearing in the *CCAR YB*, vol. XCV, 301-302.)
16. Olan Autobiography.
17. Ibid.
18. Michael A. Meyer, *Response to Modernity, A History of the Reform Movement in Judaism*, 301-302. (Meyer writes that the teachers of Prophetic Judaism at the College believed that religion was essentially reverence for human personality, and that it should be concerned more with high aspirations and noble purposes than with dogma or ritual. After the appointment of Abraham Cronbach to a newly created chair of Jewish social studies, students had the opportunity not only to study the Prophets but to consider ways of applying prophetic morality to current social problems.)
19. Olan Autobiography. (Meyer, in *Response to Modernity*, 301-302, describes Prophetic Judaism as significant in the curriculum at the Hebrew Union College in Cincinnati. "Moses Buttenwieser" he writes, taught the prophetic literature with critical competence and great enthusiasm for the subject.")
20. Commentary on Amos, *The Holy Scriptures According to the Masoretic Text*, p. 479.
21. Ibid.

22. Ibid.
23. Levi A. Olan, "A Troubler of the People," WFAA Radio, March 12, 1967.
24. Olan, "Philanthropy and the Modern World," 4.
25. Levi A. Olan, "The President's Message to the 80th Annual Convention."
26. Saxon, Levi Olan: Oral History Interviews. 9.
27. Worcester Telegram & Gazette Newspaper, August 4, 1948 (Copy of article furnished by the Worcester Historical Museum.) [*Statistics of Jews—1929*, by H. S. Linfield, PhD, Appearing in the American Jewish Year Book. (ajcarchives.org/ajc_data/files/1930_1931_7_statistics), estimated Jewish population of Worcester to be 13,000].
28. Saxon, Levi Olan: Oral History Interviews, 6 and 12 and Cristol, *A Light in the Prairie*, 155. (Wolfson outlined a course of study after Olan introduced himself by saying "I just became a rabbi and don't know what to do." Olan also began weekly study sessions of Talmud with Braude, a rabbi in Providence, Rhode Island.)
29. Saxon, Levi Olan: Oral History Interviews, 5.
30. Weiner, *Jewish Stars in Texas*, 218.
31. Jonathan D. Sarna, *American Judaism*, 219-220.
32. Richard S. Levy, *Anti-Semitism in the Modern World, An Anthology of Texts*, 168. (In the Aish.com Jewish History Series, Part 59 of 68, Rabbi Ken Spiro mentions the *Protocols* became the second biggest selling book in the United States in the 1920s and 1930s, second only to the Bible.)
33. Levy, *Anti-Semitism in the Modern World*, 168.
34. Levi A. Olan, "Beware of False Messiahs," WFAA Radio, February 18, 1968.
35. Levy, *Anti-Semitism in the Modern World*, 168. (In "What Shall We Do About Demagogues?" Olan believed that Coughlin's sincere preaching represented an insufferable arrogance filled with prejudice and hate. Olan continued by saying that Coughlin had "not hesitated again and again to resort to shameful innuendos and vile slanders to make a point and achieve an end.")
36. Sarna, *American Judaism*, 219.
37. Leonard Dinnerstein, *Anti-Semitism in America*, 85-86.

References Cited in Chapter 1

38. Sarna, *American Judaism*, 219.

39. Levi A. Olan, "Hitlerism—The Grave of Liberalism," undated, (Olan believed Hitler was just another serpent biting a struggling mankind.)

40. Levi A. Olan, "The Business of Religion is Peace," WFAA Radio, November 13, 1949.

41. Levi A. Olan, "The Jew in Germany — Whose Problem is He?" (Dated before the 1936 Berlin Olympics.)

42. Ibid.

43. Ibid.

44. Sarna, *American Judaism*, 308-309.

45. Gary P. Zola, *The Four Ideological Pronouncements of Reform Judaism in America*, a seminar led by Dr. Gary P. Zola, The Jacob Rader Marcus Center of the American Jewish Archives, 2001.

46. Ibid.

47. Levi A. Olan, "Steadiness in an Unsteady World," WFAA Radio, January 9, 1949.

48. Olan Autobiography, 7.

49. Ibid., 8.

50. Editorial, Jewish Civic Leader Newspaper, Worcester, Massachusetts, December 10, 1948. (From the Archives of Temple Emanuel, Worcester.)

51. "Rabbi Levi A. Olan," in *Jewish Civic Leader* Newspaper, 1, December 10, 1948.

52. "Civic Groups Honor Rabbi Olan," in *Jewish Civic Leader* Newspaper, 3, December 10, 1948.

53. Rabbi Joseph Klein (Temple Emanuel, Worcester, Massachusetts) to Rabbi Gerald J. Klein (Temple Emanu-El, Dallas, Texas), May 15, 1970, Jacob Rader Marcus Archives of the UAHC.

54. "Organizational Activities," in *Jewish Civic Leader* Newspaper, 3, December 10, 1948.

55. Levi A. Olan, "The Rabbi Speaks to You," *Jewish Civic Leader*, 1 (Olan alludes to the major program as the new house of worship and the school.

References Cited in Chapter 1

Unfortunately, he could not stay for the dedication of the building, saying "I must submerge this personal desire for the challenge of the new call.")

56. A. J. Bradley to Levi A. Olan, Archives of Temple Emanu-El, Dallas, Texas, 1949-1950.

57. Archibald Hillman to Levi A. Olan, October 15, 1951, Archives of Temple Emanu-El, Dallas, Texas, 1949-1950.

58. Weiner, *Jewish Stars in Texas,* 220. [Michele Alperin of JointMedia News Service (May 8, 2012 post to *ejewishphilanthropy.com*), in her interview with America's first female rabbi, Sally Priesand, points out that Nelson Glueck and his successor president of the HUC, Dr. Fred Gottschalk, supported Priesand's admission and ordination (1972), despite opposition from some faculty members.]

59. Cristol, *A Light in the Prairie,* 11.

60. The Temple Emanu-El annual report for the 2012-2013 year presented a total budget approximating $8,882,000. The June 2013 membership approximated 2,600 family members. Through the use of future value tables, an operating budget of $100,000 in 1949 equates to approximately $680,000, $1,250,000, and $2,400,000 sixty-four (1949 to 2013) years later at rates of three percent, four percent, and five percent, respectively. The American Jewish Year Book estimates the 1948 Jewish population in Dallas to be 10,000.

61. Classical alludes to the Reform movement's early changes which consisted of reforming synagogue services, eliminating certain Jewish laws, abridgement of the prayer service, and other moderate religious innovations. Examples include men and women sitting together in mixed pews, bareheaded men without prayer shawls, organ music and a mixed choir of men and women (Jews and non-Jews), a Hebrew prayer book opening from left to right (rather than the traditional right to left), and social activism as the central demand of its followers.

62. Weiner, *Jewish Stars in Texas,* 222.

63. Judge Irving Goldberg, President of Temple Emanu-El 1955-1957, interviewed by Joseph Rosenstein, August 22, 1974 (Archives of Temple Emanu-El, Dallas.)

64. Olan Autobiography, 8-9. (Olan referred to himself as a preacher and to Lefkowitz as a pastor).

References Cited in Chapter 1

65. Weiner, *Jewish Stars in Texas*, 220.
66. Will Herberg, *Protestant-Catholic-Jew, An Essay in American Religious Sociology*, 186.
67. Cristol, *A Light in the Prairie*, 205.
68. Ibid.
69. Ibid., 63-164 (In his letter of July 27, 1962, to Mrs. Edward C. Stern, Olan wrote that Temple's focus should include intensification of members' participation in education and worship, added opportunity for more Jews to affiliate with the Reform Movement, transfer of prophetic ideals into active programs in the greater community, and creation of more personal relationships between the leadership of Temple and its members.)
70. Ibid., 182.
71. Ibid., 191 and Cristol, "Levi A. Olan, Conscience of the City," 51.
72. Cristol, *A Light in the Prairie*, 175.
73. Olan Autobiography, 9.
74. Levi A. Olan, Guest Editorial, Marque, a publication of the St. Mark's School of Texas, Spring, 1969 (Jacob Rader Archives of the HUC-JIR.)
75. Ibid.
76. Cristol, *A Light in the Prairie*, 183. (Cristol continues by writing that over 900 attended the first review while the following year 1,900 people purchased series tickets and 700 more bought single tickets. The Significant Book Series became a sought after North Dallas social and intellectual event attracting an active and enthusiastic following.)
77. Olan Autobiography, 11.
78. Jeffrey Weiss, "Religious Leaders Honor Outspoken Rabbi's Legacy," *The Dallas Morning News, Religion Section D*, September 2, 2006, p. 3.
79. Levi A. Olan, "From Birmingham to Memphis," WFAA Radio, April 28, 1968.
80. Levi Olan, letter of March 11, 1970 to Reverend Peter Johnson, Regional Representative of the Southern Christian Leadership Conference, responding to the reverend's request for support of the world premier movie *Montgomery to Memphis*. According to the initial request (March

References Cited in Chapter 1

4, 1970) to Reverend Johnson from the presiding bishop of the Dallas-Fort Worth area of the United Methodist Church, the world premier was shown in 300 cities and 1,000 theaters in the U. S., Canada and Europe.

81. Olan, "From Birmingham to Memphis."
82. Ibid.
83. Ibid.
84. Gerry Cristol, *A Light in the Prairie*, p. 186 (quoting from Levi A. Olan's WFAA radio broadcast reprinted in *The Texas Observer*, June 7, 1957).
85. Levi A. Olan, "Religion and the Goals for Dallas," WFAA Radio, October 30, 1966. (The Goals for Dallas was a civic agenda orchestrated by city leaders.)
86. Levi A. Olan, "Civil Rights and Civil Disobedience," WFAA Radio, February 19, 1967. (This sermon was also included in *Maturity in an Immature World*, 266.)
87. Michael Phillips, *White Metropolis (Race, Ethnicity, and Religion in Dallas, 1841-2001)*, 144.
88. Ibid.
89. Olan Autobiography, 10.
90. Phillips, *White Metropolis*, 152.
91. Ibid. 159.
92. Ibid.
93. Levi A. Olan, in a statement dated November 22, 1963. (Provided by the Jacob Rader Marcus Archives of the HUC.) (From a February 22, 1964 statement released by the John F. Kennedy Citizens Memorial Committee, Olan, along with many other prominent leaders and citizens of the Dallas establishment, were members of that Committee, the purpose for which was to raise funds for the proposed John Fitzgerald Kennedy Library in Boston and the creation of a dignified and modest memorial near the assassination site in Dallas.)
94. Cristol, *A Light in the Prairie*, 196-197.
95. Levi A. Olan, "The First Anniversary of a Tragedy," WFAA Radio, November 22, 1963.

References Cited in Chapter 1

96. Ibid.
97. Ibid.
98. Ibid.
99. Cristol, "Levi A. Olan, Conscience of the City," 53.
100. Saxon, Levi A. Olan: Oral History Interviews, 55.
101. Telephone interview of April 2, 2008 with Dr. William Jennings Bryan III, Director of Internship, Program and Professional Formation at the Perkins School of Theology, SMU.
102. Cristol, *A Light in the Prairie*, 198.
103. Information of Olan's participation in organizational activities came from numerous sources while researching information included within this project. These sources, provided by the Jacob Rader Marcus Archives of the HUC and Temple Emanu-El Archives in Dallas, include numerous letters, newspaper articles, congregational bulletins, Olan's autobiography (1981), and the texts of Gerry Critsol (*A Light in the Prairie, Temple Emanu-El of Dallas*) and Hollace Ava Weiner (*Jewish Stars in Texas, Rabbis and Their Work.*)
104. The World Union for Progressive Judaism website describes itself as the international umbrella organization of the Reform, Liberal, Progressive and Reconstructionist movements, serving 1,200 congregations in 45 countries in 2014.
105. Olan, "Called to Preach," 3-7.
106. Levi A. Olan, interview by Rabbi B. Schachtel, CCAR Oral History Interviews with Members of the CCAR, Cassette No. 1247, CCAR 90th Annual Convention, March 29, 1982.
107. Levi A. Olan, "Called to Preach," 1959, in *CCAR Journal* 1960, 3-7.
108. Hal M. Lewis, *Models and Meanings in the History of Jewish Leadership*, 311.
109. Levi A. Olan, "Is Religion Without Ritual Possible?" WFAA Radio, March 26, 1961.
110. Lewis, *Models and Meanings*, 237.
111. Arthur Hertzberg, *Being Jewish in America, The Modern Experience*, 99.
112. Olan to Rabbi George Zepin, August 30, 1948.

113. Peyton Davis, "Rabbi Levi Olan: A Conscience of the City."

114. Jane Bock Guzman, *David Lefkowitz of Dallas, A Rabbi for All Seasons*, 38 (Guzman writes that, in addition to his pastoral duties, Lefkowitz served as chairman of the United Charities, the Community Chest, the Boy Scouts, the Girl Scouts, the Camp Fire Girls, the Dallas Astronomical Society, and the Jewish Federation for Social Service. He also held memberships in the Critic Club, the Athletic Club, the University Club, the Masons, the Pythians, the Elks, the Rotary Club, and B'nai B'rith. Lefkowitz was also a member of the executive board of directors and later chairman of the Dallas Chapter of the American Red Cross. Lefkowitz was also awarded an honorary Doctor of Law degree from Southern Methodist University, the first time a Jew had ever received such an honor from that institution.)

115. Saxon, *Levi Olan: Oral History Interviews*, 69.

116. Gerald J. Klein, in the introduction of *A Rational Faith: Essays in Honor of Rabbi Levi A. Olan*, x.

117. Weiner, *Jewish Stars in Texas*, 232 (Weiner continues by writing that although Olan never earned a Ph.D., except for honorary doctoral degrees, "his intellect and philosophical reach were a match for many of those among the faculty.")

118. Gerry Cristol Interview with Levi A. Olan on July 22, 1974.

119. John A. Linder, "A Snapshot in Time," 8. (Written for American Jewish History-403 class, HUC, January 17, 2001.)

120. Sidney L. Regner, Memorial Tribute remembering Levi A. Olan, *Central Conference of American Rabbis, Ninety-Sixth Annual Convention*, June 24 to June 27, 1985, Vol. XCV, 302.

Chapter 2

1. David Rudavsky, *Emancipation & Adjustment*, 167.

2. Ibid.

3. Steven S. Schwarzschild, "Modern Jewish Philosophy," in Arthur A. Cohen and Paul Mendes — Flohr, *20th Century Jewish Religious Thought*, 631.

References Cited in Chapter 2

4. Eugene Borowitz, *Studies in the Meaning of Judaism*, 48.
5. Ibid.
6. Simon Noveck, *Great Jewish Personalities in Modern Times*, 62.
7. Ibid., 63.
8. Ibid.
9. Meyer, *Response to Modernity*, 75.
10. Levi A. Olan, "Judaism and Modern Theology," in CCAR Yearbook, vol. LXVI, 1956, 204. (Robert G. Goldy, in *The Emergence of Jewish Theology in America*, 85, writes that "Hegelian and other schools of historicism…reduced God to an evolving process in history, and defined human redemption in terms of the inevitable progress of reason in history.")
11. Ibid.
12. Meyer, *Response to Modernity*, 286-287.
13. Ibid., 288 (Michael A. Meyer writes that in 1918, the CCAR adopted a Declaration of Principles, the first social justice platform of Reform Judaism. It called for a more equitable distribution of the profits of industry, a minimum wage, and an eight hour day, a safe and sanitary working environment with particular reference to the special needs of women, abolition of child labor, proper housing for workers, and other benefits. The ideal of social justice, the document declared, has always been an integral part of Judaism.)
14. Olan, "Judaism and Modern Theology," 203-204.
15. Revelation may be described as "progressive revelation," which is the classical Reform view that claims that as history unfolds, society automatically moves to a higher perception of truth than previous generations, enabling the more current generations the authority to reform past traditions and teachings. This is compared to "continuous revelation," which is embraced by the Conservative Movement that stresses the continuation of divine revelation through the community of Israel. Sinai is supplemented by an ongoing revelation manifesting itself throughout history. Orthodoxy's approach to revelation places Sinai at the highpoint of religious truth where greater authority rests with those closest to the revelation at Sinai. (See Byron L. Sherwin, *Studies in Jewish Theology*, 325-326 and Louis Jacobs, *A Jewish Theology*, 202.)

References Cited in Chapter 2

16. Byron L. Sherwin, *Studies in Jewish Theology*, 326.

17. Nathaniel Katzburg and Walter S. Wurzburger, *Encyclopedia Judaica*, Vol. 15, 2nd ed., 493-500, Gale Virtual Reference Library, Spertus Institute for Jewish Learning and Leadership. (The writers explain that as it relates to Judaism, the term "Orthodoxy" first appeared in 1795 and became widely used from the beginning of the 19th century in contradistinction to the Reform movement.)

18. Sherwin, *Studies in Jewish Theology*, 325-326.

19. Ibid.

20. Auerbach, *Rabbis and Lawyers*, 74-75.

21. Olan, "The President's Message to the 80th Annual Convention."

22. Levi A. Olan, "Is Liberal Judaism Zionist or Anti-Zionist?" December 31, 1943.

23. Roland B. Gittelsohn, "No Retreat from Reason," CCAR Seventy-Fifth Annual Convention, Atlantic City, NJ.

24. Rudavsky, *Emancipation & Adjustment*, 294-295.

25. Meyer, *Response to Modernity*, 265 and Levi A. Olan, "Reform Judaism In A Post-Modern World," in *Journal of Reform Judaism, Volume XXVIII, No. 1, Winter 1981*, 2.

26. Sherwin, *Studies in Jewish Theology*, 322. (In concluding that Kohler "may be considered the first significant American Jewish theologian," Sherwin is referring to Kohler's *Jewish Theology Systematically and Historically Considered*, published by the Macmillan Company in 1918.)

27. Meyer, *Response to Modernity*, 265.

28. Benny Kraut, *From Reform Judaism to Ethical Culture: The Religious Evolution of Felix Adler*, 153-154. (For an in depth study of Kohler's views, see *Jewish Theology Systematically and Historically Considered*, The Macmillan Company, 1918, New York, New York.)

29. Levi A. Olan, quoting Dr. Isaac Mayer Wise in "The President's Message to the 80th Annual Convention of the Central Conference of American Rabbis, Houston, Texas, June 16, 1969."

30. Dr. Gary P. Zola, "The Common Places of American Reform Judaism's

References Cited in Chapter 2

Conflicting Platforms," in the *Hebrew Union College Annual*, Volume LXXII, 2001, 160.

31. Zola, "The Common Places," 171. (Additional information on the Pittsburgh Platform of 1885 and the Columbus Platform of 1937 can be found in *Response to Modernity* (Michael A. Meyer) and *American Judaism* (Jonathan D. Sarna).

32. Ibid. 170-171.

33. Ibid. and Meyer, *Response to Modernity*, 269.

34. Zola, "The Four Ideological Pronouncements of Reform Judaism in America;" Meyer, *Response to Modernity*. 387-388; and Rudavsky, *Emancipation & Adjustment*, 298-300.

35. The banquet following the ordination of Hebrew Union College's initial class of four rabbis in Cincinnati on July 11, 1883, included four biblically forbidden foods (clams, crabs, shrimp, and frogs' legs), considered as Levitical abominations, as well as mixed meat and dairy products. This was known as the *trefa* (nonkosher) banquet which traditionalists viewed as a "public insult."

36. Levi A. Olan, "A New Prayer Book — Conservative Judaism Defines Itself," *Judaism: A Quarterly Journal of Jewish Life and Thought*, Fall Issue, 1973. (Olan discussed the first official prayer book of the CCAR issued in 1895. "The Union Prayer Book," he wrote, "excised all prayers referring to the sacrificial service of the ancient Temple. The Kol Nidrei was eliminated entirely and the use of Hebrew reduced to a very bare minimum. The radicalism of Reform lay as much in this break with the tradition of the prayer book as it did in its rejection of the authority of Halakhah as binding.")

37. Zola, "The Common Places," 171.

38. Jonathan D. Sarna, *American Judaism*, 195.

39. Meyer, *Response to Modernity*, 280.

40. Sarna, *American Judaism*, 194. (Michael A. Meyer, *Response to Modernity*, 280, also points out that while the vast majority of rabbis in Reform synagogues still read from the Torah scroll, some rabbis merely showed the scroll to the congregation. Emil G. Hirsch's Sinai in Chicago went so far as to remove both scroll and ark from the synagogue.)

41. Ibid.
42. Ibid. [Rabbi Joseph Krauskopf (1858-1923) was a leader of radical Reform, and one of the more prominent rabbis introducing Sunday services. As a leading figure in the leadership of American Reform, he served as vice president of the conference that adopted the Pittsburgh Platform in 1885.]
43. Meyer, *Response to Modernity*, 264.
44. Sarna, *American Judaism*, 132.
45. Levi A. Olan, "Felix Adler, Critic of Judaism and Founder of a Movement," Union Anniversary Series, UAHC, New York, 3.
46. Ibid.
47. Levi A. Olan, review of *From Reform Judaism to Ethical Culture: The Religious Evolution of Felix Adler,* by Benny Kraut, in the *Journal of Reform Judaism*, Spring 1980, 89-92.
48. Meyer, *Response to Modernity*, 297.
49. Sarna, *American Judaism*, 214.
50. Steven M. Cohen and Arnold Eisen, *The Jew Within*, 191-193.
51. Zola, "The Common Places," 173.
52. Meyer, *Response to Modernity*, 319.
53. Zola, "The Common Places," 173.
54. Sarna, *American Judaism*, 253.
55. Zola, "The Common Places," 181. (Dr. Zola quotes Rabbi Abraham J. Felman's call for a new platform at the CCAR convention in 1934.)
56. Meyer, *Response to Modernity*, 390-391.
57. Ibid. 389 and Zola, The Columbus Platform.
58. Meyer, *Response to Modernity*, 390.
59. Ibid.
60. Sydney E. Ahlstrom, *A Religious History of the American People*, 952.
61. Ibid.

References Cited in Chapter 2 and Chapter 3

62. Meyer, Response *to Modernity*, 355.
63. Ibid.
64. Sarna, *American Judaism*, 279-281.
65. Meyer, *Response to Modernity*, 353. (It should be noted that other expressions of religious resurgence included the addition of the phrase "under God" to The Pledge of Allegiance on Flag Day in 1954 and the adoption in 1956 of the phrase "in God we trust" as the official motto of the United States as an alternative or replacement to the unofficial motto *E pluribus Unum*.)
66. Moshe Shraga Samet, *Encyclopedia Judaica, Vol. 15, 2nd ed.*, pp. 82-83, Gale Virtual Reference Library, Spertus Institute for Jewish Learning and Leadership, and Arthur A. Cohen and Paul Mendes-Flohr, *20th Century Jewish Religious Thought*, 1090.
67. Levi A. Olan, "Forward to the Fundamentals," *Judaism Quarterly 26-3*, Summer 1977.
68. Ibid. (Olan continued by emphasizing the Conservative Movement's desire to place final authority in matters of law and practice in Catholic Israel, the total Jewish Community. Catholic Israel is translated from the phrase *Kelal Yisrael*, the whole of the Jewish community, and represents Solomon Schechter's view that decisions on Jewish Law are largely determined by the practices of the total Jewish community - *Kelal Yisrael*.)
69. Levi A. Olan, "Putting First Things First," undated.
70. Rudavsky, *Emancipation & Adjustment*, 185.
71. Sherwin, *Studies in Jewish Theology*, 324.
72. Ibid.

Chapter 3

1. *Encarta 'World English Dictionary*, 1,039.
2. Levi A. Olan, "The Faith of an Untired Liberal," *The Torch*, volume XXII, No. 4, October 1949 and April 24, 1949.
3. Ibid.

References Cited in Chapter 3

4. Levi A. Olan, "Rethinking the Liberal Faith," *Reform Judaism, Essays by Hebrew Union College Alumni*, 1949, 32.
5. Ibid.
6. Olan, "The Faith of an Untired Liberal."
7. Olan, "Rethinking the Liberal Faith," 32 and "The Faith of an Untired Liberal," undated.
8. Auerbach, *Rabbis and Lawyers*, 50 and 52. (Auerbach is quoting from Julius Wellhausen, *Prolegomena to the History of Israel*, pp. 398 ff).
9. Olan, "The Faith of an Untired Liberal," *The Torch*.
10. Olan, "Rethinking the Liberal Faith," 32-33.
11. Levi A. Olan, "A Preliminary Summing Up," *A Rational Faith: Essays In Honor of Levi A. Olan*, edited by Jack Bemporad, 185.
12. Regner, Memorial Tribute, 301 and Evan Moffic, "Levi Olan: Champion of Liberalism," Independent Reading Course, HUC, Spring 2005, 3.
13. Levi A. Olan, "Over-Anxious Jewish Theologians," *Chanuko*, 1953, 19.
14. Levi A. Olan, "Liberal Judaism in a Reactionary World," CCAR Fifty-Third Annual Convention, CCAR Yearbook, Vol. LII, p. 309.
15. Ibid.
16. Ibid.
17. Ibid., 309-310.
18. Ibid., 310.
19. Olan, "A Preliminary Summing Up," 188.
20. Levi A. Olan, "The New Liberalism - An Interpretation of the Scientific Revolution," undated, 85 and "A Preliminary Summing Up," 188.
21. Levi A. Olan, "An Unrepentant Liberal Jew," undated, 3.
22. Olan, "Rethinking the Liberal Faith," 3.
23. Olan, "An Unrepentant Liberal Jew," 3.
24. Olan, "The Faith of an Untired Liberal," in *The Torch*.
25. Olan, "Rethinking the Liberal Faith," 38-39.

References Cited in Chapter 3

26. Ibid., 49-50.
27. Olan, "The Faith of an Untired Liberal," in *The Torch*.
28. Ibid.
29. Olan, "Rethinking the Liberal Faith," 35-36.
30. Levi A. Olan, "New Resources for a Liberal Faith," CCAR Seventy-Third Annual Convention, June 1962, 236-237 and "The Future of Man," November 12, 1962.
31. Olan, "The Future of Man."
32. Olan, "The New Liberalism," 17.
33. Ibid., p. 30
34. Eugene Borowitz, "Reason," *20th Century Jewish Religious Thought*, edited by Arthur A. Cohen and Paul Mendes-Flohr, 750-751 (Borowitz explains the departure from classic Jewish faith by negating unique revelation to the Jews and Judaism, and like other religions, Jews and Judaism would be thought of in terms of human spiritual search and development.)
35. Olan, "New Resources for a Liberal Faith," 226.
36. Olan, "Rethinking the Liberal Faith," 35. (In "Judaism and Modern Theology," 208, presented to the Sixty-Seventh Annual Convention of the CCAR, Olan commented: "Faith and reason are essential to a liberal epistemology: faith to lay the first postulates, to arouse a passionate commitment; and reason to evaluate the possibilities of ultimate concern and always to guard against a blind irrationalism by which we may never know whether we are worshipping God or the devil.")
37. Levi A. Olan, "Is Religion without Ritual Possible," *Maturity in an Immature World*, 162.
38. Olan, "A Preliminary Summing Up," 190.
39. Ibid., 190-191.
40. Levi A. Olan, "New Recourses for a Liberal Faith," CCAR Seventy-Third Annual Convention, June 1962, 236.
41. Olan, "The New Liberalism," 33.
42. Ibid., 34.
43. Ibid., 35.

44. Olan, "Judaism and Modern Theology," 215.
45. Olan, "Rethinking the Liberal Faith," 33.
46. Ibid. p. 38.
47. Ibid., 50-51.
48. Olan, "The Faith of an Untired Liberal," *The Torch*.
49. Ibid.
50. Levi A. Olan, "On the Nature of Man," *CCAR Yearbook*, vol. LVIII, 1948, 261.
51. Olan, "A Preliminary Summing Up," 200.
52. Olan, "The New Liberalism," 26.
53. Ibid., 17.
54. Ibid., 18-19.
55. Ibid., 88.
56. Ibid., 88-89.
57. Ibid., 93.
58. Ibid., 89.
59. Ephraim Fischoff, "Judaism and Modern Theology, Discussion," (Fischoff discusses Olan's "Judaism and Modern Theology," in CCARYB, Sixty-Seventh Annual Convention, 1956, 223.)
60. Goldy, *Emergence of Jewish Theology*, 81.
61. Olan, "Rethinking the Liberal Faith," 46.
62. Ibid., 47.
63. Olan, "An Unrepentant Liberal Jew," and "Requirements of Reform Jews — Liberalism," undated.
64. Ibid.
65. Joseph L. Blau, "Liberal Judaism in a Reactionary World," *Reform Judaism: A Historical Perspective*, 85D. (Blau's essay appeared in a collection of essays from the 1973 yearbook of the CCAR, edited by Blau.)
66. Levi A. Olan, "Liberal Judaism in a Reactionary World (From the Point of View of Philosophy)," *CCARYB*, vol. LII (52), 299.

References Cited in Chapter 3

67. Ibid., 324. [In his response to Rabbi Solomon B. Freehof's comments, Olan distinguished between the "philosophy of religion" (concepts) and religion (beliefs). "There are basic problems in both fields," Olan said, "but they need not be antagonistic to each other. In fact, they are essentially necessary, one to the other."]

68. Meyer, *Response to Modernity*, 324.

69. Blau, "Liberal Judaism in a Reactionary World," 85D.

70. Ibid.

71. William G. Braude, "Liberal Judaism in a Reactionary World (From the Point of View of History)," *CCARYB*, vol. LII (52), 285.

72. Ibid., 290-291.

73. Bernard Martin, "Reform Jewish Theology Today," *Contemporary Reform Jewish Thought*, 196.

74. Arnold Jacob Wolf, "On God and Theology," *Contemporary Reform Jewish Thought*, edited by Bernard Martin, 40-41.

75. Ibid., 47.

76. Ibid., 46.

77. Olan, "Rethinking the Liberal Faith," 54-55.

78. Ibid., 45.

79. Olan, "Judaism and Modern Theology," 208.

80. Olan, "Rethinking the Liberal Faith," 56.

81. Olan, "The New Liberalism," 92 and "The Future of Man.,

82. Olan, "The New Liberalism," 100-101.

83. Olan, "On the Nature of Man," 261.

84. Olan, "An Unrepentant Liberal Jew," 1.

85. Blau, *Reform Judaism: A Historical Perspective*, 85D.

86. Olan, "The Faith of an Untired Liberal," in *The Torch*.

Chapter 4

1. Levi A. Olan, "A Theology of Jewish Liberation" ("Jewish Liberation Theology"), *Judaism: A Quarterly Journal of Jewish Life and Thought*, vol. 27, No. 1, Issue #105, Winter 1978, 28.

2. Levi A. Olan, "The Outlook for Religion in a Democracy," April 7, 1940 and "The Business of Religion is Peace," November 13, 1949 (Speech given two days after the 30th anniversary of the Armistice of World War I.)

3. Levi A., Olan, "Religion and the Social Crisis," WFAA Radio, March 24, 1968.

4. Isaiah 2.4.

5. Olan, "The Majority Can Be Wrong."

6. Olan, "Religion and the Social Crisis." (Abraham Joshua Heschel, in *God in Search of Man,* 198, describes the prophetic act as an event in the life of God and His insight into the life of man.) 7. Levi A. Olan, "Religion and the New Deal," undated but sometime after Franklyn Roosevelt's New Deal in 1932.

8. Olan, "Religion and the Social Crisis."

9. Levi A. Olan, "Steadiness in an Unsteady World.

10. Levi A. Olan, "The Religious Basis of Brotherhood," WFAA Radio, February 20, 1949.

11. Levi A. Olan, "Reflections on the Meaning of Life," undated.

12. Levi A. Olan, "A Religious Anti-Poverty Program," WFAA Radio, February, 12, 1967.

13. Olan, "The President's Message to the 79th Annual Convention."

14. Levi A. Olan, "On Changing Human Nature," WFAA Radio, January 30, 1949.

15. Levi A. Olan, "Faith for These Days," WFAA Radio, October 30, 1949.

16. Olan, "The Majority Can Be Wrong."

17. Olan, "Religion and the Social Problem."

18. Genesis 1:27.

References Cited in Chapter 4

19. Levi A. Olan, "Aspirations for Ethnic Minorities," (Presented to the National Conference on Social Welfare, Columbus, Ohio.) reprinted from *Social Welfare Forum, 1971*, 38.
20. Olan, "Called to Preach," 4.
21. Olan, "The President's Message to the 79th Annual Convention."
22. Olan, "Civil Rights and Civil Disobedience."
23. Levi A. Olan, "The Religious Community." (1969 presentation to the Supermarket Institute Midwinter Executive Conference, Bal Harbour, Florida.)
24. Olan, "From Birmingham to Memphis."
25. Levi A. Olan, "As a Rabbi Sees It." [Presented to the General Assembly of the Council of Jewish Federations and Welfare Funds, February 1, 1947. (Another force shaping the pattern of American Life was individual freedom, which is discussed elsewhere in this document.)]
26. Levi A. Olan, "The Religious Basis for Brotherhood," and "Goodwill is an Urgent Matter," WFAA Radio, February 20, 1949 and February 26, 1950, respectively.
27. Levi A. Olan, "Who is a Religious Person," WFAA Radio, February 12, 1950 and "The Religious Basis for Brotherhood."
28. Olan, "Putting First Things First." (In the 1968 presidential address to the Central Conference of American Rabbis, Olan spoke of man as a significant being who reflects in miniature the rational, free, creative nature of God. "Thus it is that the Brotherhood of Man under the Fatherhood of God is not a whim or a caprice of men lost in subjectivity. It is rooted in the very essence of being itself.")
29. Olan, "Civil Rights and Civil Disobedience."
30. Ibid.
31. Olan, "The Religious Basis for Brotherhood."
32. Olan, "From Birmingham to Memphis.
33. Ibid.
34. Ibid.

References Cited in Chapter 4

35. Ibid.
36. Ibid.
37. Levi A. Olan, "The Myth of the Melting Pot." (Presented to the National Conference of Social Work, Dallas, Texas, May 20, 1971.)
38. Levi A. Olan, "Marrying a Person of Another Faith," WFAA Radio, December 11, 1960 and "Is Inter-Marriage a Problem?" WFAA Radio, December 2, 1962.
39. Olan, "The President's Message to the 79th Annual Convention."
40. Olan, "From Birmingham to Memphis."
41. Olan, "Aspirations for Ethnic Minorities," 37.
42. Union for Reform Judaism Website. (Reform Movement Perspective of the Religious Action Center of the Union of Reform Judaism.)
43. Ibid.
44. Levi A. Olan, "Philanthropy and the Modern World," January 28, 1965, 2 and "Philanthropy and the Modern World (Scene)," June 7, 1965.
45. Ibid.
46. Olan, "Philanthropy and the Modern World," 2.
47. Ibid., 3.
48. Ibid.
49. Ibid., 14.
50. Ibid., 4.
51. Ibid., 4.
52. Levi A. Olan, "Some Causes and a Possible Cure for the Depression," undated but probably written after 1939 since he discusses the Depression of 1939.
53. Ibid.
54. Danielle Kurtzleben, "50 Years Later, A War Over the Poverty Rate," U.S. News & World Report, January 6, 2014.
55. Olan, "The President's Message to the 79th Annual Convention."

References Cited in Chapter 4

56. Olan, "Beyond Cheap Thanksgiving."
57. Olan, "The President's Message to the 79th Annual Convention."
58. Levi A. Olan, review of *From Reform Judaism to Ethical Culture: The Religious Evolution of Felix Adler*, by Benny Kraut, Cincinnati, Hebrew Union College press, 1979, *Journal of Reform Judaism*, Spring, 1980.
59. Psalms 71:18.
60. Ruth 4:15.
61. Exodus 20:12.
62. Isaiah 3:5.
63. Levi A. Olan, "Treatment of the Aged — A Test of our Civilization," (Presented to the Governor's Committee on Aging, Dallas, Texas, May 1971.)
64. Ibid.
65. Ibid.
66. Ibid.
67. Ibid.
68. Ibid.
69. Olan, "Some Causes and a Possible Cure for the Depression."
70. Olan, "Religion and the Social Problem."
71. Olan, "Some Causes and a Possible Cure for the Depression."
72. Olan, "Reform Judaism in a Post-Modern World," 6-7.
73. Olan, "Some Causes and a Possible Cure for the Depression."
74. Levi A. Olan, "Man, His Nature and Destiny," undated and "The Nature of Man," 1964.
75. Olan, "Called to Preach," 7.
76. Olan, "Religion and the Social Problem." (The essence of his thoughts can also be found in Olan's broadcasts of March 24, 1968, "Religion and the Social Crisis," and February 19, 1967, "Civil Rights and Civil Disobedience.")
77. Olan, "Aspirations for Ethnic Minorities," 34.

References Cited in Chapter 4

78. Olan, "Reform Judaism in a Post-Modern World," 6-7.
79. Ibid., 7-8.
80. With an assist from Deborah Bodin Cohen, "Real Life / Real Food," in *The Sacred Table, Creating a Jewish Food Ethic*, edited by Mary L. Zamore, pp. 343-344, I now fast forward to 2011 for infusing Olan's wrath against Centerra Wine Company, the maker of Manischewitz Passover wines, and Mogen David Winery. This is the same company that produces two of the most popular fortified wines, Cisco and Richards Wild Irish Rose that are not kosher and have an alcohol content and lower price tag than Manischewitz. Richards Wild Irish Rose has been the leading product of the company since 1954. Centerra shares a fortified wine market with two other wineries: Mogen David and E. & J. Gallo. In comparison, the kosher wine market is about one-fifth the size of the fortified wine market. Annual sales of kosher wines in the United States approximate $27 million with Manischewitz and Mogen David comprising 88 present of those sales. Fortified wines, also called "bum wine" and "hooch," are available exclusively in poor urban areas and college campuses and are shunned by most popular package stores in middle class and affluent neighborhoods. These wines are sold at cheap prices (375-milliliter for less than $3) and contain the equivalent of four to five shot of vodka; its high sugar content satisfies hunger, an important consideration when choosing between a meal and a drink. The word "wino" came into use during the depression to describe those unfortunate individuals who turned to fortified wine to forget their troubles. For Reform Jews, wine is one of the few kosher products universally purchased. Fortified wines make it easy for street alcoholics and young people to get drunk — hardly a holy or just mission. As Jews, made in the image of God and co-workers in the pursuit of social justice, how does one condone these activities? Kosher wine is used to sanctify our most sacred events — marriage, Passover, Shabbat, and b'rit milah. The root of *Kiddush*, the blessing over the wine, means "holiness." Furthermore, MD 20-20, also called "Mad Dog 20-20," is a fortified wine produced by Mogen David Winery. Rappers sing about its potency and on college campuses, fraternity members force prospective recruits to drink a bottle quickly. With *Magen David* meaning "Star of David," the holy symbol of our people, can the profaning of such a symbol be considered kosher? Some of these practices certainly existed during Olan's pulpit years but apparently have become more widespread with the growth of population centers and those in poverty. Needless to say, Olan would

References Cited in Chapter 4

certainly have something to say about the ethics of these companies as well as their products.

81. Olan, "Treatment of the Aged." (Similar sentiments were expressed in numerous Olan commentaries including WFAA radio broadcast of March 12, 1967, "A Troubler of the People.")
82. Levi A. Olan, "God in a Secular World," WFAA Radio, November 16, 1969.
83. Letter dated January 30, 1963 from the chairman of the Texas State Committee, Lloyd M. Bentsen, Jr. (senator, Secretary of the Treasury, and 1988 candidate for Vice President) to Olan and the undated public relations release of the National Development Program of the Sam Rayburn Foundation to the Associated Press and United Press International.
84. Vice-President Lyndon B. Johnson to Levi A. Olan, October 22, 1963.
85. Ibid.
86. Levi A. Olan to Vice President Lyndon B. Johnson, October 28, 1963.
87. Levi A. Olan, "Disarm!" 1933 or 1934.
88. Ibid.
89. Ibid.
90. Ibid.
91. Ibid.
92. Levi A. Olan to Dr. Allan Knight Chalmers, June 4, 1941.
93. Levi A. Olan to Rabbi Joseph Rauch, June 17, 1941.
94. Ibid.
95. Olan, "A Troubler of the People."
96. Levi A. Olan to Rabbi Joseph Rauch, June 17, 1941.
97. Ibid.
98. Levi A. Olan, "The High Cost of Peace," WFAA Radio, October 3, 1943.
99. Levi A. Olan to Herbert Hoover, the honorary chairman of the National Committee on Food for the Five Small Democracies, December 19, 1940.
100. Levi A. Olan to Dr. David de Solo Pool, Spanish and Portuguese Syna-

gogue, New York, New York, October 3, 1941. (Olan responded to Dr. Pool's accusation in a September 29, 1941 letter that feeding the starving civilians aids the Nazi's cause and represents anti-Roosevelt and anti-British sentiment.)

101. Ibid.

102. Levi A. Olan, review of *Christianity Through Jewish Eyes — A Quest for Common Ground*, Walter Jacob, *Perkins Journal*, Summer 1976, 40.

103. Levi A. Olan, review of *We Jews and Jesus*, Samuel Sandmel, *Perkins Journal*, Winter 1973, 34.

104. Rabbi Levi A. Olan, "The Nation is Not God," WFAA Radio, October 9, 1966.

105. Levi A. Olan, "No Messiah, Please," WFAA Radio, January 19, 1969.

106. Levi A. Olan, "All Problems Begin With Me," WFAA Radio, March 29, 1970.

107. Edward K. Kaplan, *Spiritual Radical, Abraham Joshua Heschel in America, 1940-1972*, 302-303.

108. Olan, "Disarm!"

109. Levi A. Olan, "Statement on U. S. Viet Nam Policy," 1968. (Olan references the plight of the people supporting a regime and choosing a way of life not approved by the U. S. He cites our country's disapproval of the Communist leaders of Viet Nam rather than viewing the war as a war of liberation by the Viet Cong and people of Viet Nam. In his March 29, 1970 WFAA radio sermon, Olan referred to the Viet Nam War as a useless massacre in which not even many U.S. leaders believed.)

110. Olan, "The President's Message to the 79th Annual Convention." (This was an apparent reference to the domestic economic advantages gained by American industry.)

111. Ibid.

112. Olan, "Called to Preach," 7.

113. Levi A. Olan, "God in a Secular World."

114. Olan, "Statement on U. S. Viet Nam Policy."

115. Levi A. Olan, "The Faith of an Untired Liberal."

References Cited in Chapter 4

116. Ibid.
117. Ibid.
118. Levi A. Olan, "Who Shall Fight the War," WFAA Radio, February 26, 1967.
119. Ibid.
120. Levi A. Olan, "Morality and Nuclear Testing," WFAA Radio, April 15, 1962.
121. Ibid.
122. Ibid.
123. Olan, "The President's Message to the 79th Annual Convention."
124. Ibid., 14.
125. Levi A. Olan to Texas Local Board No. 30, Selective Service System, August 6, 1969.
126. Olan, "Reflections on the Meaning of Life."
127. Levi A. Olan, "The Future of Judaism in America (A Tercentenary Address)," delivered in 1954 at Washington, D.C. (This comment centered on Asser Levy who insisted upon his right to serve in the military after arrival of the Jews in America).
128. Ibid.
129. Olan, "Steadiness in an Unsteady World."
130. Levi A. Olan, "Judaism as a Religion of Life," undated.
131. Olan, "Man, His Nature and Destiny."
132. Jeremiah 9:23.
133. Olan, "The New Liberalism — An Interpretation of the Scientific Revolution," 7.
134. Ibid., 8.
135. Levi A. Olan, "The Christian-Jewish Encounter," WFAA Radio, October 26, 1969.
136. Abraham Joshua Heschel, *I Asked for Wonder, A Spiritual Anthology*, 87.

Chapter 5

1. Zola, "The Four Ideological Pronouncements of Reform Judaism in America."
2. In the 1880s Zionism meant the return of the Jewish people to their homeland and the resumption of Jewish sovereignty in the Land of Israel. Later, Zionism took many forms, including Political Zionism (the original movement), Labor Zionism (advocating immigration and socialist ideals), Cultural Zionism (maintaining the core of Jewish history and culture), Christian Zionism (Jesus will return as the Messiah), and Progressive Zionism (focusses on *Tikhun Olam*).
3. Rudavsky, *Emancipation and Adjustment*, 301.
4. Sarna, *American Judaism*, 96.
5. Rudavsky, *Emancipation and Adjustment*, 301.
6. Ibid.
7. Sarna, *American Judaism*, 250.
8. Zola, "The Four Ideological Pronouncements of Reform Judaism in America.
9. Levi A. Olan, "Israel — State and Diaspora," 1968-1969.
10. Levi A. Olan, "Address to Rabbinical Assembly Convention," (Conservative and Reform Movements), June 10, 1969.
11. Olan, "Israel — State and Diaspora."
12. Olan, "Address to Rabbinical Assembly Convention" and Olan's presidential messages to the 79th and 80th annual convention of the CCAR in Boston, Massachusetts and Houston, Texas, June 20, 1968 and June 16, 1969, respectively.
13. Ibid.
14. Levi A. Olan, address to the World Union of Progressive Judaism, 1968, and "Israel — State and Diaspora."
15. Olan, presidential message to the 79th Annual Convention of the Central Conference of American Rabbis.
16. Olan, address to the World Union of Progressive Judaism, 1968, and "Israel — State and Diaspora."

References Cited in Chapter 5 and Chapter 6

17. Olan, "Address to Rabbinical Assembly Convention" and presidential message to the 80th annual convention of the CCAR.
18. Olan, "Address to Rabbinical Assembly Convention" and presidential message to the 79th Annual Convention of the Central Conference of American Rabbis.
19. Olan, Presidential message to the 79th Annual Convention of the Central Conference of American Rabbis.
20. Ibid.
21. Olan, Presidential message to the 80th annual convention of the CCAR.
22. Ibid.
23. Ibid.
24. Olan, "Address to Rabbinical Assembly Convention."
25. Ibid.
26. Olan, "The President's Message to the 80th Annual convention of the Central Conference of American Rabbis.
27. Olan, alluding to the words of Mordecai Kaplan, in "Address to Rabbinical Assembly Convention."
28. Levi A. Olan, "Is Liberal Judaism Zionist or Anti-Zionist?" December 31, 1943.
29. Ibid.
30. Ibid.
31. Olan, "An Unrepentant Liberal Jew.
32. Zola, "The Four Ideological Pronouncements of Reform Judaism in America.
33. Ibid.
34. Olan, "A New Prayer Book — Conservative Judaism Defines Itself."

Chapter 6

1. *Encarta World English Dictionary*, 1,848.
2. Kaufmann Koeher (Kohler), *Jewish Theology Systematically and Histori-*

cally Considered, 1. (Metaphysics may be described as the division of philosophy that is concerned with the fundamental nature of reality and being.)

3. *Encarta World English Dictionary*, 1,848 and Merriam-Webster.com/dictionary.

4. Byron L. Sherwin, *Toward A Jewish Theology*, 6 and 26, footnote 3 and *Studies in Jewish Theology*, 17-18, footnote 3. (Dr. Sherwin continues by indicating the inappropriateness of the term "theology" when dealing with the nature and implications of Jewish faith. "Jewish teachings emphasize that the nature of God is beyond the ken of human understanding or analysis; we can speak about the ideas, perceptions, and experiences of God that we might have and that the classical sources discuss.")

5. Levi A. Olan, "The Need to Re-Think Jewish Theology," undated.

6. Goldy, *The Emergence of Jewish Theology in America*, 64.

7. *Encarta World English Dictionary*, 966.

8. Sherwin, *Toward A Jewish Theology*, 9.

9. Levi A. Olan, review of *Understanding Jewish Theology*, edited by Jacob Neusner, *Perkins Journal*, Spring 1974, 57.

10. Louis Jacobs, *A Jewish Theology*, 1.

11. Ibid., 3.

12. Olan, "Judaism and Modern Theology," 200, "The Need to Re-Think Jewish Theology," and review of *The Story of Jewish Philosophy*, Joseph L. Blau, *Perkins Journal, Fall 1972*, 61.

13. Ibid. (Kaufmann Kohler, in *Jewish Theology Systematically and Historically Considered*, 2, wrote that philosophy of religion deals with the same subject matter as theology, but treats religion from a general point of view as a matter of experience without any foregone conclusion. "Consequently it submits the beliefs and doctrines of religion in general to an impartial investigation, recognizing neither a divine revelation nor the superior claims of any one religion above any other.")

14. Olan, "Judaism and Modern Theology," 200.

15. Levi A. Olan, "Comment on Dr. Fackenheim's Call for a Reform of Reform Theology," undated and written for *American Judaism Magazine*.

References Cited in Chapter 6

16. Abraham Joshua Heschel, *Moral Grandeur and Spiritual Audacity*, 154.

17. Jacobs, *A Jewish Theology*, 15. (Jacobs called this the traditional view and at the time referred to as theism.)

18. Michael L. Morgan, *Beyond Auschwitz*, 45. (The goal of Protestant theology was to reconstruct the essential content of Christian faith in ways that were compatible with modernity. This required a return to a God centered faith which opposed religion's accommodation to the prevailing materialistic culture and tendency toward mediocrity. Robert G. Goldy, in *The Emergence of Jewish Theology in America*, 53, referred to Harry Emerson Fosdick, one of the most influential spokesmen for Protestant liberalism, referring to his preaching against "liberal religion's excessive preoccupation with rationalism, it's naïve optimism, sentimentalism, and ethical meliorism, and it's watered-down, deistic conception of God. In accommodating itself to a man-centered, secular culture, it had often lent its support to nationalism, capitalism, and even racism and imperialism.")

19. Sherwin, *Studies in Jewish Theology*, 3 and 42 and *Toward A Jewish Theology*, 9.

20. Rabbi Samuel E. Karff, "The Agada as Source of Contemporary Jewish Theology," 74th Annual Convention, Central Conference of American Rabbis, June 19, 1963, Philadelphia, Pennsylvania.

21. Jacobs, *A Jewish Theology*, 4.

22. Ibid., 8.

23. Goldy, *The Emergence of Jewish Theology*, 58. (This is Goldy's concise interpretation of Will Herberg's commentary on theology.)

24. Ibid., 9.

25. Simon Noveck, *Great Jewish Thinkers of the Twentieth Century*, 213. (Noveck specifically mentions Ahad Ha-am, Simon Dubnow, and Martin Buber.)

26. William E. Kaufman, *The Evolving God in Jewish Process Theology*, 127.

27. Ibid.

28. Goldy, *The Emergence of Jewish Theology*, 12.

29. Ibid., 13.

30. Ibid., 12. (Quoting from Jacob Petuchowski, "The Question of Jewish Theology," 53.)

31. Ibid., 44 (These reasons can be compared to those submitted by Jonathan D. Sarna, *American Judaism*, 279-282. The synagogue boom, expansion of Jewish education, renewed interest in Biblical study, renewed interest in Jewish religious thought, and reduction of secularism.)

32. Ibid., 45.

33. Ibid., 50.

34. Ibid., 25.

35. Ibid., 57.

36. Ibid., 1-3.

37. Ibid., 3. (Goldy refers to the law of Marcus Lee Hansen, *The Problem of the Third Generation Immigrant*, by explaining the first generation of American immigrants arrived with its religious heritage largely intact; the second generation wished to become more modern and American by either abandoning religion altogether or by adopting a kind of religious liberation which would show how to overcome the conflict between religion and science, tradition and modernity. According to this sociological principle, the third generation was less enamored with modern science and technology and more secure as Americans, longing to re-appropriate for itself much of the traditional heritage of the first generation.)

38. Sarna, *American Judaism*, 275.

39. Goldy, *The Emergence of Jewish Theology*, 51.

40. Bernard Martin, "Reform Jewish Theology,"183.

41. Sherwin, *Studies in Jewish Theology*, 327.

42. Olan, "Theology Today."

43. Olan, "Judaism and Modern Theology," 197-198.

44. Levi A. Olan, "Democracy and the Atomization of the Individual," Undated. (In describing the Maladjusted Man of the twentieth century, Olan alludes to the Creative Man of the Renaissance, the Natural Man of the eighteenth century, and the Economic or Political Man of the nineteenth century.)

References Cited in Chapter 6

45. Olan, "Judaism and Modern Theology," 198.

46. Goldy, *The Emergence of Jewish Theology*, 3-4 and 90. (Goldy also points out that at the same time, it must be noted that the two historical events most often associated with the war — the Holocaust and the reborn Jewish state — were not important theological issues until after the 1967 Arab-Israeli War.)

47. Morgan, *Beyond Auschwitz*, 47. (Morgan presents the most pressing issues to be the issues of faith and autonomy, revelation, and halakhah.)

48. Olan, "Judaism and Modern Theology," 200.

49. Levi A. Olan, "The Attack on Reason," 10.

50. Olan, "Judaism and Modern Theology," 200.

51. Ibid. and "The Need to Re-Think Jewish Theology." (Mendelssohn distinguished between religion and law and Judaism was not a religion in the strict sense of the word. Religious tenets, such as the belief in the existence and unity of God, His providence, and the immortality of the soul, are principles of Deism, the general religion of reason. They were "self-evident to reason and required no proof, no mysterious supernatural act of revelation in order to be intelligible to men of reason everywhere. Judaism had not discovered them. Reason had. Judaism merely reaffirmed them." See Alfred Jospe, "Moses Mendelssohn," in *Great Jewish Personalities in Modern Times*, 30-31.)

52. Olan, Judaism and Modern Theology" 200.

53. Ibid., 201 and "The Need to Re-Think Jewish Theology."

54. Olan, "Judaism and Modern Theology," 201.

55. Ibid.

56. Jacobs, *A Jewish Theology*," 1.

57. Olan, "Judaism and Modern Theology," 201.

58. Ibid., 201.

59. Ibid., 202.

60. Ibid.

61. Morgan, *Beyond Auschwitz*, 48.

62. Borowitz, *Studies in the Meaning of Judaism*, 8. (Quoting from "Theology Today" by Levi Olan," undated but after 1960, 1).

63. Morgan, *Beyond Auschwitz*, 49.

64. Ibid., 49-50.

65. Olan, "Judaism and Modern Theology," 197.

66. Ibid.

67. Sherwin, *Studies in Jewish Theology*, 23-24.

68. Ibid., 15.

69. Olan, "Judaism and Modern Theology," 199.

70. Olan, "The need to Re-Think Jewish Theology."

71. Olan, "Comment on Dr. Fackenheim's Call for a Reform of Reform Theology."

72. Olan, "Judaism and Modern Theology," 205. (During the 74th Annual Convention of the Central Conference of American Rabbis, June 19, 1963, and during the session discussing "The Role and Limits of Reason in Contemporary Jewish Theology," Rabbi Steven S. Schwarzchild interpreted Barth's writings regarding the Jewish people to represent a lack of sociological culture — language, civilization, and literature.)

73. Ibid.

74. Ibid.

75. Ibid., 202.

76. Ibid., 202-203.

77. Byron L. Sherwin, *Kabbalah, An Introduction to Jewish Mysticism*, 17.

78. Olan, "Judaism and Modern Theology," 203. (*Sefer Ha-Yashar* is an anonymous work, probably written in the 13th century and one of the most popular ethical books in the Middle Ages.)

79. Ibid.

80. Michael A. Meyer, *Response to Modernity*, 362.

81. Ibid., 362-363.

References Cited in Chapter 7

Chapter 7

1. Bible Scholar CD-Rom, Torah Educational Software, Inc., New York, New York, (The words "truth" and "true" appear 111 and 27 times, respectively.)
2. The Soncino Talmud, CD-Rom version, Davka Corporation, 1991-1995. (The words "truth" and "true" appear 464 and 419 times, respectively.)
3. Rashi Commentary, Zephaniah 3:5, *Complete Tanach With Rashi*, CD-Rom version 1.2, Davka Corporation, The Judaic Press.
4. Isadore Twersky, *A Maimonides Reader*, 420-421. (Maimonides' Eighth Fundamental Principle states that "the Torah came from God, perfect, pure, holy and true.")
5. Abraham Joshua Heschel, *A Passion for Truth*, 45.
6. Zechariah 8:16.
7. Malachi 2:6.
8. Genesis 24:49.
9. Zechariah 7:9.
10. Psalms 25:5.
11. Levi A. Olan, "Some Directions for Reform Judaism," *CCAR* Journal, January 1958.
12. Olan, "The New Liberalism," 86-87 and "A Preliminary Summing Up," 190-191.
13. Olan, "Theology Today."
14. Levi A. Olan, review of *Rediscovering Tradition, Reflections on a New Theology*, edited by Arnold Jacob Wolf, *Judaism*, in *A Quarterly Journal*, vo. 15, number 2, Spring 1966, 254-255.
15. Olan, "Judaism and Modern Theology," 206.
16. Sherwin, *Studies in Jewish Theology*, 293.
17. Olan, "Theology Today."
18. Ibid.
19. Ibid.

20. Levi A., Olan, "Mitzvoth — Authority and Freedom," UAHC November 1973. (The last decades of the twentieth century and first decade of the twenty first century witnessed an American Jewish awakening with the quest for more Jewish learning and a return by many to traditional ritual. This period included the expansion of educational programs on Jewish education and the growth in number of Jewish day care centers, supplementary schools, Sunday Schools, Jewish Day Schools, Jewish studies programs at the college level, and Talmudic and rabbinical schools.)
21. Olan, "Theology Today."
22. *A Portrait of Jewish Americans, Findings from a Pew Research Center Survey of U.S. Jews,* October 1, 2013.
23. Olan, "Judaism and Modern Theology," 206.
24. Ibid. and "Theology Today."
25. Levi A. Olan, "Comments on "No retreat from Reason!," Roland B. Gittelsohn, Central Conference of American Rabbis, Seventy-Fifth Annual Convention, June 16 to June 20, 1964, Atlantic City, New Jersey, 205.
26. Olan, "The Future of Man," 10.
27. Olan, "Some Directions for Reform Judaism."
28. Ibid.
29. Olan, "Theology Today."
30. Ibid.
31. Olan, "Judaism and Modern Theology," 206.
32. Ibid.
33. Ibid.
34. Ibid., 207.
35. Ibid.
36. Ibid.
37. Ibid.
38. Ibid.
39. Ibid.

References Cited in Chapter 7

40. Ibid.
41. Ibid., 208.
42. Ibid.
43. Ibid.
44. Ibid.
45. Ibid., Olan, "The Attack on Reason," 8-9.
46. Olan, "Judaism and Modern Theology," 208.
47. Ibid.
48. Olan, Comments on "No Retreat from Reason!" 206.
49. Levi A. Olan, "Reinhold Niebuhr and the Hebraic Spirit; A Critical Inquiry," *Judaism: A Quarterly, vol. 5, #2, Spring 1956*, 114.
50. Steven T. Katz, *Jewish Philosophers*, 254.
51. Jacob Dienstag and Arthur Hyman, *Encyclopedia Judaica*, CD-Rom Edition, no page number.
52. Samuel Hugo Bergman, *Encyclopedia Judaica*, CD-Rom Edition, no page number [Hermann Cohen (1842-1918) was a German philosopher.]
53. Yehoshua Amir (Neumark), *Encyclopedia Judaica*, CD-Rom Edition, no page number.
54. Olan, "Reinhold Niebuhr and the Hebraic Spirit; A Critical Inquiry," 114. (Olan believed Niebuhr's theology was not in the Hebraic spirit and distorted the rationalistic character of Judaism, 122.)
55. Ibid.
56. Ibid., 115.
57. Kaufman, *The Evolving God in Jewish Process Theology*, 10.
58. Gittelsohn, "No Retreat from Reason!" (Although Judaic history believed the faith element firmly and unquestioningly, for Gittelsohn faith ceased to be an essential core-message when it became demonstrably false. In this same document, 193, he continued his assertion that reason, along with science, provides the most useful strainers for necessary removal of that which was essential to Judaism at an earlier stage of development but

References Cited in Chapter 7

which may now need to be removed or at least refined if Judaism is to be kept viable for the future.)

59. Ibid., 194 (Gittelsohn refers to *Anatomy of Faith*, 213 and 230ff by Conservative Rabbi Milton Steinberg.)
60. Alfred North Whitehead, *Process and Reality, An Essay in Cosmology*, 14.
61. Rabbi Steven S. Schwarzchild (1924-1989) (Lynn, Massachusetts), "The Role and Limits of Reason in Contemporary Jewish Theology," 74th Annual Convention of the CCAR, June 19, 1963.
62. Ibid., 204-205.
63. Olan, "New Liberalism," 7. Levi A. Olan, "Some Sources for the Philosophy of Reform Judaism," undated, 20 and "The Philosophic Foundations of Reform Judaism," undated, 15.
64. Olan, "Being Honest With Oneself," undated.
65. Olan, "The Jewish Will to Live," undated.
66. Olan, "The Failure of Nerve."
67. Olan, "Literature and the Condition of Modern Man," undated.
68. Olan, "Religion is One — Religions are Many," WFAA Radio, March 27, 1949.
69. Moses Mendelssohn, *Jerusalem*, *A Treasury of Jewish Quotations*, edited by Joseph L. Baron, 25 and Alfred Jospe, "Moses Mendelssohn," *Great Jewish Personalities in Modern Times*, 30.
70. Olan, "But, What Does God Do Today?," WFAA Radio, April 30, 1967.
71. Olan, "Bargaining with God," WFAA Radio, December 13, 1964.
72. Olan, "The Attack on Reason," 10.
73. Olan, "From Birmingham to Memphis."
74. Olan, "A Preliminary Summing Up," 190 and "The New Liberalism," 87.
75. Olan, "The New Liberalism," 87.
76. Olan, "Judaism and Modern Theology," 208.
77. Koeher (Kohler), *Jewish Theology Systematically and Historically Considered*, 136-137.

References Cited in Chapter 8

Chapter 8

1. Levi A. Olan, "Is There Really a God?" April 1962 sermon to the Unity Church and "The God We Worship, an Organicist View," *Dimensions Magazine*, Fall 1967. (In his radio address of March 26, 1950, "Why do the Righteous Suffer," Olan referred to these gods as "whimsical creatures, who needed to be appeased and flattered into doing good and not harm." Therefore, suffering was a sure sign that the gods were displeased, a simple answer that satisfied primitive man.)

2. Levi A. Olan, "The Theological Foundations of Prayer, A Reform Jewish Perspective," 54-55. (Presented to the 48th Biennial of the UAHC. (Published by the Union of American Hebrew Congregations, 1967) and "The God We Worship, an Organicist View," Dimensions Magazine.

3. http://en.wikipedia.org/wiki/isaac_newton's religious views and writings on Newton by Stephen David Snobelen at issac-newton.org.

4. Ibid.

5. Ibid.

6. Ibid.

7. *Encarta World English Dictionary*, 439.

8. Levi A. Olan, "The Prophetic Faith in a Secular Age," *The Journal of Reform Judaism*, Spring 1979, Central Conference of American Rabbis, 1.

9. Ibid. and "The Doctrine of the Chosen People Reaffirmed," *Judaism: A Quarterly Journal of Jewish Life and Thought*, vol. 29, No. 4 Fall 1980, 466.

10. Olan, "The Theological Foundations of Prayer," 54-55.

11. Olan, *Prophetic Faith and the Secular Age*, xiii.

12. Olan, "The Religious Community."

13. Levi A. Olan, "God is Real," WFAA Radio, February 11, 1968.

14. Olan, "God in a Secular World," and "If There is No God," January 28, 1968.

15. Olan, "God is Real."

16. Olan, "God in a Secular World." (In his WFAA Radio sermon of January 28, 1968, "If There is no God," Olan suggested that if God does not exist,

References Cited in Chapter 8

then why should a person be moral or keep a promise. The immediate answer, he said, is that promises and morality are necessary for a just society or anarchy would occur.)

17. Levi A. Olan, "How Can We Believe in God in a World Like This?" WFAA Radio, January 13, 1963 and April 5, 1964.

18. Levi A. Olan, "Teaching Religion in a Secular Age," WFAA Radio, March 26, 1967.

19. Olan, "How Can We Believe in a World Like This," and "Is Anything Too Hard for God?" WFAA Radio, December 16, 1951.

20. Ibid.

21. Levi A. Olan, "Life With or Without God," WFAA Radio, October 15, 1967.

22. Olan, "The Prophetic Faith in a Secular Age," 5.

23. Olan, "God in a Secular World."

24. Levi A. Olan, review of *A Faith for Moderns*, Robert Gordis, *Judaism: A Quarterly Journal*, Spring 1961.

25. Ibid.

26. Derro Evans, "Rabbi Levi Olan: A Conversation," *Sunday Magazine, Dallas Times Herald*, October 11, 1970.

27. Olan, "Life With or Without God."

28. Olan, review of *A Faith for Moderns*. 1961.

29. Ibid.

30. Ibid.

31. Olan, "Judaism and Modern Theology," 210.

32. Henry Slonimsky, *Essays*, 15. (Slonimsky continues to explain the Midrash as a vast post-biblical Bible written on the margin of the Bible to account for the sufferings of God and man in their efforts to reclaim and uplift an unfinished and emerging world.)

33. Olan, "The Theological Foundations of Prayer," 58.

34. Rabbi Henry Cohen, *Why Judaism? A Search for Meaning in Jewish*

References Cited in Chapter 8

Identity, 1973. (Cohen also attributes "theistic finitism," in one form or another, to Milton Steinberg and, in addition to Olan, other Reform theologians.)

35. Levi A. Olan, "God and Auschwitz," WFAA Radio, February 25, 1968.
36. Olan, "Why do the Righteous Suffer and the Wicked Prosper?"
37. Olan, "An Unrepentant Liberal Jew," 4-5.
38. Ibid. (In his radio sermon of November 6, 1966, "Will God Keep His Promise," Olan preached that atheism is a philosophy of despair. The plans of man cannot be realized without order or law, or purpose and mind. These views lead to despair and to the corrosion of the moral will.)
39. Olan, "God is Real."
40. Ibid.
41. Ibid.
42. Ibid.
43. Ibid. and "God and Auschwitz."
44. Saxon, "Levi Olan, Oral History Interviews." 37.
45. Olan, "The Prophetic Faith in a Secular Age," 3, 5.
46. Ibid.
47. Levi A. Olan to Rabbi Erwin L. Herman, Director of Regional Activities, UAHC, New York, January 17, 1966. (The Jacob Rader Marcus Archives) (In his review of *Rediscovering Tradition: Reflections on a New Theology*, edited by Arnold Jacob Wolf, Olan emphasized that ultimate reality (truth) may be sought through the four stages referenced in Herman's letter. See *Judaism, A Quarterly Journal*, vol. 15, #2, Spring 1966.)
48. Olan, "The Prophetic Faith in a Secular Age," 5-6.
49. Sandra B. Lubarsky, "Introduction," *Jewish Theology and Process Thought*, 1. (In *A Light in the Prairie, Temple Emanu-El of Dallas 1872-1997*, 215, Temple Emanu-El archivist Gerry Cristol mentions Hartshorne as the 1976 and first Sam R. Bloom Scholar in Residence of the adult education committee of Temple Emanu-El.) (Coincidently, Hartshorne was appointed to a philosophy chair at the University of Texas in 1962, a semester before Olan began a six year term on the university's Board of

Regents. Olan cultivated a scholarly friendship with Hartshorne, who later contributed an essay - "Whitehead's Metaphysical System" - in Olan's honor included in *Essays in Honor of Rabbi Levi A. Olan*.)

50. Ibid.
51. Heschel, *God in Search of Man: A Philosoph6y of Judaism*, 210.
52. Olan, "If There is No God."
53. Kaufman, *The Evolving God in Jewish Process Theology*, 70-71.
54. Charles Hartshorne, *A Rational Faith: Essays in Honor of Rabbi Levi A. Olan*. 109-110.
55. Kaufman, *The Evolving God in Jewish Process Theology*, 68.
56. Ibid.
57. Ibid.
58. Olan, "The Doctrine of the Chosen People Reaffirmed," 467.
59. Olan, "God is Real."
60. Olan, "Why do the Righteous Suffer?"
61. Ibid.
62. Olan, "Putting First Things First."
63. Kohler, *Jewish Theology Systematically and Historically Considered*, 176.
64. Olan, "How Can We Believe in a World Like This?"
65. Levi A. Olan, "Free Will and Moral Responsibility," undated.
66. Olan, "Reinhold Niebuhr and the Hebraic Spirit: A Critical Inquiry," 108.
67. Olan, "On the Nature of Man," 262.
68. Levi A. Olan, "The Right to Do Wrong," WFAA Radio, November 13, 1955.
69. Levi A. Olan, "Freedom and Responsibility," *CCAR Year Book*, 1965, 134.
70. Genesis 4:7.
71. One may look to Deuteronomy 30:15-19 and Jeremiah 21:8, as well as rabbinic commentary in the Talmud. ("Everything is seen, and freedom of choice is given" - Aboth 3.15.)

References Cited in Chapter 8

72. Olan, "Man, His Nature and Destiny," "The Jewish View of Man," and The Nature of Man," 165-181.
73. Ibid.
74. Ibid.
75. Olan, "On the Nature of Man."
76. Olan, "Man, His Nature and Destiny," "The Jewish View of Man," and "The Nature of Man."
77. Ibid. (This reasoning originated during Judaism's classical period in a Midrash comprising a collection of ancient homiletical interpretations of the Book of Genesis. The specific Midrash, Genesis Rabbah, was attributed in the third century CE to the Amora Hoshaiah.)
78. Olan, "Why do the Righteous Suffer?"
79. Ibid.
80. Olan, "Man, His Nature and Destiny," "The Jewish View of Man," and "The Nature of Man."
81. Olan, "Man, His Nature and Destiny," 27.
82. Ibid. and "The Jewish View of Man," "The Nature of Man." (Olan quoting Hosea 14:2).
83. Ibid. and Exodus 34:6.
84. Olan, "Man, His Nature and Destiny," "The Jewish View of Man," and "The Nature of Man."
85. Ibid.
86. Ibid. (While this assessment of repentance is rather brief, Jewish thinking generally holds that *teshuva* consists of multiple stages that include: the sinner's recognition of his sin; the feeling of remorse; undoing any damage done by the sinner; appeasing the victim of his wrongdoing; and resolving never to commit the sin again. These five steps could certainly be compressed into Olan's three categories, depending upon one's understanding and viewpoint.)
87. Olan, "Judaism and Modern Theology," 211.
88. Olan, "If There is No God."
89. Olan, "Judaism and Modern Theology," 212.

90. Ibid.
91. Ibid.
92. Micah 6:8.
93. Olan, "The Prophetic Faith in a Secular Age," 6.
94. Olan, "Why do the Righteous Suffer and the Wicked Prosper?"
95. Ibid.
96. Ibid.
97. Ibid. and "If We Could Ask of God Only one Question," WFAA Radio, April 7, 1957.
98. Ibid.
99. Olan, "If We Could Ask of God Only one Question." (Olan provides examples of Helen Keller turning "the darkness of her own life into a bright flame of hope and faith for millions of people" and Franklin Roosevelt adjusting "the braces of his crippled legs" during a speech to the nation.)
100. Olan, "Why do the Righteous Suffer?"
101. Olan, "Putting First Things First."
102. Ibid.
103. Ibid.
104. Borowitz, *Studies in the Meaning of Judaism*, 67.
105. Olan, "An Unrepentant Liberal Jew."
106. Lubarsky, "Introduction," *Jewish Theology and Process Thought*, 12.
107. Olan, "Is Anything Too Hard for God?"
108. Peyton Davis, "Rabbi Levi Olan: A Conscious of the City," *Dallas Times Herald*, October 10, 1976.
109. Olan, "Judaism and Modern Theology," 210.
110. Ibid., 211.
111. Levi A. Olan, address to the Super Market Institute Midwinter Executive Conference in Florida, January 1969.

References Cited in Chapter 9

Chapter 9

1. Psalms 8:5-7.
2. Levi A. Olan, "The Nature of Man," in *Great Jewish Ideas*, 1964, 166 and "Man, His Nature and Destiny," 4.
3. Olan, "On the Nature of Man," 255.
4. Ibid.
5. Ibid.
6. Ibid.
7. Olan, "New Recourses for a Liberal Faith," and "The Future of Man."
8. Levi A. Olan, "The Mission of Israel in a Nuclear Age" and "Why do the Righteous Suffer and the Wicked Prosper," WFAA Radio, January 13, 1952, and "Crisis and Faith," undated but probably written at the beginning of the final quarter of the 20th century.
9. Levi A. Olan, "Prophecies of Doom — A Critical Examination," undated.
10. Levi A. Olan, "The New Liberalism - An Interpretation of the Scientific Revolution," 4.
11. Ibid.
12. Ibid., 35.
13. Ibid., 26.
14. Ibid., 36.
15. Levi A. Olan, "Theology Today," undated.
16. Levi A. Olan, The Window, Temple Emanu-El Bulletin, December 13, 1978.
17. Olan, "Crisis and Faith."
18. Ibid.
19. Levi A. Olan, "Ethics in a New Key," *Journal of Reform Judaism*, Fall 1982 (In "Prophecies of Doom — A Critical Examination," Olan referred to the artists and scientists as today's prophets alerting us of the doom ahead. "While they draw upon two very different sources of experience, they are one in their unveiling of the explosively dangerous human condition.")

References Cited in Chapter 9

---

20. Levi A. Olan, "Science — Another False Messiah," WFAA Radio, April 27, 1969.
21. Olan, "Ethics in a New Key."
22. Olan, "The New Liberalism."
23. Olan, "Prophecies of Doom."
24. Ibid.
25. Ibid.
26. Olan, "The Future of Man."
27. Olan, "The New Liberalism," 27.
28. Olan, "The President's Message to the 79th Annual Convention."
29. Ibid.
30. Ibid. (In an address to the Super Market Institute Midwinter Executive Conference in Florida, January 1969, Olan suggested that one must ask the basic questions of life: Who am I? What is my relationship to the universe in which I live? Do my aspirations, my loves, my hopes have a reality? If we begin to ask the right questions about ourselves, we will move towards answering the questions that plague the cities, the nation, or the world.)
31. Olan, "God in a Secular World." (Previous to this address, in his radio sermon of February 11, 1968, entitled "God is Real," as well as other commentaries currently excluded from mention, Olan preached that evidence of science's success is demonstrated by the "sickness being conquered in the laboratory, not the chapel. Hunger and drudgery are fast becoming memories. It was only yesterday that men beseeched God to save them from the scourge of polio. The answer, however, came from the scientist.")
32. Olan, "The Religious Community" and The Christian-Jewish Encounter, WFAA Radio, October 26, 1969.)
33. Olan, "The Mission of Israel in a Nuclear Age." and "Why do the Righteous Suffer and the Wicked Prosper."
34. Sidney L. Regner, "Levi A. Olan," 301.
35. Levi A. Olan, "Crisis and Faith." and "The President's Message to the 79th Annual Convention.

References Cited in Chapter 9

36. Olan, "Crisis and Faith."
37. Ibid.
38. Olan, "Putting First Things First.
39. Olan, *Prophetic Faith and the Secular Age*, 138.
40. Olan, "The President's Message to the 80th Annual Convention."
41. Amos 2:6
42. Olan, "The Mission of Israel in a Nuclear Age" and "Why do the Righteous Suffer and the Wicked Prosper."
43. Olan, "Crisis and Faith.
44. Wolf, "On God and Theology," 46.
45. Levi A. Olan, "Hope for Man," 1954.
46. Levi A. Olan, "Creative Hope, (The Essence of Purpose)" (Sermon preached in Rockefeller Memorial Chapel of the University of Chicago, Sunday, February 11, 1962.)
47. Olan, "The New Liberalism," 61.
48. Ibid., 48.
49. Olan, "Man, His Nature and Destiny," and "The Jewish View of Man," undated.
50. Olan, "Prophecies of Doom." (In "The New Liberalism — An Interpretation of the Scientific Revolution," Olan suggested the mood of despair pervading the arts was characteristic of the more formal disciplines of philosophy, science, psychology, and religion. "When modern man turns from the discouragement he experiences at an art gallery, a theater, or a symphony concert to the writings of the philosophers and theologians he is confronted with an academic confirmation of his despondent mood. Historians, or more accurately, philosophers of history are today prophets of doom. They find the parallel for our era in the last days of the Roman Empire, and predict for us the decline and fall of our civilization.")
51. Levi A. Olan, "A National Purpose for America," WFAA Radio, October 29, 1961. (In this radio sermon, Olan emphasized the moral culture of the day dominated by corporate success while eternal moral principles, reason, and freedom are gradually being diluted.)

52. Olan, "Theological Foundations for Guiding Principles for Reform Judaism."
53. Olan, "A New Prayer Book — Conservative Judaism Defines Itself," 419.
54. Olan, "Theological Foundations."
55. Olan, "The New Liberalism," 7.
56. Ibid., 23.
57. Levi A. Olan, "The Failure of Nerve," undated.
58. Olan, "The New Liberalism." 23.
59. Ibid., 101-102.
60. Olan, "Hope for Man."
61. In his 1980 Baccalaureate address "And Not to Yield" to St. Marks School in Dallas, Texas, Olan explained the mystery of life, saying "from minute to minute, hour to hour, day to day, year to year we face the unknown. This is the mystery of life without which life becomes dull. Life is beautiful because it is a venture into the unknown, each day a new creation."
62. Olan, "Ethics in a New Key."
63. Olan, "Crisis and Faith."
64. Olan, "Prophecies of Doom."
65. Olan, "Ethics in a New Key."
66. Olan, "Prophecies of Doom."
67. Saxon, April 6, 1983 interview with Levi A. Olan, 66.
68. Olan, "Man, His Nature and Destiny." (It should be noted that, within limitations, asceticism has existed in Judaism over the course of history.)
69. Olan, "On the Nature of Man," 271.
70. Ibid.
71. Levi A. Olan, "The Jewish Will to Live," undated.
72. Levi A. Olan, "The New Jewish Irrationalists," undated and "The Attack On Reason" in *The American Zionist*, 7. (In his WFAA Radio sermon of November 9, 1969 Olan said the search for one's self is the essence of the existential challenge of our time.)

References Cited in Chapter 9 and Chapter 10

---

73. Levi A. Olan, "Judaism and Modern Theology," 199.
74. Ibid.

Chapter 10

1. Olan, *Judaism and Immortality*, ix.
2. Robert Gordis to Robert Garvey, September 10, 1670. (Gordis was a professor at Jewish Theological Seminary of America from 1940 to 1992.)
3. Olan, *Judaism and Immortality*, 6.
4. Leo Baeck, "The World Beyond," *Contemporary Jewish Thought*, edited by Simon Noveck, 190, Louis Jacobs, *The Book of Jewish Belief*, 231, and Olan, *Judaism and Immortality*, 8.
5. Louis Jacobs, *The Book of Jewish Belief*, 231.
6. Byron L. Sherwin, "A Jewish View of Death and Dying," *CCAR Journal: A Reform Jewish Quarterly*, Fall 1999, 13.
7. Olan, *Judaism and Immortality*, 10. (This represents God breathing the spirit into the body of man as the foundation for the belief that the soul is eternal.)
8. Ibid., 10.
9. Ibid.
10. Ibid., 16.
11. Ibid., 18.
12. Ibid., 19.
13. R. Travers Herford, B.A., D.D., *Talmud and Apocrypha, a Comparative Study of the Jewish Ethical Teaching in the Rabbinical and Non-Rabbinical Sources in the Early Centuries*, 179 and Martin Goodman, *The Oxford Handbook of Jewish Studies*, 55.
14. Herford, *Talmud and Apocrypha, a Comparative Study*, 178-179.
15. Olan, *Judaism and Immortality*, 21.
16. Ibid., 23.
17. Ibid., 26.

18. Ibid., 29-30.
19. Ibid., 32.
20. Ibid., 33.
21. Ibid., 34.
22. Ibid.
23. Ibid.
24. Ibid., 37-38.
25. Ibid., 35.
26. Ibid., 38.
27. Avoth 4:16-17.
28. Ecclesiastes 9:4.
29. Avoth 4:22.
30. Olan, *Judaism and Immortality*, 40-41.
31. Ibid., 46.
32. Eiruvin 19a.
33. Olan, *Judaism and Immortality*, 51.
34. Ibid., 52.
35. Ibid.
36. Byron Sherwin, Lecture Tape 2, Spertus' Medieval Judaism Course.
37. Olan, *Judaism and Immortality*, 56.
38. Trude Weiss-Rosmarin, "Saadia Gaon," *Great Jewish Personalities in Ancient and Medieval Times*, 170.
39. Olan, *Judaism and Immortality*, 56.
40. Ibid. (Olan interprets the position of Saadia Gaon.)
41. Isadore Twersky, *A Maimonides Reader*, 416.
42. Olan, *Judaism and Immortality*, 67 (Quoting from Joseph Albo, *Sefer Ha-Ikkarim*.)
43. Ibid., 69.

References Cited in Chapter 10

44. Sherwin, *Kabbalah, An Introduction to Jewish Mysticism*, 24.
45. Olan, *Judaism and Immortality*, 71.
46. Moshe Hallamish, *An Introduction to the Kabbalah*, 9.
47. Olan, *Judaism and Immortality*, 71.
48. Ibid.
49. Sherwin, *Kabbalah, An Introduction to Jewish Mysticism*, 25.
50. Berachoth 10a.
51. Olan, *Judaism and Immortality*, 72-73.
52. Ibid., 73.
53. Ibid.
54. Ibid., 73-74.
55. Ibid., 76.
56. Ibid., 78.
57. Ibid., 79.
58. Shmuel Feiner, *Haskalah and History*, 1.
59. Olan, *Judaism and Immortality*, 81.
60. Allan Arkush, "Immortality," *20th Century Jewish Religious Thought*, 480.
61. Olan, *Judaism and Immortality*, 81.
62. Ibid., 81-82 and Arkush, "Immortality," 480.
63. Olan, *Judaism and Immortality*, 83-84.
64. Ibid., 85.
65. Ibid.
66. Leo Baeck, *The Essence of Judaism*, 184.
67. Olan, *Judaism and Immortality*, 96.
68. Ibid. and Michael A. Meyer, *Response to Modernity, A History of the Reform Movement in Judaism*, 388.
69. Olan, *Judaism and Immortality*, ix.

70. Ibid., 98.
71. Ibid., 99.
72. Ibid., 100.
73. Ibid., 100-101.
74. Ibid., 101.
75. Ibid.
76. Ibid.
77. Levi A. Olan, "Is There Life after Death," WFAA Radio, January 20, 1952.
78. Ibid.
79. Olan, *Judaism and Immortality*, 102.
80. Levi A. Olan, "Our Secret of Eternity is Revealed, Sharing through Love," WFAA Radio, October 24, 1965.
81. Olan, *Judaism and Immortality*, 103.
82. Ibid., 104.
83. Ibid.
84. Ibid.
85. Ibid., 98.
86. Olan, "Theological Foundations for Guiding Principles for Reform Judaism."

Chapter 11

1. Levi A. Olan, "Forty Sermons. (Presented after his first year at Temple Emanu-El, Dallas, Texas.)
2. Olan, "Called to Preach," 4.
3. Ibid., 3-4.
4. Ibid., 7.
5. Sidney L. Regner, memorial tribute to Levi A. Olan, in the 96th Annual Convention of the Central Conference of American Rabbis, June 24 to

References Cited in Chapter 11

       June 27, 1985, volume XCV, 302.

6.   Olan, "Some Directions for Reform Judaism," 22.
7.   Ibid.
8.   Ibid.
9.   Ibid., 21
10. Ibid.
11. Ibid., 22
12. Levi A. Olan, "On Being a Success or Failure," WFAA Radio, January 16, 1949.
13. Olan, "Some Directions for Reform Judaism," 20.
14. Ibid., 20
15. Levi A. Olan, "Jewish Cultural Trends in America," undated.
16. Olan, "The Future of Judaism in America."
17. Ibid.
18. Dallas Times Herald, October 20, 1984. (On the passing of Levi Olan.)
19. Levi A. Olan to Miss Mary E. Clary of Framingham, Massachusetts, December 19, 1950.
20. Levi A. Olan to Mr. Bernard Pines, Worcester, Massachusetts, April 11, 1950.
21. Peyton Davis, "Rabbi Levi Olan: A Conscience of the City."
22. Rabbi Joseph Klein, Senior Rabbi, Temple Emanuel, Worcester, Massachusetts to Rabbi Gerald Klein, Temple Emanu-El, Dallas, May 15, 1970.
23. Aviezer Ravitzky, quoting from JT Ta'an 4:2, in "Peace," *20th Century Jewish Religious Thought*, 687.

General Resource List and Bibliography

Primary Sources

The Levi A. Olan Collection at the Jacob Rader Marcus Center of the American Jewish Archives, Hebrew Union College, Cincinnati, Ohio.

The Levi A. Olan Papers at the Archives of Temple Emanu-El, Dallas, Texas.

The Levi A. Olan Collection at the Perkins School of Theology, Southern Methodist University, Dallas, Texas.

Extensive Collection of Levi A. Olan's WFAA Radio Sermons from 1949-1971.

Extensive Collection of Levi A. Olan's unpublished commentaries and compositions.

Dallas Public Library. *(Levi Olan: Oral History Interviews Conducted by Gerald D. Saxon on February 4 and April 6, 1983).*

Spertus Institute for Jewish Learning and Leadership, Chicago, Illinois.

Books

Ackroyd, P.R., A.R.C. Leaney and J.W. Parker. *The Wisdom of Solomon.* Cambridge, England: Cambridge University Press, 1973.

Ahlstrom, Sydney E. *A Religious History of the American People.* Binghamton, NY: Ballou Press, Inc., 1973.

Auerbach, Jerold S. *Rabbis and Lawyers: the Journey from Torah to Constitution.* Bloomington, Indiana: Indiana University Press, 1990.

Baeck, Leo. *The Essence of Judaism.* New York: Schocken Books, Inc., 1965.

Baron, Joseph L. *A Treasury of Jewish Quotations.* Northvale, NJ: Jason Aronson Inc., 1996.

Bemporad, Jack, ed. *A Rational Faith: Essays in Honor of Rabbi Levi A. Olan.* New York: KTAV Publishing House, Inc., 1977.

Bible Scholar, CD-ROM Edition. Torah Educational Software, Inc., New York, New York.

Blau, Joseph L., ed. *Reform Judaism, A Historical Perspective, Essays from the Yearbook of the Central Conference of American Rabbis,* New York: KTAV Publishing House, Inc., 1973.

Borowitz, Eugene B. *Studies in the Meaning of Judaism.* Philadelphia: The Jewish Publication Society, 2002.

Bright, John. *A History of Israel.* Philadelphia: Westminster Press, 1981.

Charles, R.H. *The Book of Jubilees,* Oxford, England: The Clarendon Press, 1902.

Cohen, Arthur A., ed. and Paul Mendes-Flohr, ed. *20th Century Jewish Religious Thought.* Philadelphia: The Jewish Publication Society, 2009.

Cohen, Henry. *Why Judaism? A Search for Meaning in Jewish Identity.* New York: Union of American Hebrew Congregations, 1973.

Cohen, Steven M. and Arnold Eisen. *The Jew Within.* Bloomington, IN: Indiana University Press, 2000.

Complete Tanach With Rashi, CD-ROM Edition. Version 1.2, Davka Corporation, Chicago, Illinois, 1998.

Cristol, Gerry. *A Light in the Prairie, Temple Emanu-El of Dallas 1872-1997.* Fort Worth, TX: Texas Christian University Press, 1998.

Dinnerstein, Leonard. *Anti-Semitism in America.* New York: Oxford University Press, Inc., 1994.

Dubnow, S.M. *History of the Jews in Russia and Poland.* Philadelphia: The Jewish Publication Society of America, 1920.

Encarta World English Dictionary, New York: St. Martin's Press, 1999.

Encyclopedia Judaica, CD-ROM Version 1. Judaica Multimedia (Israel) Ltd., 1997.

Encyclopedia Judaica, Jerusalem, Israel: Keter Publishing House Ltd., 2007

Essays by Hebrew Union College Alumni, Hebrew Union College Press, 1949, Cincinnati, Ohio

Feiner, Shmuel. *Haskalah and History.* Portland, OR: Littman Library of Jewish Civilization, 2002.

Goldstein, Jonathan A. *II Maccabees, Vol. 41a.* Garden City, NY: Doubleday & Company, Inc., 1983

Goldy, Robert G. *The Emergence of Jewish Theology in America,* Bloomington, IN: Indiana University Press, 1990.

Goodman, Martin. *The Oxford Handbook of Jewish Studies.* New York: Oxford University Press, 2002.

Graetz, Heinrich. *The Structure of Jewish History and Other Essays.* New York: The Jewish Theological Seminary of America, 1975.

Griffin, David Ray. *God, Power, and Evil: A Process Theodicy.* Philadelphia: Westminster Press, 1976.

Great Jewish Ideas, B'nai B'rith Department of Adult Jewish Education, 1964, Colonial Press, Inc., Clinton, Massachusetts

Greenberg, Moshe, trans. *The Religion of Biblical Israel, from its Beginnings to the Babylonian Exile.* New York: Schocken Books, 1972.

Guzman, Jane Bock. *David Lefkowitz of Dallas, A Rabbi for All Seasons.* Dallas: The Florence Foundation, 2006.

Hadas, Moses, ed. and trans. *The Third and Fourth Books of Maccabees.* New York: Harper & Brothers, 1953.

Hebrew Union College Annual, Volume LXXII (62), 2001, Hebrew Union College Press, Cincinnati, Ohio

Hallamish, Moshe. *An Introduction to the Kabbalah.* Albany, NY: State University of New York Press, 1999.

Herberg, Will. *Protestant-Catholic-Jew: An Essay in American Religious Sociology.* Garden City, NY: Doubleday & Company, Inc., 1955.

Herford, R. Travers. *Talmud and Apocrypha, a Comparative Study of the Jewish Ethical Teaching in the Rabbinical and Non-Rabbinical Sources in the Early Centuries.* New York: KTAV Publishing House, 1971.

Hertzberg, Arthur. *Being Jewish in America, The Modern Experience.* New York: Schocken Books, 1979.

Heschel, Abraham Joshua. *A Passion for Truth.* Woodstock, VT: Jewish Lights Publishing, 1995.

___ *God in Search of Man, A Philosophy of Judaism.* New York: The Noonday Press, 1983.

___ *I Asked for Wonder, A Spiritual Anthology.* New York: The Crossroad Publishing Company, 2000.

___ *Moral Grandeur and Spiritual Audacity.* New York: Farrar, Straus and Giroux, 2001.

___ *The Insecurity of Freedom.* Philadelphia: The Jewish Publication Society of America, 1996.

Jacobs, Louis. *A Jewish Theology.* West Orange, New Jersey: Behrman House, Inc., 1973.

___ *The Book of Jewish Belief.* Springfield, NJ: Behrman House, Inc., 1984.

Kaplan, Edward K. *Spiritual Radical, Abraham Joshua Heschel in America, 1940-1972.* New Haven, CT: Yale University Press, 2007.

Katz, Steven T. *Jewish Philosophers.* New York: Bloch Publishing Company, 1975.

Kaufman, William E. *The Case for God.* St. Louis: Chalice Press, 1991.

___ *The Evolving God in Jewish Process Theology*. Lewiston, NY: The Edwin Mellen Press, 1997.

Koeher (Kohler), Dr. Kaufmann. *Jewish Theology Systematically and Historically Considered*. New York: The Macmillan Company, 1918.

Kraut, Benny. *From Reform Judaism to Ethical Culture: The Religious Evolution of Felix Adler*. Cincinnati, OH: Hebrew Union College Press, 1979.

Levy, Richard S. *Anti-Semitism in the Modern World*. Lexington, MA and Toronto: D. C. Heath and Company, 1991.

Lewis, Hal M. *Models and Meanings in the History of Jewish Leadership*. Lewiston, NY: The Edwin Mellen Press, 2004.

Liebman, Charles S. *The Ambivalent American Jew*. Philadelphia: The Jewish Publication Society of America, 1973.

Lubarsky, Sandra B. and David Ray Griffin. *Jewish Theology and Process Thought*. Albany, NY: State University of New York Press, 1996.

Martin, Bernard. *Contemporary Reform Jewish Thought*. Chicago: Quadrangle Books, 1968.

Meyer, Michael A. *Ideas of Jewish History*. Detroit: Wayne State University Press, 1987.

___ *Response to Modernity, A History of the Reform Movement in Judaism*. Detroit: Wayne State University Press, 1988.

Morgan, Michael L. *Beyond Auschwitz*. New York: Oxford University Press, 2001.

Neusner, Jacob. *Understanding Jewish Theology*, Jacob Neusner, New York: KTAV Publishing House, Inc., 1973.

Noveck, Simon. *Contemporary Jewish Thought*. Clinton, MA: The Colonial Press Inc., 1966.

___ *Great Jewish Personalities in Ancient and Medieval Times*. Clinton, MA: The Colonial Press, Inc., 1969.

___ *Great Jewish Personalities in Modern Times*. Clinton, MA: The Colonial Press, Inc., 1969.

___ *Great Jewish Thinkers of the Twentieth Century*. Washington, DC: B'nai B'rith Books, 1985.

Olan, Levi A. *Judaism and Immortality.* New York: Union of American Hebrew Congregations, 1971.

___ *Maturity in an Immature World.* New York: KTAV Publishing House, Inc., 1984.

___ *Prophetic Faith and the Secular Age.* New York: KTAV Publishing House, Inc., 1982.

Phillips, Michael. *White Petropolis, (Race, Ethnicity, and Religion in Dallas, 1841-2001).* Austin, TX: University of Texas Press, 2006.

Reform Judaism, Essays by Hebrew Union College Alumni. Cincinnati, OH: Hebrew Union College Press, 1949.

Rudavsky, David. *Emancipation & Adjustment.* New York: Diplomatic Press, Inc., 1967.

Sachar, Abram Leon. *A History of the Jews.* New York: Alfred A. Knopf, Inc., 1964.

Sarna, Jonathan D. *American Judaism.* New Haven, CT: Yale University Press, 2004.

Schechter, Solomon. *Aspects of Rabbinic Theology.* Woodstock, VT: Jewish Lights Publishing, 1993.

Scherman, Rabbi Nosson, trans. *The Complete ArtScroll Siddur,* Brooklyn: Mesorah Publications, Ltd., 1999.

Schorsch, Ismar. *From Text to Context, The Turn to History in Modern Judaism.* Hanover, NH: Brandeis University Press, 1994.

Schwartz, Leo W., ed. *Great Ages and Ideas of the Jewish People.* New York: Random House, Inc., 1956.

Sherwin, Byron L. *Kabbalah, An Introduction to Jewish Mysticism,* Lanham, MD: Rowman & Littlefield Publishers, Inc., 2006.

___ *Studies in Jewish Theology.* Portland, OR: Vallentine Mitchell, 2007.

___ *Toward a Jewish Theology.* New York: The Edwin Mellen Press, 1992.

Slonimsky, Henry, ed. *Essays.* Cincinnati, OH: Hebrew Union College Press, 1967.

Soncino Talmud, CD-ROM Edition. Davka Corporation, Judaic Press, Inc., Chicago, Illinois, 1991-1995.

Tanakh, The Holy Scriptures, 1985, The Jewish Publication Society, Philadelphia, Pennsylvania and Jerusalem, Israel

Tanach, The Stone Edition of the Torah, Prophets, and Writings, ArtScroll Series, 2000, Mesorah Publications., Ltd., Brooklyn, New York

The Holy Scriptures According to the Masoretic Text. Melrose Park, IL: Delair Publishing Company, 1988.

The Solomon Goldman Lectures, Volumes I (1977) through VIII (2003), Spertus Institute of Jewish Studies, Chicago, Illinois

Twersky, Isadore. *A Maimonides Reader*. Springfield, NJ: Behrman House, Inc., 1972.

Weiner, Hollace Ava. *Jewish Stars in Texas, Rabbis and Their Work*. College Station, TX: Texas A&M University Press, 1999.

Whitehead, Alfred North. *Process and Reality, An Essay in Cosmology*. New York: The Macmillan Company, 1929.

___ *Process and Reality, An Essay in Cosmology,* (Corrected Edition by David Ray Griffin and Donald W. Sherburne). New York: The Free Press (Macmillan Publishing), 1978.

Zamore, Mary L. *The Sacred Table, Creating a Jewish Food Ethic*. New York: CCAR Press, 2011.

Zeitlin, Solomon, ed. *The Second Book of Maccabees*. New York: Harper & Brothers, 1954.

Journals

Blau, Joseph L. "Liberal Judaism in a Reactionary World." *Reform Judaism: A Historical Perspective*. CCAR Yearbook, 1973.

Cristol, Gerry. "Levi A., Olan, Conscience of the City." *Legacies, A History Journal for Dallas and North Central Texas,* vol. 17, no. 2, Fall 2005.

Gittelsohn, Roland B. "No Retreat from Reason." CCAR Seventy-Fifth Annual Convention, Atlantic City, NJ, 1964

Karff, Rabbi Samuel E. "The Agada as Source of Contemporary Jewish Theology." 74th Annual Convention, Central Conference of American Rabbis, Philadelphia, Pennsylvania, June 19, 1963.

Kraut, Benny, "From Reform Judaism to Ethical Culture: The Religious Evolution of Felix Adler," *Hebrew Union College Press*, 1979.

Olan, Levi A. "A New Prayer Book – Conservative Judaism Defines Itself." *Judaism: A Quarterly Journal of Jewish Life and Thought*. Fall 1973.

___ "A Theology of Jewish Liberation." *Judaism: A Quarterly Journal of Jewish Life and Thought*, vol. 27, no. 1, Issue #105, Winter 1978.

___ "Called to Preach." *CCAR Journal*, January 1960.

___ "Doctrine of the Chosen People Reaffirmed." *Judaism: A Quarterly Journal of Jewish Life and Thought*, vol. 29, No. 4 Fall 1980.

___ "Ethics in a New Key." *Journal of Reform Judaism*, Fall 1982.

___ "Felix Adler, Critic of Judaism and Founder of a Movement." New York, *Union Anniversary Series*, Union of American Hebrew Congregations, 1950.

___ "Freedom and Responsibility." *CCAR Year Book*, 1965

___ "Judaism and Modern Theology." *CCAR Yearbook*, vol. LXVI, 1956.

___ "Kaplan – A Product of Post-Hegelian Nationalism and Pragmatism." *CCAR Journal*, June 1956.

___ "Liberal Judaism in a Reactionary World." *CCAR Yearbook*, vol. LII, 1942

___ "Mitzvoth – Authority and Freedom." UAHC, November 1973.

___ "New Resources for a Liberal Faith." *CCAR Seventy-Third Annual Convention*. June 1962.

___ "Reform Judaism in a Post-Modern World." *The Journal of Reform Judaism*, No. 1, Winter 1981.

___ "Reinhold Niebuhr and the Hebraic Spirit; A Critical Inquiry." *Judaism: A Quarterly Journal of Jewish Life and Thought*, vol. 5, #2, Spring 1956.

___ "Rethinking the Liberal Faith." *Reform Judaism, Essays by Hebrew Union College Alumni*. Cincinnati, OH, UAHC, 1949.

___ "Some Directions for Reform Judaism." *CCAR Journal*, January 1958.

___ "The Faith of an Untired Liberal," *Reform Judaism, Essays by Hebrew Union College Alumni*, Cincinnati, OH, UAHC, 1949.

___ "The Faith of an Untired Liberal." *The Torch* (International Association of Torch Clubs, Inc.), vol. XXII, no. 4, October 1949.

___ "The Mission of Israel in a Nuclear Age." *Judaism: A Quarterly Journal of Jewish Life and Thought*. Winter 1983.

___ "On the Nature of Man." *CCAR Yearbook*, vol. LVIII, 1949

___ "The President's Message to the 79th Annual Convention of the CCAR." Boston, MA, June 17-20, 1968.

___ "The President's Message to the 80th Annual Convention of the CCAR." Houston, Texas, June 16, 1969.

___ "The Prophetic Faith in a Secular Age." *Journal of Reform Judaism*, Spring 1979.

___ "Who is a Jew Symposium." *Judaism: A Quarterly Journal of Jewish Life and Thought*, Winter, 1959.

___ Review of *A Faith for Moderns*, by Robert Gordis, *Judaism: A Quarterly Journal of Jewish Life and Thought*, Spring 1961.

___ Review of *Christianity Through Jewish Eyes – A Quest for Common Ground*, by Walter Jacob. *Perkins Journal* (SMU), Winter 1975

___ Review of *Rediscovering Tradition, Reflections on a New Theology,"* edited by Arnold Jacob Wolf, *Judaism, A Quarterly Journal*, vol. 15, no. 2, Spring 1966.

___ Review of "The Need to Re-Think Jewish Theology," by Joseph Blau, *Perkins Journal* (SMU), Fall 1972.

___ Review of *Understanding Jewish* Theology, by Jacob Neusner. *Perkins Journal* (SMU), Spring 1974.

___ Review of *We Jews and Jesus*, by Samuel Sandmel. *Perkins Journal* (SMU), Winter 1973.

Regner, Sidney L. Memorial Tribute remembering Levi A. Olan. *Central Conference of American Rabbis, Ninety-Sixth Annual Convention*, vol. XCV, 1985.

Sherwin, Byron L. "A Jewish View of Death and Dying," *CCAR Journal: A Reform Jewish Quarterly,* Fall 1999.

The Reconstructionist Journal, Wyncote, Pennsylvania, Reconstructionist Rabbinical Association, July 4, 1969.

Schwarzschild, Rabbi Steven S. "The Role and Limits of Reason in Contemporary Jewish Theology," 74th Annual Convention of the CCAR, June 19, 1963.

Texas Library Journal. Waco, Texas, Texas Library Association, 1954.

Zola, Dr. Gary. "The Common Places of American Reform Judaism's Conflicting Platforms." *Hebrew Union College Annual,* vol. LXXII, 2001.

Magazines

Kurtzleben, Danielle. "50 Years Later, A War Over the Poverty Rate." *U.S. News & World Report,* January 6, 2014

Olan, Levi A. "The Attack on Reason." *American Zionist Magazine,* February 15, 1954.

___ "The God We Worship, an Organicist View." *Dimensions Magazine,* Fall 1967.

Ritz, David. "Inside the Jewish Establishment." *D Magazine,* November 1975.

___ "The Way It Was. *D Magazine.* November 2008.

Smith, Richard Austin. "How Business Failed Dallas." *Fortune Magazine,* July 1964.

Newspapers

Editorial Comments. "Dedicated to Rabbi Levi A. Olan, Humanitarian, Philosopher, Educator." *Jewish Civic Leader,* Worcester, MA, December 10, 1948.

Davis, Peyton. "Rabbi Levi Olan: A Conscience of the City." *Dallas Times Herald,* October 10, 1976, Q & A Section.

Evans, Derro. "Rabbi Levi Olan: A Conversation." *Dallas Times Herald,* Sunday Magazine, October 11, 1970.

Weiss, Jeffrey. "Religious Leaders Honor Outspoken Rabbi's Legacy." *Dallas Morning News,* September 2, 2006.

The Window, Temple Emanu-El Bulletin. December 13, 1978

Worcester Telegram & Gazette Newspaper, August 4, 1948

Internet Sources

A Portrait of Jewish Americans, Findings from a Pew Research Center Survey of U.S. Jews. PewResearch.org/Religion, October 1, 2013, Washington, DC.

www.ellisisland.org/research/passRecord.asp?:MID=007938074

Samet, Moshe Shraga. *Encyclopedia Judaica*, vol. 15, 2nd ed. Gale Virtual Reference Library, Spertus Institute for Jewish Learning and Leadership.

Unpublished Materials and Other Sources

Linder, John A. "A Snapshot in Time." American Jewish History Course, HUC, Cincinnati, OH, January 17, 2001.

Moffic, Evan. "Levi Olan: Champion of Liberalism." Independent Reading Course, HUC, Cincinnati, OH, Spring 2005.

Olan, Levi A. Olan. "Address to Rabbinical Assembly Convention." (Conservative and Reform Movements), June 10, 1969.

___ "Address to the World Union of Progressive Judaism." 1968.

___ "And Not to Yield." Baccalaureate address to St. Marks School in Dallas, Texas, 1980.

___ "As a Rabbi Sees It." presented to the General Assembly of the Council of Jewish Federations and Welfare Funds, February 1, 1947.

___ "Aspirations for Ethnic Minorities." presented to the National Conference on Social Welfare, Columbus, Ohio, 1971.

___ "Creative Hope, (The Essence of Purpose)." Sermon preached in Rockefeller Memorial Chapel of the University of Chicago, Sunday, February 11, 1962.

___ *Levi Olan Autobiography*. Written in the 50th anniversary year of marriage (1931-1981).

___ "Philanthropy and the Modern World." A talk given at a dinner with faculty consultants to the Hogg Foundation for Mental Health, The University of Texas, 1965.

___ "The Future of Judaism in America." An address in Washington, DC on the 300th anniversary of Jews in America, 1954.

___ "The Myth of the Melting Pot." Presented to the National Conference of Social Work, Dallas, Texas, May 20, 1971.

___ "The New Liberalism - An Interpretation of the Scientific Revolution." Undated.

___ "The Religious Community." Presented to the Supermarket Institute Midwinter Executive Conference, Bal Harbour, Florida, 1969.

___ "The Theological Foundations of Prayer, A Reform Jewish Perspective." Presented at the UAHC 48th Biennial, 1967.

___ "Treatment of the Aged – A Test of our Civilization." Presented to the Governor's Committee on Aging, Dallas, Texas, May 1971

A Portrait of Jewish Americans, Findings from a Pew Research Center Survey of U.S. Jews, October 1, 2013.

Proceedings. Seminar. "Faith and Method in Contemporary Jewish Theology." 74th Annual Convention of the CCAR, June 19, 1963

Zola, Dr. Gary P. "The Four Ideological Pronouncements of Reform Judaism in America" (a seminar led by Dr. Zola).

Photos

Photographs for the cover, title page, and pages 29 and 102 are courtesy of The Jacob Rader Marcus Center of the American Jewish Archives, Cincinnati, Ohio (americanjewisharchives.org).

The photograph on page 103 is courtesy of the archives of Temple Emanu-El in Dallas, Texas.

www.ingramcontent.com/pod-product-compliance
Lightning Source LLC
Chambersburg PA
CBHW070049080526
44586CB00013B/977